B. H. ⸻

July
1935

WALKING
IN THE GRAMPIANS

Robert M. Adam

BEINN DOIREANN

WALKING
in the
GRAMPIANS

by
CHARLES PLUMB

*With 19 sketch-maps and
16 illustrations*

LONDON
ALEXANDER MACLEHOSE & CO.
58 Bloomsbury Street
1935

PRINTED IN GREAT BRITAIN BY ROBERT MACLEHOSE AND CO. LTD.
THE UNIVERSITY PRESS, GLASGOW

TO

ALL WHOSE NAMES ARE HERE TAKEN IN VAIN

AND IN PARTICULAR

TO

JOCK AND MARJORY STEWART

FROM WHOM THE WRITER CONTRACTED

AN INCURABLE AFFECTION

FOR HIS SUBJECT

PREFACE

THIS note really exists to thank Miss Seymour, my first and most flattering reader, for her sketches; Mr. Adam, Mr. Beattie and the L.M.S. for the use of the photographs (in the proportion of 12 : 2 : 1, if I may subject gratitude to arithmetic); and Miss D'Arcy and Mr. Adam jointly for the Siamese-twin-flowers, whose elegance deserves, but cannot command, more than one of these iron-shod pages. I take the chance of thanking also my wife, without whose constant help this book would either have been finished several months earlier or not at all; Mr. Morris for literary, and Mr. George Smith for musical criticisms; and my publisher for patience.

To *The Romance of Poaching in the Highlands*, by McCombie Smith, I owe the story at the end of Chapter XII; the text admits all other literary obligations of which I am conscious. *Hill Paths in Scotland*, by Walter A. Smith (MacNiven and Wallace), does however deserve a special mention; not so much because I have made any great use of it as because you may well do so. It is a most practical guide to all the good passes.

I only wish the honours list had been at least one or two Smiths longer. I have in fact been at some disadvantage in writing away from Scotland and without any knowledgeable person handy to consult on points of detail, but these are as accurate as my own memory and notes can make them.

The map assumed throughout is the one-inch Ord-nance Survey. I should add that the printing of the Pope quotations is in accordance with the earliest editions I have been able to lay hands on in each case ; that of the passage from *The Iliad* has the best authority.

C. T. P.

May, 1935.

CONTENTS

ILLUSTRATIONS

MAPS

CHAPTER I

ROMANCE is always round the corner—except in Scotland. There it is in the very air and soil. It is under your feet and in your lungs. It has become a mere matter of experience within the grasp even of the unimaginative. As a good reactionary from the nineteenth century, I am aware of some inconsistency in making these remarks, for where mountains were concerned, ' horrid ' was quite the favourite epithet of the age of reason. But emotions change with the times. In those days man did not need mountains, because his normal surroundings gave little or no cause for complaint ; and an industrial age has, I think, justified our taste for escape into a wilder nature. It is a taste which the hills of Scotland, and perhaps the Cairngorms in particular, can satisfy more perfectly than any other part of the British Isles—for that matter, more than any other part of the world. I do not except Switzerland, nor (in a lordly ignorance) the Rockies or the Himalayas. The difference in appeal is that between a perfect mistress and an army of the noblest specimens of predatory female : which type of indulgence you prefer depends simply upon your taste in love.

Taken for all in all, then, walking in the Highlands has probably meant more to me in enjoyment, and even perhaps in excitement, than any other kind of experience ; and I write in order to recapture some of it, and if possible to share it with any to whom the same or like interests

A

appeal. For hedonism is as hard a creed as another, and the only way to make a success of it is to create the pleasure.

But I am eager for an early start to the hills, and generalisations are tiresome before breakfast. So I hope good taste will accommodate itself with just that one deep breath for a preface, and turn attention to the destination for the day, chosen, as it must be, overnight—of the countless possibilities——

BEINN A BOURD

I can't justify my choice, but there are plausible reasons for it. In the first place, it is descriptively named ' a Table ', which besides being the first word in the Latin grammar, and therefore the foundation, historically, of our sense of order in things, is a necessary condition, gastronomically, of the enjoyment of such courses as are to follow. In the second, it is the nearest of the big Cairngorms to Braemar, appearing fairly close on the right as you come from Aberdeen by road, soon after you cross the Invercauld bridge, disappearing behind the small hill of Carn na Drochaide as you approach the village, and returning into sight above Glen Quoich, two miles further to the west ; while Beinn A'an, with which it stands in neighbourly connection and for purposes of walking is almost inseparably linked, can be seen at even less distance from the village. It must be late in an exceptional summer if this southern bluff of Beinn a Bourd is not marked with a large horse-shoe of snow, or at least the two patches, the frogs of the shoe, remaining, which it is almost possible to use as a calendar for the time of

2

year. I believe the ancient Downie, the shepherd of that name, could have done so—who passed most of his ninety years, day and night in the summer, in those smooth green fields, they may be the ' policies ', of Invercauld.

But my preface has committed me to a romantic reason also. Mine is one of sentiment, springing from what the French should call (I am sure they do not) *la nostalgie de jeunesse*. For personal recollections to acquire a *patina*, an imaginative value, a few years are proportionate, within the course of a lifetime, to the three thousand years of Troy within that of world-history, the twice three thousand of Egypt, the God knows how many which have buried Ur of the Chaldees ; from which came a small cup and saucer of the common rosy clay which was given to my father and used to stand on his writing-table. It was with him that I first climbed Beinn a Bourd, and of the more distinguished hills it was the only one which I ever visited in his company ; and this has a peculiar significance in my *recherche*, because my first recollections of the hills are linked with him, my pleasantest of him with them.

I have a natural shrinking from the clerical collar, whether by aesthetic instinct or association—if the latter, it is a fact which the most casual glance at Freud seems to explain, but which I prefer to account for by thinking that my unusual fortune in having known some of those clergymen, who may be counted amongst the best and not the worst of mortals, has trained my eye to see with a painful certainty through the usual pretensions. Only on holiday—which meant, in the Highlands—did my father discard that distasteful adornment, and at least matriculated into the lay world, in a tweed suit of the profoundest grey. I remember the suit with affection, though I always rather disapproved of it at the time ; it showed up

3

so far on the hillside—as bad as white. Then he also smoked out of doors, which he did not at other times ; and to this day the smell of tobacco out of doors, commonplace for others, retains for me this individual association. Smells seem to have this ineffaceable quality more than other sensible impressions. His particular brand was of the mildest, put up in a tin box as garishly inept as the sign of a public-house called ' THE ROSEMARY ' which I once noticed, the word of such softly fragrant associations standing out in block-capitals upon an illuminated field of scarlet.

There is something pleasantly ludicrous in the thought that the effect upon my childish mind of these trifling personal liberties upon the part of my father contributed largely in my case to the creation of that sense of utter freedom which the hills so readily provoke in people of a certain temperament ; perhaps the more so because I do not remember many precise details of particular days.

The only part of that first Beinn a Bourd day which I can actually recall is our return over the top of the Slugain glen, the last look back to the hill, and the fast last miles home begun, he in his raven plumage and his fragrant cloud ahead, and I behind, singing brassy bits of *Tannhäuser* at the top of my voice. It was in a burn a couple of miles down to the left from here that I bathed, the last time I was that way, in a patch of sunshine on a day of storm. What more than legendary monster does a man feel himself when running across the windy side of a mountain, naked but for a pair of tremendous boots—too wet already to be worth taking off !

I have said that Beinn a Bourd and Beinn A'an are hidden from Braemar by the hill of Carn na Drochaide, called ' of the Bridge ' from its resemblance to a bridge

4

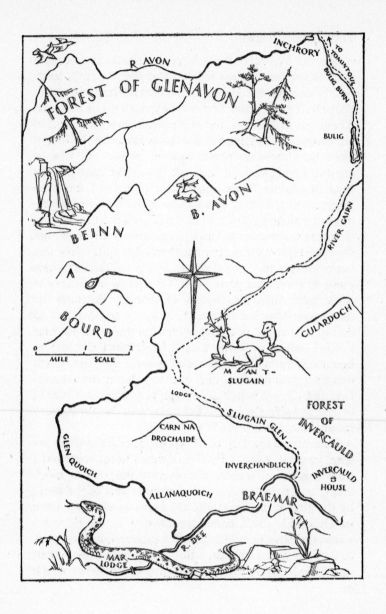

of the old ' General Wade ' type, certainly not because there is any bridge close at hand ; for there was till lately no bridge over the Dee between that of Invercauld and the private one to Mar Lodge four miles west of Braemar. There was in old days, and still remains in mind, an air of remoteness in the fringe of fine Scots firs along the foot of Carn na Drochaide which seemed to me like that of another world; such an undertaking was the fording of the river in Charlie Sim's dog-cart or on one of the farm waggons with a beast or a load of hay. The low water-meadows along the river on this side are a further defence. (Expensive attempts to drain them have been made, but they remain to a great extent undrained in spite of the turf banks at their edge and the deep and broad ditches which intersect them, and parts are still the freehold of the wild duck rather than the tenancy of sheep.) But now the timbermen have come, like Fairson, to murder and to ravish, and there is a foot-bridge for them below Mar Castle ; which only the most high-minded traveller to Beinn a Bourd will none the less disdain. Formerly it was necessary to shout for a boat over the Dee at Inverchand-lick, and often it took long enough before one was heard ; or else to wade the river—but this must be further up-stream before it is joined by the Cluny.

Once across the Dee at the appropriate point there are three possible routes : by Glen Quoich to the west, but I leave this out of account for practical purposes as much longer and tiresome going in the upper part of the glen ; by the glen of the Slugain to the east ; or else over Carn na Drochaide itself, either by the nick in the ridge to-wards the Slugain, which makes a picturesque little pass, or over the actual summit. But I recommend this ascent, up a hillside covered with bell-heather and redolent, which

6

can be started anywhere between the houses of Allanmore or Allanaquoich, rather as gentle exercise for a spare afternoon, as the top is an excellent point from which to make a preliminary survey. The whole range of Beinn a Bourd and Beinn A'an appears at very close quarters, and although even from here, no more than the bear of the classic jingle can you see more than one side of the mountain at one time, the view of that side is good enough to afford an excellent text for one of those geographical descriptions to which readers of this class of book must be resigned.

The two hills, lying almost in isolation to the east of the main body of the Cairngorms, to which they properly belong, form a continuous range (except for the drop to the pass between them) which provides what must be the longest high-level walk in the British Isles—about six miles at over 3500 ft., taking perhaps three hours to cover from end to end. Beyond them the River Avon forms the northern frontier of the Cairngorm region.

Starting from the south top above the snow-field visible from the valley, the ridge of Beinn a Bourd runs back for about two miles to its highest point (3924 ft.) and then turns sharply to the east, enclosing a dark precipitous corrie whose recesses are as secret from human eye, unless you go deliberately inside to explore, as the crater of a volcano. By contrast, the outer sides slope steeply but uneventfully away into bogs (so that from Loch Etchachan to the west the mountain has the appearance of a gigantic chesterfield) except for the jutting prong of Stob an t-Sluichd, which, with the side of Beinn A'an, and its answering protuberance, Stob Bac an Fhuarain, encloses the fine open corrie which heads the glen running north from the bealach between the two mountains.

7

Beinn A'an is every way gentler, more feminine, than Beinn a Bourd, with neither his uncompromising massiveness, nor his abrupt lines in all three dimensions, nor quite his height. It is a chain which swings in a graceful semi-circle and tapers from the summit (3843 ft.), the nearest to Beinn a Bourd of the strange-looking knobs that appear at intervals, like colossal boils, along the spine of the ridge, and are the distinctive characteristic of the hill when seen from a distance. Beyond the far eastern end of Beinn A'an lies Loch Bulig, to which there is a kind of road from the south, extended northward by a footpath to Inchrory Lodge and on to Tomintoul, the only village in Scotland which is higher than Braemar.

From the bridge of sighs at Inverchandlick the shortest way into the Slugain glen is to follow the upper cart-track towards Invercauld for a few hundred yards, until you come to a heavy wooden gate into the plantation on the left, through which a path leads past the site of an old saw-mill and out over a stile. Here there is a plank-bridge over a fine pool in the burn. On the other side you join a broad shooting-track which goes the length of the glen. The going is luxurious, until near the top it becomes steeper as the glen narrows to a ravine, where the water has disappeared underground, leaving patches of smooth green turf amongst the rocks to mark its course. Just below the top of the pass you come rather surprisingly on a small stone lodge. It has always seemed to me a little strange that such a place should have been thought necessary only four miles or so from Invercauld House, but I suppose that in the days of more zealous stalking it was an advantage as a base for the pursuit of the stag on to the high tops. When I was last there the roof was in the course of demolition ; so, even were it likely to be open,

8

it is idle to make a mental note of this place as a possible shelter.

At the watershed, Beinn a Bourd comes into sight ahead (Beinn A'an, more to the right, being obscured by its own outpost of Carn Eas) and to reach it you have to cross the upper glen of the Quoich, which lies between, having curled right round to the back of Carn na Drochaide from the west. The Slugain is a pretty, sheltered glen, with birch-trees and basking-places for the adder ; the Quoich, by contrast, is of the more magnificent, the true Cairngorm type, and I fancy there is an eyrie in one of the stragglers of the wood of Scots firs which fills its lower reach. This wood, I may add, since the subject of fauna has been introduced, rejoices in an exceptionally talented species of cleg, which I am happy to say I have not elsewhere encountered.

For Beinn a Bourd there is a bridge and a path, which it is well not to miss, as it saves some time over this rather broken ground where the heather is deep, and being pitched at the angle most sparing of effort, is very useful in the ascent later. It turns at right angles from another which goes farther along the south side of the glen, leading past Beinn A'an to Loch Bulig, or (if you take the next left-hand fork) to the bealach between Beinn a Bourd and Beinn A'an, or into the great corrie. Across the Quoich the path is easy to miss ; it turns left-handed round to the inside of the spur marked on the map as Carn Fiaclach, and then goes straight up, within sight, but well to the right, of the burn called Allt an t-Sneachda. This, as the name implies, proceeds from the field of almost perpetual snow which I have mentioned ; and past the snow to the south top, rather further to the left, is a steady but direct climb of about an hour from the Quoich—an hour well spent, for

9

all climbing is practically over for the day, and you will find yourself at the summit at, say, eleven o'clock (if you have left Braemar at eight), just in time to catch the clearest of the view even in hot weather, and with the prospect of an hour of easy and level walking in which to watch it variously unfold. The smooth gravelly surface of this plateau frees the feet and with them the spirit from preoccupation with their earthly ties ; and you may fancy yourself pacing the rampart of some Titanic fortress, not so very badly crumbled by the years in which three generations of gods have passed away.

But one is not always lucky in weather and nothing is more certain than that in a mist Beinn a Bourd is a most inconvenient neighbourhood, not only because of the misleading flatness of its top, but also because the precipices are very easy to walk over. They do not start abruptly, but fall by geometric progression from the most seductive of gently sloping banks into the perpendicular ; while a forced descent even in a safer direction will land you in the midst of forlorn and forgotten wastes, probably without landmarks and certainly at an immense distance north, south, east or west from any habitable part of the earth's surface.

I speak for those with compasses and the habit of compasses ; for those foolish virgins (as they mostly are) who go into the high hills without either, if they must do so in anything but entirely reliable weather—supposing there to be such a thing in Scotland—no words of wisdom can avail. But there must be many walkers wise enough not to go without a compass and fortunate enough never to have really needed it. To them the recommendation I would like to make may sound superfluous : it is that when you are finding your way by compass, you should follow it in humble obedience and blind faith, surrendering your reason to the dictation of the needle as if it were the finger of an angel. This is not as easy as it sounds, and, if you do not agree, I have little hope that you will do so until the human passion for self-determination and the tendency of the right and left legs to take paces of different lengths have led you astray as often as they have done me, and so proved me right in my preaching—if even yet not always so in practice.

The last time I was up Beinn a Bourd, a hill I have always been unlucky with so far as conditions of weather are concerned, is the first I shall mention of a good many cases in point. For the whole length of the plateau we had to put up with an unusual combination of mist and a furious cold rain, which would have been blinding, dead against us, but was fortunately driving from the forest of Athole well on our left flank. As it was, apart from soaking us to the skin in that quarter, it made the compass necessary. We reached the north top without mistake, but thereafter were lured by the compass-disregarding devil, posing as the lie of the ground, the least bit too far north, and so by degrees along the ridge leading to Stob an t-Sluichd. It did not take us long to realise that something was wrong, but it took us a little time to discover what; and though we had picked up the right line again at the cost of ten or fifteen minutes wasted, we were not very sure of ourselves till, at a lifting of the mist, we caught a glimpse of Cnap a' Chleirich, the big rock at the east end of the ridge. We climbed back to that point before making the descent towards Beinn A'an, in order to skirt the crags which run northward from that point.

There is a drop of six hundred feet over screes to the col, known locally as 'the Sneck'—I have hitherto

referred to it by the Gaelic name *bealach*—a lovely place.
On the north is a short and steep, indeed almost a precipitous fall into the desolate corrie or glen of the Slochd
Mor. I well remember the pretty sight of a hind and a
fawn lying together on the grassy ledge fifty feet or so
down this side, a group so well composed that heraldry
might envy. There are plenty of big rocks about if you
care to lunch in their shelter, before taking the southward path home down the glen or going on to Beinn
A'an.

This means only a short steep climb equivalent to the
descent from Cnap a' Chleirich which you have just made.
It is as well to keep as close as possible to the northern
crags. Half an hour will bring you to the top, and what
a monument of a top—that black tongue of rock, granite
moulded by time into the appearance of lava, thrusting
high from the crown of the ridge. The first part of the
ascent is a stiff pull, but that fantastic trophy, once in
sight, will draw you onwards with the magnetism of an
architectural perspective. It is called Leabaidh an
Daimh Bhuidhe, the Bed of the Yellow Stag, after what
famous or fabulous beast I know not. It may be climbed,
with care, but without any great difficulty or any particular advantage.

From here the most direct routes home are, either to
return on your steps a little way, and then to go south
along the buttress of Carn Eas, which takes its name from
the cascades of the burn immediately below Leabaidh an
Daimh Bhuidhe, and so back to the top of the Slugain ;
or else to follow the burn itself, in which case you will save
nearly two miles by taking a short cut into the Slugain,
through the little trackless glen between Meall an t-
Slugain and Meall Glasail Beag.

12

But the most tempting course is to complete the circuit of Beinn A'an by the series of minor stacks of rock upon the ridge; and this is also your direct way in case you should happen to have any means of transport at Loch Bulig, or wish to go on to Donside or Tomintoul. You have only to turn east at the last of the stacks—the next after that marked on the map as Clach Choutsaich—in order to reach the loch in an hour or so.

From parts of the ridge the verdant swathe of Glen Cluny, and the edge of Braemar village can be seen; and there is an incomparable prospect over the floating miles of moor and bog to the north, with Beinn Rinnes, near Dufftown, conspicuous in the distance. I have seen this country at its best under the rim of a cloud-bank suspended not more than a hundred feet overhead, an endless sea of blue rising and falling to the horizon; to mountaineers obscure but not inglorious, for from its edge issues the water which goes to make the finest of all pure malt whisky. It is pleasant to have some with you to mix for a libation with the pure water from some spring flowing towards the sacred valley of its birth.

It is perhaps fortunate that our ideals are so rarely fulfilled, or we should miss many pleasures, and perhaps not discover how much better the world is than our conceptions of it. The ideal mountain is no doubt a soaring peak; but what idealist with such an image frozen in his mind is likely to imagine, or even to appreciate, these singular and very different ' characters ', Beinn a Bourd and Beinn A'an. ' Ideal weather ' means conventionally a cloudless sky and temperate air; but to refuse the hills in any weather is to sacrifice many individual kinds of enjoyment and all chance of ever knowing them as they are at heart. Which remarks are my excuse

13

for ending this chapter with an account of a memorable expedition to these hills on one of the few occasions upon which I have taken them from the Loch Bulig end.

This was done with Ronald McNair Scott in July of 1926, on the whole a brooding sulphurous month and on this day especially so. I cannot remember for what reason, partly no doubt because it is only just possible to get a car to Loch Bulig at all, we did not leave there till twenty minutes before midday. There is a plain track, winding and wet and rather uninteresting, all the way up to the ridge of Beinn A'an ; but in the oppressive conditions we found the long steady climb very exacting, and took two hours, sweating freely, to reach the summit, where we lunched beside the springs of Allt an Eas Mhoir. Even on the heights there was no breath of wind, and our own expiring in the languid air, we ate our sandwiches like the very lotus-plant.

It was as late as four o'clock when we arrived at the north top of Beinn a Bourd. Here mist fell in patches from the impending storm-cloud which pressed down like a thatched roof over our heads. Against the grey back-cloth of the southward line of hills from Lochnagar to Beinn a' Ghlo, the serpentine black contour of A'Chioch, the southern cornice of the great corrie, stood out fiercely. Snow-drifts on the main Cairngorm group were momentarily disclosed and concealed again by the now perceptible motion of the clouds from that quarter.

I am not sure whether our original plan was to make the northern descent into Glen Avon, and so down the glen and back to Loch Bulig ; but we thought it as well to be off the heights as soon as possible, and this was the course we took in point of fact—and without much further loss of time. We set off round Stob an t-Sluichd, crossing on the

14

way a snow-bridge, a patch fifty yards long, well-preserved in the shades of this sunless hollow of Cul na Bruaich. As we made our way down the very steep hillside from that point to the path that leads to the ford and bridge at the junction of the Allt an t-Sluichd and the Avon, the rain began to fall in a soaking torrent. Near the bridge there is a shed with a tin roof, and as there was no lightning, nor much thunder either, we took advantage of its shelter to calculate our distances on the map. It was then ten minutes past six. The streams were all rising at such a pace that, had it been an hour later, I suppose, though we did not realise it at the time, that we should have been cut off before reaching this spot, and have been forced to spend a more than uncomfortable night on the hills. As it was, the next stage was simply a walk of four miles in the incessant rain along the shooting-track towards Inchrory Lodge. The Linn of Avon is admirable. I wish we could have waited to see it a little later in the evening.

By half-past seven, we were on the southward path to Loch Bulig, well on the way home. But here our real troubles began. The Bulig burn runs in a gorge, and the path beside it was more or less impossible to trace, so we took our own. The rocks close to the edge made it necessary to cross the burn several times : the first was a simple matter, the water no more than ankle-deep, but the second, which we should never have made had there been any apparent alternative, was a very different proposition, the water running waist-high perhaps. Unfortunately a third and last crossing was necessary, not of the main burn now but of its main tributary, the Feith Laoigh, which comes down from Beinn A'an. Normally you could step over this little stream, but at this moment it was a cataract running as deep as to the arm-pits. We

15

stripped off our clothes and threw them over, more as a formality than anything else, for already we had hardly a dry stitch on. The water made no impression on Ronald's tall Nordic body, but it actually carried me off my feet for a few yards. We did not reach the car till nearly half-past nine, having taken two hours over the last two miles.

The rest is not appropriate for a book written for walkers ; but we noble creatures like to score over the machine on those rare occasions when it gives us the opportunity, so I will not rob you of this pleasure. We found that the car had a puncture and the jack had an obscure complaint that made it useless. We had thus great difficulty in removing the wheel and setting things to rights. The rain had now stopped, and our clothes were spread out to dry to what small extent was possible. Meanwhile we were being devoured by a ravening horde of insects, nor had we any means of lighting our pipes for consolation and defence ; so that we began to get really impatient with the situation for the first time in the day, which hitherto I at least had thoroughly enjoyed. However we got away in time, refreshed by the relics of a sandwich and a piece of chocolate, warmed by brandy and the heat of the engine, and cheered with the assurance of good work well done and thoughts of hot baths and sorrowing families.

The drive itself was a curious one. The road down to Crathie was corrugated with gullies of water, and streams ran across the open fields. The Dee was a turbid yellow flood, most unlike itself, and a part of the main Aberdeen road had been swept away and was barely passable. It was nearly dark when we reached Braemar at rather before eleven o'clock, and we found the discussion of our probable fate in full swing. We read in the papers next

Robert M. Adam

I. THE LOCHNAGAR RANGE FROM BEINN A BOURD

day that there had been a cloud-burst on Beinn A'an, which was the centre of what was considered to have been the worst storm on Deeside for fifty years.

But these sudden torrents are by no means uncommon amongst the high tops. When I was talking about this day's wetting to Macdonald the greenkeeper at the golf-course, who is a great man for the hills, he told me that only a few days before he had been caught on Beinn Muichdhui in what he vividly described as ' a storm with great lumps of ice in it and lightning you could feel warm on your face '. He said the little burn which has to be crossed between the summit and Loch Etchachan became almost impassable in a few minutes.

CHAPTER II

LOCHNAGAR

SINCE my capricious start in the direction of Beinn a Bourd, these rather random papers have acquired a purpose, and must now live up to the unforeseen dignity of inclusion in this series. A proper sense of responsibility would no doubt, at this stage at least, insist upon a more systematic arrangement of my subject with definitions and axioms complete ; but I refuse quite to spoil my own pleasure for your mere information, and as I have done without them so far, I propose to put these serious thoughts off still further, and instead to turn at once across the valley of the Dee to that group of ' mild flourishing mountains ' standing about the borders of the counties Aberdeen and Angus, of which Lochnagar is the lofty north-eastern termination.

Lochnagar itself is a hill which I really rather dislike. It is too popular (the sardine-tins on the top are witness) and too accessible. Besides the name is a ridiculous one— why should a mountain be called a loch ? I must say the obvious explanation only occurred to me lately : we are now in the region where Scots names are beginning to take the place of Gaelic, and no doubt the name must formerly have been Lochnagar *Hill* (after the loch), and have been abbreviated to the present form with increasing currency. Its older name was Beinn nan Cichean, the Mountain of

18

the Paps, which accounts for the mysterious appearance of a
' Bin Chichnes ' upon Gordon of Straloch's A.D. 1662 map.

It owes its celebrity to Byron, whose just adequate line
has been too often quoted. In his time the Highlands
were coming into literary fashion so strongly that it is at
first sight surprising that their inspiration was so rarely a
happy one. Keats is feeble in face of them and so even is
Wordsworth—whose friend at Kilchurn could think of
nothing better than ' cove ' for one of the corries of Beinn
Cruachan. They have fared no better in painting ; although those rather rare beasts, Highland cattle, set in a
welter of appropriately shaggy scenery, are, through that
medium, more familiar in effigy to the average middle-
class townsman than the commonplace features of the
countryside within a few miles of his home.

The reason, it seems, is that ideas which present themselves naturally in artistic forms, appearances naturally
expressive, set up a resistance against the power of the
creative hand, to which chaos and void are malleable. It
would require a giant of the imagination to assimilate in
his poetic digestion these massive symbols ; indeed I can
think of none but Blake to whose mind the hills might
have been servant and not master. Or perhaps it is that
hills alone happen to fall outside the range and variety of
English, and that the solution is to be found in Gaelic, a
language which contains in its small vocabulary I think
thirty-three descriptions of mountain.

None the less I have been up Lochnagar very many
times, and had many fine days amongst them. The two
main routes are from Loch Callater to the west, and from
Loch Muick to the east. It would also be possible to
reach it from Glen Clova to the south, though I have never
done this myself. There are besides two direct approaches

19

from the north through the miniature but well-stocked forest of Balmoral; but this royal preserve admits no one further than the pretty falls of Garrawalt, a mile or two up from the bridge of Invercauld. Even so far is worth a spare afternoon, for the sake of the splendid old trees, perhaps the finest relic of the original forest of Caledonia.

I have only once obtained very special permission to approach Lochnagar through the royal forest, the part of it called the forest of Ballochbuie, and it was a very long time ago. We did not get up Lochnagar itself because of mist, but visited the Sandy Loch, and climbed one of the foothills, I am not now sure which, but I remember an amusing incident which happened on it. We had put down our lunch and maps on the ground before walking a little further over the side to see anything there was to be seen, and when we came back we could not find them again. We had to patrol the ground for a surprising length of time before we did so, to our great relief. Why we should have been so foolish I cannot imagine. Since then I have always marked anything I leave for a few minutes on a stony hillside very very carefully, otherwise it is remarkably difficult to pick it up.

Of the normal routes, the way from Loch Muick is the quicker, and the nearer to Ballater, to which it is about ten miles by road; from Braemar the road-approach is unreasonably long to walk, being about eighteen miles (whereas the distance from Braemar to Loch Callater is not much over five). From Loch Muick the climb is steep and impressive, and reveals all the best of the mountain. No directions are needed as the path is clear from the gate across the road, which closes the way to the King's lodge of Alltnaguibhsaich.

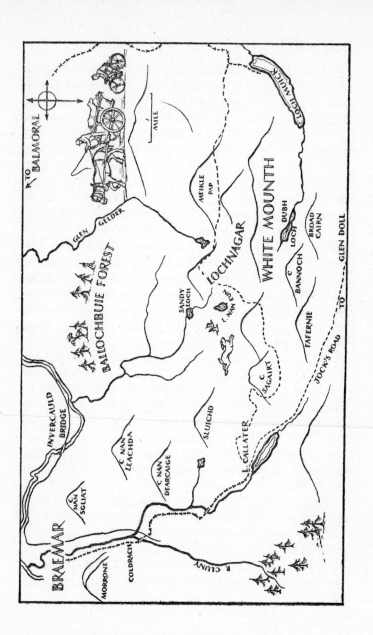

The first part is not very interesting, but after rounding the Meikle Pap, the point which rises at the eastern corner of the big corrie, you come to the edge of the corrie itself, and from there on may follow it pretty closely, if you so desire, and enjoy the views down the steep gullies and across to the crags opposite. The real Lochnagar (the loch) lies below, but is so close to the foot of the cliff that it cannot be seen from every point on the edge. The ascent as far as the south top takes about two hours. I once found a paper purporting to establish the extraordinary record of *one* hour, a feat claimed by ' a party of boy scouts from Stonehaven', but even with such credentials I cannot help being somewhat sceptical of this exploit.

The south top is on the base of a triangular plateau, faced with the precipices on one side, which runs north-wards to reach its apex at the real summit, the natural cairn, Cac Carn Beag (3786 ft.). This is the sharp peak which shows so handsomely not only from Deeside and the surrounding hills, but from parts of the country at least as far distant as the Riggin of Fife. The view is famous, and there is an indicator set up by the Cairngorm Club to explain it to you. You can certainly see the Firth of Tay and the Lomonds clearly, and I believe the Firth of Forth, and I have heard a very definite claim made for Hadding-ton Tower. But the old guide Downie, who spoke always as one of the prophets, positively refused to admit even the Forth.

This old man, the brother of the shepherd whom I have mentioned, lived with their two sisters at the Croft of Muickan above Braemar, which is the highest cultivated land in Scotland. He gave up Beinn Muichdhui a few years before he died, but still went to Lochnagar occa-sionally until at least his eightieth year. These were the two hills for which, though with the least need, he was most constantly engaged, and he should have known all there is to be known about them—and had he followed the general custom of guides, a good deal more—although I have known him to be wrong about some which are more rarely in demand.

In order to see Lochnagar from Braemar, it is well to climb Morrone, a hill like a great pair of buttocks, just under the three thousand feet level, which few visitors to Braemar, even the tennis-enthusiasts, altogether avoid. (The resemblance I have mentioned may account for its name—' *mor thon*'. This is sometimes supposed to be a corruption of ' *mor sron*', but is certainly not equivalent to Morven (*mor bheinn*), as is also suggested.)

It can be done, up and down, at the very shortest in an hour and a half, but it is an extensive hill and the exploration of its various ramifications can be made into quite a long and interesting tour. The ascent is equally good for a reconnaissance of the Cairngorms.

So far as Lochnagar is concerned, the lower and less frequented Carn nan Sgliat to the south of Glen Cluny is a useful alternative, and, having no paths, it is about the same length of climb. This hill suffered some years ago from a heather fire started by some wretched picnicker, from which it has never recovered. The blaze was just checked from spreading over the march into the Balloch-buie forest, but ate deep into the peat, so that, for a week or two afterwards a subdued smouldering, ' no light but rather darkness visible', showed up the hillside infernally against the midnight sky.

Carn nan Sgliat is at the end of a line of hills, foothills of the Lochnagar group, which run out from above Loch Callater to Braemar, and its ascent can be turned into a fine afternoon's excursion, equivalent in point of effort, though not of honour and glory, to either of the short ascents of Lochnagar itself, by continuing southwards along the ridge up and down the summits successively of Creag nan Leachda, Creag nan Dearcaige, and then perhaps either Creag Phadruig, or else Meall an t-Slugain or t-Sluichd, whichever it should properly be called. From either of the latter hills one can come down pleasantly beside Loch Phadruig, one of the type of small hill-loch perched at a good height but on an open hillside which is not found on the steeper slopes north of Glen Dee. I believe it is good for trout, but the fishing of course is preserved. Descending into the very pretty glen of the Callater you can be back in Braemar in five hours or so for the whole round ; but it can well be turned into a whole day if the weather is tempting and you are not in the mood to go far afield.

Loch Callater, at the head of the glen, is an attractive mile of water, not too narrow for its length. The hills descend into it directly but not too steeply, so that it is well-set without being forbidding. The valley that extends two miles from its head, ending in a circle of mild crags and steep grass slopes, is closed by the rounded form of the Tolmount. Lochs are not a feature of Deeside, which may be why this used to be such a favourite expedition, accomplished, when we were children, in that now legendary vehicle known as a waggonette. I may mention, for anyone who can still enjoy a bicycle, that to ride over the three miles of rough road from Loch Callater down to the main road in Glen Cluny is a good piece of sport. There are plenty of twists and bends and plenty of flying stones, and in some places the burn is immediately below you on the right, but there is no angle that cannot

Robert M. Adam

GLEN CLOVA

II.

just be taken without brakes—which is of course a rule of the game. But, unless you walk all the way, you are most likely nowadays to come to Loch Callater by car.

Although it has been known for an unfortunate man who had been lost in the mist to be found dead within a few yards of the lochside, in summer the Callater, with its neat keeper's house and kennels at the foot, is civilisation itself by comparison with most places in these hills. Yet I can imagine that the stalker Lamont and his sister are glad enough not to have to live there through the winter ; their minds could not be better stocked and restocked than they are with Shakespeare, but when snow-drifts block the glen that would not feed them in body.

It was a day of winter-in-summer which I most enjoyed in Lochnagar, and it is pleasant to be able to say so, because my companion on that day was the publisher of this book. The first part of September is early for a fall of snow which will lie, but this morning it lay white on Carn an Tuirc, the only top of a height of over three thousand feet which can be seen actually from the village of Braemar.

There was sharp frost and a cold north wind as we left there at a few minutes before eight o'clock. We took the old road to the west side of the Cluny, which is the best for walking. This is part of the old military road from Coupar-Angus, by Braemar, Corgarff on Donside, Tomintoul and Grantown-on-Spey, to Fort George. It was constructed between 1749 and 1763 by Governor Caulfeild, a grandson of the first Viscount Charlemont, who was chief surveyor of the military roads in the Highlands for many years after General Wade left Scotland. The bridge by which it joins the present main road three or four miles up Glen Cluny is therefore not quite correctly known as Wade's Bridge. We crossed the river a mile or more short of this point by what is called the Shepherd's Bridge at the Coldrach. There is no path leading to this —you must climb a fence and go across a field through a clump of birches to find it. The pool here is fine for bathing, though not so big as one could wish, and is well enough out of sight of the road from either side to satisfy anyone who does not push his or her modesty to maudlin lengths. This however was not the occasion for anything of the kind, and proceeding with due speed we arrived at Loch Callater, I should rather say, the gate leading to Lamont's house a little before the loch, at about quarter-past nine.

From here you skirt the wall until the path up the hill on the left becomes plain. This ascends for a short distance directly, and then turns and rises gradually across the face of Creag an Loch (the southward ridge of Meall an t-Slugain), curving round this to the left about opposite to the far end of Loch Callater. In another mile you come to the remains of a fence marking the boundary of the Invercauld and Balmoral estates, at the col between Creag an Loch and Carn an t-Sagairt. Just before this is the only point where the path is easy to miss : there is a tendency to keep too much to the left ; it is therefore well to watch carefully for a series of small cairns towards the right which will lead you on the way. At the fence the path doubles back round Carn an t-Sagairt (the hillside still being kept on the left hand) and soon there is a fine direct view into the gulf of Loch Kander on the opposite side of the Callater glen, to which we shall return. At about three thousand feet, you are now level with the hills around its edge ; and on every side the prospect begins to open out. It is also possible, though so far as I can see by comparing recorded times for various days, a little longer, to climb Carn an t-Sagairt (3430 ft.) and regain the path on the far side. If you wish to do this, simply keep along the fence instead of the path. This variation has no great merit, apart from that of adding another peak to your collection. The view down into the wild Dubh Loch, with its flanks of glistening rock, is certainly good, but very little better than from the path. This loch is a high level reservoir for Loch Muick, which is quite a big expanse of water, fed by all the southward drainage of Lochnagar. Both lochs are on the King's property.

When MacLehose and I reached this neighbourhood we found ourselves in what might have been mid-winter ; in every direction the snow lay thick enough to cover the ground, and it continued to fall quite heavily for a good part of the day. In the hollow above the Dubh Loch were a herd of about fifty deer and an immense congregation of ptarmigan, gathered here perhaps for shelter from the north wind.

After you cross the last burn flowing into the Dubh Loch comes what is almost the final ascent, and you find yourself on the plateau of the White Mounth, looking down into the northern corrie in which lie Loch nan Eun, and, farther away, the Sandy Loch. All the way the slope has been gentle enough, but from here till just before the summit of Lochnagar it is imperceptible. There is a mile or so which could be used as a race-track.

We reached the south top at a quarter to twelve, and found ourselves in mist. I took a bearing for Cac Carn Beag and then put the compass in my pocket, considering how short the distance is and that the precipices of the great north-east corrie would guide us safely to the top if we missed the exact line. But this incident shows how quickly a mistake made in a mist throws one out ; though it must be admitted that, knowing the mist was only the fringe of a high cloud, and did not reach far down hill, we were careless. We did not reach the top in the expected ten minutes, so inclined deliberately more towards the right to find the crags, which we then followed, keeping them on our right hand. What was our surprise to find ourselves walking *down* hill instead of *up*, and then, suddenly right out of the mist and back along the White Mounth ! We had turned completely round in the few hundred yards before we became suspicious, and the crags which we had come to on our right hand were not those of the Lochnagar corrie at all but those above Loch nan Eun on the other side of the ridge. At the time it produced a strange feeling of bewilderment : the same sense of pure miracle which occurs to anyone who cannot find something which he has searched for several times in the same place —and which turns up in that very place the next time he looks.

Our vanity dislikes to admit that more highly valued experiences of the cosmic mystery than these are also due not to the strength but to the weakness of our faculties.

When we reached the main top, with this diversion the ascent had taken three hours ; it should normally take about two and a half, and I have done it in two. Meanwhile the mist cleared off and we had a long clear view in each direction. The snow-clad Cairngorms especially held the eye, but my amateur attempts to photograph them, though in the most favourable conditions, were unsuccessful. There are two good springs near the summit, one half-way between the two cairns near the edge of the eastern corrie, and one near the route towards the Callater, rather below the south top ; but we were not thirsty and therefore lunched at the Cac Carn : the view tempting us to spend one half-hour more on the heights in spite of the extreme cold.

Of the several descents which are possible, on this day we had no thoughts of any but to return to Callater as we had come, arriving there at a sound pace by a quarter to three, and at Braemar—this time by the main road and across the golf-course—by something after four o'clock. If you should wish to complete the traverse of Lochnagar, I should advise you to do so in the reverse direction, first the steep climb from Loch Muick and then the gentle grassy descent towards Loch Callater. I prefer this sequence anywhere, and here particularly for what lies in front of you ; but obviously this is a matter of taste (by which expression we are accustomed to signify that those who do not agree with us are fools). By way of variation it is possible to find a way down into the western corrie of Loch nan Eun (which means ' the Loch of the Birds ' but is also the haunt of the brown hare, that rarer person in these regions), and so to work round the south side of Carn an t-Sagairt, across screes and boulders, through moss and obstructive heather, and to rejoin the path to Callater at the point where it touches the fence and doubles back round Carn an t-Sagairt on the other side.

If, on the other hand, you wish to go south towards Glen Clova, you will descend across the White Mounth as we came from Callater, and branch off to the left when the path gets to the turn of Carn an t-Sagairt, or a little before, to the rising point just to the right of the Dubh Loch, which is Cairn Bannoch (3314 ft.) ; or else to the next summit-by-courtesy again to the right, which has the name of Fafernie (3274 ft.). From Cairn Bannoch proceed above the Dubh Loch to the Broad Cairn (3268 ft.). From this ridge the view down and across the crags has

29

plenty of character, and from the Broad Cairn Loch Muick comes into sight round the shelving mass of Lochnagar and the White Mounth. It would now be possible to come down into the eastern fork of the Clova, joining the path which comes over from the head of Loch Muick to Bachnagairn—or at least is so marked, for in fairness I must give due warning that I have never tested this route myself. (But the main right-of-way, the Capel Mounth, is considerably more to the south, crossing the ridge from the lower end of Loch Muick to a point farther down towards Milton of Clova.)

Better, from Fafernie, to join the well-known track called Jock's Road, leading from Loch Callater into Glen Doll, the other fork of Glen Clova. This route lies through the large expanse of peat-hags known as the Knaps of Fafernie, and is quite untraceable as a path. The line however is partly marked by means of sticks, and the general direction is clear enough in good weather. It was in this wilderness that a party coming from Clova a few years ago were caught in mist and forced to spend the night, an experience which resulted afterwards in the death of one of them. It might indeed be a bad place in such conditions, because the northern descent, though not actually precipitous, is sufficiently craggy to be a danger. But personally I should prefer this risk to the prospect of a night on the hill. The crags would at least be what an Irish lady once described as ' such a healthy death ' !

CHAPTER III

THE BRAES OF ANGUS

THE walking over the grassy steppes south from Lochnagar is some of the pleasantest and easiest in the world.
These hills—no longer of granite, which comes to an end
at Loch Callater—are covered with an abundant peaty
soil, which provides pasture for great numbers of deer,
and, on the dry parts of the ground, forms an elastic turf.
In the wetter parts—the hollows, such as that between
Tolmount and Fafernie, and the long level stretches
which occur mostly on the ridges west of the Tolmount—
the peat is broken up into hags with deep soft beds between. After much rain these must be impassable, and
even in dry weather they are tiring to cross.

We are now entering upon the Braes of Angus. This
tangle of hills, the last defences of the Highlands before
they descend, though gradually, into the coastal plain, is
broken up into multitudinous ridges which have no
clearly definable common plan. They are on the whole
green and lacking in heather, and differ very markedly in
type from both neighbouring mountain-tracts, the Cairngorms and the hills of Perthshire, bearing some resemblance rather to the less striking fells of the English Lake
District.

There is little here of either splendour or grace, for
the lack of which they are in their own way the more
impressive; unless it is truer to say that, except for mourn-

ful ' Celts ' and natural historians, such abject visual desolation, which to common humanity does not offer so much
as a challenge, goes beyond the normal range of impressions to which we are emotionally responsive, and
therefore shocks. I certainly require the encouragement
of sunshine to make me take much pleasure in walking
these hills alone. And yet a single, though an elusive,
personality persists from the Dubh Loch to the Cairnwell
Pass. Across that line of division objective form begins to
reassert itself.

There is however one main ridge, broken on either side
of the Tolmount, but otherwise an entity, into whose
southern flanks the glens of Angus thrust dark passionate
heads. This fluctuates, with a south-westerly movement,
from Fafernie and over Tolmount, and on over Cairn na
Glasha and the Glas Maol, forming so far the line of the
county march ; and then along Creag Leacach and Carn
Aighe down to the Spital of Glenshee. It can be followed
out from end to end, if that is your destination. Otherwise you will turn north from Cairn na Glasha to Carn
an Tuirc, and so descend.

The Tolmount (3143 ft.) has a very winning way with
it. In itself it is merely a grandiose hummock, but it
happens to be splendidly posted right at the head of the
steep-sided glacial valley in which Loch Callater lies. On
the south side it would be improved by the absence of its
twin neighbour, Tom Buidhe (3140 ft.), to which however
it is worth while to make an excursion in order to get
something of a view of the converging branches of Glen
Clova and Glen Isla, the famous crevices of the Doll and
Caenlochan, on either hand.

Southward again from Tom Buidhe extends an un-
kempt range which ends in Mayar, Driesh, and the Hill

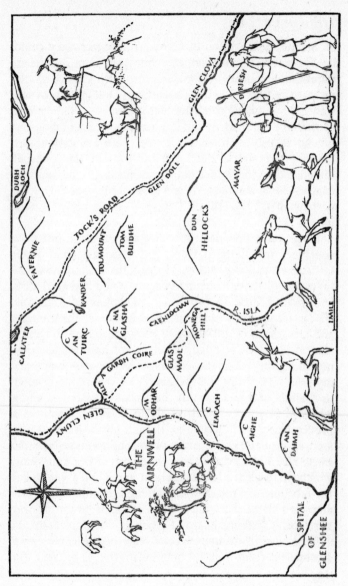

of Strone, near Milton of Clova, from which they could be climbed pleasantly enough : but from Tom Buidhe an unprofitable journey. If making into Glen Clova I would rather take Jock's Road through Glen Doll (which by the way is pronounced to rhyme with ' droll '). This is one of the rare cases when the low road as well as being the quicker is also the finer route. Yet I am not sorry that I have been tempted along the hill-tops in this unusual direction by the appealing strangeness of the names : Mayar—is it *maothar*, ' the Gentle Hill '—and Driesh, perhaps *dris*, ' the Hill of Thorns '—as certainly I found it ?

It was on a fine clear day with a north wind but little sunshine that Bernard Cook and I started from Loch Callater on this expedition. I made the mistake of wearing a pair of shoes which had been wet and had hardened, and yielded little to prodigal applications of Mars oil. (Boots are on the whole much the best wear for the hills and are almost essential where rock and screes and steep angles cannot be avoided, which is not however the case in this region.) The consequence was that after two miles my heel was neatly skinned, before I was properly alive to the fact and had got out the sticking-plaster—a thing which it is always worth while to carry with you as a preventive of such accidents, though not of much use as a cure. But the day was too promising to go to waste so easily : so I carried my shoes to the top of the Tolmount, which we reached in about an hour and a half ; I then left them behind in a pile of stones on the west side, on the line along which we intended to return, and went on my way barefoot. Walking in this fashion is not unpleasant on soft or smooth ground—I had once before come down Lochnagar from top to bottom in the same way for

34

experiment—so we were not much delayed by the slight handicap on this occasion ; although in any circumstances these four miles across broken peat are weary to endure.

Fortunately there had been a long spell of hot weather and we kept up quite a good pace, holding rather to the right of Tom Buidhe and across the Dun Hillocks. In this part of the walk, especially in the folds and hollows around the head of the Canness Burn, we saw extraordinary numbers of deer. No sooner had we sighted one large herd than another would come into view, and as they all moved in the same direction, upwind towards Cairn na Glasha, eventually that side of the glen was fairly ' creeping' with them : so far as we could reckon, of those we had seen alone there must have been quite a thousand. Once we came upon a parcel of stags directly in our path, and they started off at full speed straight for where we stood, so that for a discouraging moment we could not help imagining that they were deliberately charging on us. Nor did they swerve aside till they were well within fifty yards, and Bernard took two or three snapshots of them as they passed.

As you approach Mayar, which it took us two hours to reach from the Tolmount, the view to the south and west opens out more and more. From the summit (3043 ft.) half the Scottish lowlands lay clearly before us, with wide Strathmore stretched across the middle distance, behind it the Sidlaws, with a glimpse of the smoke of Dundee, and farther away to the right, the Tay, the Ochils and the Firth of Forth. Below, the hill breaks cleanly down into Glen Prosen, at the foot of which, but out of sight, lies Kirriemuir. We spent some time deciphering various landmarks with glass and map—one of the most conspicuous being the tower of red sandstone which, so far as I remember, stands not far from Cortachy Castle—before starting the descent towards Driesh (3105 ft.).

Here the ground is dry and stony and covered with blaeberries ('blasphemies', a typist's error !). Better walking could not be—but not for bare feet. There were a few ptarmigan about and scores of hares, both blue and brown. I have not seen so many except upon a mountain called Trostan in Ireland ; but there they are sacred and do not count much in this world.

A painful twenty minutes got us as far as the col, and we looked down the brisk precipices into Glen Doll, where the white lodge just showed through its trees, like one of those little churches lying apart in some Alpine valley. It seems a pity that I should have denied myself the bombast of an epic feat, but heroism was not the order of the day. As a matter of fact the additional hour of extreme discomfort, which would have been required for the ascent of Driesh and the return, was out of the question, and, if undertaken, might indeed have made it impossible to make the journey back over the great moss which lay between us and home. Richard before Jerusalem turned not less readily ; but ' the fates so accomplished'.

On the return we parted company, I following the lower and softer parts of the hill, and Bernard the firmer ground. I had the best of the transaction, for my route led me close to the crags, which are worth seeing. It happened also that a plump black vole surprised me face to face at the edge of a runnel in the peat ; into which he promptly disappeared—for the surprise was mutual. The line was not altogether easy to pick up even in full daylight—in a mist this range could be an unimaginable horror—and it was a quarter-past six by the time we reached the place where I had left my shoes. Just beyond, in a patch of scrubby grass, we came on an eagle, squatting unpresentably like a hen on a cabbage-stalk : a mean introduction to this autocrat, for whom the tourist is accustomed to search the most promising heavens, so often without satisfaction. The monkey's paw again ! He shuffled uneasily into his element, and soon swung off with recovering dignity into the north. We took the first burn north-west of Tolmount down into the glen, and so were back at Callater Lodge by half-past seven.

The whole time for the day was ten hours, a time which in proper conditions should easily include Driesh.

This has been a disproportionate digression. The main ridge of the Braes is more deserving of such prolonged attention, though it must now be content with less. For the more normal route from Tolmount over Cairn na Glasha and Carn an Tuirc back to Callater, which completes the circuit of the loch upon the hilltops, makes a great day's walking.

Cairn na Glasha, a broad flat hill of considerable height (3484 ft.) which, with the better-known Glas Maol, forms the highest ground of the range, Lochnagar apart, can be reached in half an hour or so from Tolmount. This ' Hill of Greyness', typical of the Braes of Angus in its melancholy dignity, on its southern side overhangs the black rift of Caenlochan, and in that direction has the same prospect to offer as the Glas Maol, except for the section which that higher mountain obscures. To some it will be a further recommendation to say that Queen Victoria and Prince Albert once lunched here. Carn an Tuirc (3340 ft.) is also flat, but that much lower and very much less extensive. As I think has already been noticed, it is the only hill of over three thousand feet in height to be seen from Braemar, from which its profile is dead level against the sky.

Northward from Carn an Tuirc there is a direct way down to Callater by an easy path made for shooting purposes. But it is more interesting to descend on the northern, the least precipitous, side of the little glen at the head of which lies Loch Kander, a circular tarn deep in the bent arm of Carn an Tuirc, with sheer sides falling for a thousand feet, where the sheep, which are allowed to share the rich pasture of these hills with the deer, perversely clamber, and look down at you casually with their pleasant Bourbon faces. The top, no doubt for their sake in intention, but more effectively for yours in case there is a mist, is protected by a low wall. Its construction was perhaps suggested by the plentifulness of material, the summit of Carn an Tuirc being fairly strewn with loose stones of a convenient building size, out of which a number of fox-butts have also been built here and there.

Glen Kander, like the other glens about here, is known for various Alpine plants, but the only botanical singularity which it has presented to my lay mind is the ' grass of Parnassus', an ivory cup veined with green which is rare, if not altogether unknown, in other parts of the eastern Highlands, although I have found it in luxuriance in the west, especially beside the banks of Loch Awe. In Glen Kander, July is the month in which it blooms ; if that word can be used of what emerges like a star from darkness. This flower is well worth looking for, even if you are no botanist. It deserves a name taken from Greece, for it has an Attic delicacy.

' The Grey Bare Hill', the Glas Maol (3502 ft.) lies in the other direction, south-west from Cairn na Glasha.

The summits are about two miles apart, divided by a narrow col, falling sharply to the head of Caenlochan on one side and that of the Allt a' Gharbh Choire on the other, along which runs a dyke—a very desolate spot. The summit-cairn of the Glas Maol lies in Angus, but close by is the point where the three counties of Perth, Aberdeen and Angus meet. Apart from this distinction, the view, which is unobstructed towards the lowlands, is very highly praised, and not without cause ; although I should imagine that the much lower hill of Mount Blair, on the Drumore estate between Glen Shee and Glen Isla, seven miles due south as the crow flies, would be nearly its equal in this respect.

Mount Blair has been considered to be the site of Agricola's northernmost battle against the Caledonians, so obscurely mentioned in Tacitus under the name of Mons Graupius. Accuracy compels me to record the contempt of most antiquarian authorities for this theory. At the same time local tradition has so often enjoyed her gentle triumphs over the self-confidence of reasonable history that the fact that the Gaelic word *blar* can mean a battle, as well as a field or plain in a more general sense, should not be overlooked ; and even with the shocking example of Lochnagar before us, we can hardly believe that any people in their senses could have decided to call a hill by a name which describes the direct opposite of a hill. On the other hand ' vixerunt fortes ante Agamemnona', and men fought battles in Scotland before and since Agricola's time.

The Glas Maol can most easily be climbed from Glen Cluny : either by the old drove-road, no doubt by far the highest of its kind, which crosses the very top and descends over Monega Hill into Glen Isla, leaving the modern main road just before it crosses the river two miles south of Glen Cluny Lodge ; or else from the top of the Cairnwell Pass over the projection of Meall Odhar, where there is no path. In either case an hour or so will suffice. The path is straightforward enough ; it runs parallel to the new road on the other side of the Cluny for half a mile or so, and then crosses the Allt a' Gharbh Choire, and goes up a long bluff right on to the summit-plateau. The other way is not quite so simple and has its ups and downs, but all you have to do is to keep to the highest point of the ridge along the county march.

The last time I was this way I did not actually go to the top, but explored the flanks and corries fairly thoroughly. This was a day of heat and lazy walking, the more so since I did not start till midday from the Spital of Glenshee, at which the mail-car had delivered me after an early call lower down the glen. As I crossed the Shee Water from a point about a mile and a half up the road, numbers of birds of many sorts were disporting in the coolth of the glen, amongst those of which I know the names peewits, oyster-catchers and curlews ; also some young moorhen— it was charming to watch their battles with the slight current. I went at an angle across the slope of the long ridge which runs southwards from the Glas Maol, and round its points of Carn an Daimh and Carn Aighe (' the Hart ' and ' the Hind '), without undue haste ; except when my steps were three times hastened involuntarily by the unsavoury remains of stags, from which I made all speed to escape. The experience made me very careful indeed, for that day at least, only to drink at springs. Fortunately when you are at the top of a hill the springs are the most accessible points of the burns, and on the normal Scottish mountain there is little need to worry

40

III.

HEAD OF GLEN ISLA

upon that score. But my route on this day was singularly waterless, and the thirst created in me by the blazing sun emphasised this fact unpleasantly. Creag Leacach (3238 ft.) which I had climbed by two o'clock, is, as it is named, a barren and very stony point on the ridge ; indeed all these summits consist of more or less loose agglomerations of stones, which on this particular ridge thrust up with more than usual bareness, like piles of rain-washed skulls. Into these the water percolates deeply and does not see light again until far down the sides of the hills.

From Creag Leacach I made round the very steep face of the Glas Maol towards Meall Odhar and found one moderate spring ; but flies and the uncomfortable angle of the slope soon sent me to finish my lunch on the top of Meall Odhar (3019 ft.). A further search for water led me to explore first the corrie south of this point, and then that to the north, where at last I was satisfied ; yet with but ' necessary ' pleasure, for the lethargic water of these hills is not like that of the Cairngorms, which can be enjoyed, almost, like nobler drinks, without the precedent vanity of thirst. Then I climbed back on to Cairn na Glasha and over the ridge of Carn an Tuirc down to Callater, and was back in Braemar by half-past eight o'clock.

On Carn an Tuirc I was astonished to see what at the first glance at a distance most resembled a peculiar herd of deer. It took some moments to realise that they were not deer at all, but wild goats, three dark in colour and thirteen or fourteen white, as the glass made out clearly ; but like deer, they kept together in a compact body, in true wild alertness, not straggling like sheep over the hillside.

Upon enquiring later I discovered that the existence of this herd is well-known ; unearthing also a more personal connection with them even than that suspected by the intelligent reader. There had been years ago at the farm in Braemar a kid, with which I can just remember having the most desperate encounters ; and now what should I be told but that this early boon companion had in his wild infancy been captured by some boys in the neighbourhood of Loch Callater, and brought back by them to the village. This may explain why the sight of his relations filled me at the time with a particular enthusiasm, for which even the rarity of the sight seemed barely sufficient to account.

The numerous occurrences in place-names of the word *gabhar*, ' a goat', either in a pure or a corrupted form, such as ' gower' (of which Lochnagar itself is possibly an example), prove that these animals must at one time have been common enough in the Highlands ; but they now seem to be practically extinct. I at least have never come across them elsewhere. It is reported that some still find a sufficiently well guarded retreat in Beinn a' Ghlo, whose highest peak is one of those which bears their name ; and some are certainly known to exist in the island of Mull.

CHAPTER IV

HOLDEN AT BRAEMAR

I HAVE brought you back to Braemar, and there I may keep you for some little time. Scotland is in my opinion not a country for journeys from one place to another : the distances are so great, and hotels and inns so few, and on the whole so expensive, that for pleasure and economy it is much better for the walker to stay for some time in one good centre.

The growth of the Youth Hostels in the last year or two has of course made through-travelling more practicable, and they are cheap ; but their existence does not alter the fact that cross-country journeys in Scotland must normally be made by way of passes, which may be fine walking indeed but cannot be compared with the pleasures of the heights. Nor will the sophisticated overlook another consideration : which is that those ecstasies themselves are enhanced by the prospect, and perhaps no more than equal in value to the experience, of the mellower satisfaction, which attends a return homeward into the valley, with the emotions of one more long day to remember in tranquillity, or in your cups. This addition is lost when the finish of the day was not its starting-point ; then the last miles are marred by a reasonable anticipation of discomfort, which is generally realised in Scotland. Circumstances are entirely different in the case of walking

43

in continental countries, or even to some extent in England, where at least the public-houses are plentiful and the beer is generally good.

Of all such centres, Braemar is by far the best. This large spreading village—it is made up of two formerly distinct settlements, Castleton and Auchindryne—is a place of singular good fortune. Its height, for it stands well over the thousand foot level, is what most of all gives a quality to the air and immediate scenery; for the trees about are restricted to the most typical—various firs and larches in the valley, alders and rowans by the burns, and birches covering the lower heathery slopes like livelier olive-groves; the last oaks are at Ballater, a miserable suburban place at the rail-head, sixteen miles of the sixty to Aberdeen. The main approach nowadays is over the Cairnwell Pass from Perth, which is actually nearer than Aberdeen; but this is generally impassable in winter. The Cairngorms block all exit north or west except on foot.

It has the usual riotous Highland past, and retains the religious evidences of its history, the people in Auchindryne, on the west side of the village, and further up the glen of the Dee being for the most part Catholics, and the older of them Gaelic-speaking, whereas those in Castleton and along the routes to the outer world are Protestants. Even as late as my father's time there was an old lady who thought the bridge over the Cluny, connecting the two sides of the village, was the work of the Devil—or anyhow the Protestants. But these animosities have disappeared, and one thing or the other, they are, unless affection blinds my judgment, the finest and most intelligent people in the world.

Even as a resort Braemar can plead a comparatively

dignified record, first dons then courtiers. The latter are the innocent cause of its present commercially enviable reputation. It is of course more than a ' beauty spot '— the very name suggests, if not the presence, at least the menacing proximity, of tea-shops and bungalows—but I am not enough of a mystic to suggest that the *genius loci*, though a potent spirit, has been sufficiently powerful to protect it from such horrors without material aid. Is it too much to suppose that those who are so persuasive, or at least so loud, in favour of nationalising the best areas of the Highlands, might hesitate in their enthusiasm, if their attention were called to the fact that the preservation of Braemar against great odds is due chiefly to the exclusive policy of the lairds ?

The existence of a privileged class is not a bad thing at all, provided that to enter it is made really difficult. As things are in the world, however, the concatenation of the old economic inequality with a new political equality, just coming out of the stage of convenient fiction into that of less convenient fact, is absurd in the last degree, with all its well called ' non-conformist ' incongruities of taste and behaviour ; and quite possibly the next step onward, into communism, may be the best hope of saving us from a new dark age. So far as land in particular is concerned, the social advantages of communism can also be supported by especially water-tight arguments.

But nationalisation—while things are what they are, that is not the same thing by any means. At least so it seems to me. It *may* of course be possible to suggest a worse trustee for anything of beauty than a poor witless democratic nation at the mercy of every crank that blows. One is of course at liberty to admire the latest example upon a large scale of the poor monster's aptitude for giving expression to its soul, to which those ornaments of every town and village, erected in such pious, such complacent, memory of the monster's first, and so far only, war, bear strident witness. But if one does not, it must surely be admitted as likely, that the public's best interest in the Highlands may for the present after all be better served by self-interest than by public-spiritedness.

For, on the other hand, consider that, although the process, by which the Highland chiefs have turned themselves into feudal landlords and made such money as was to be made, not only out of the land itself, but out of the eviction of their own loyal clansmen, is a sad and immoral one, yet, like many other depressing causes, it has had one excellent result : it has preserved the Highlands up to the present as nothing else could have done. I go further, many will think too far, when I suggest that it has also to a great extent created the Highlander. Before the depopulation it is doubtful, sentimentalising apart, whether Highlanders were any nobler than the general run of savages. It is now one of the few accepted generalisations which are also true, that every Highlander is ' a gentleman in the best sense of the word '. Now while some credit must be given to unimpaired racial vitality and a supreme environment, I account for this chiefly by drawing a connection between the facts, that (while there must be both) the rich on the whole are not only happier but better people than the poor, and that such few Highlanders as remain are all secure in healthy and sufficient employment. It is a case of ' the higher the fewer '. When labour on a large scale is needed, as it was, for instance, in connection with the aluminium-works at Kinlochleven, it has to be brought from Glasgow.

But I become conscious of giving offence. When mem-

46

bers of Parliament are pulled up by the Speaker for a personality or an irrelevant remark, they are generally willing (having made quite clear what they mean) to withdraw anything which is required of them. Let it be taken that in order to carry you with me to less disputable ground, I will act, if you command, in the same spirit ; and return to the immediate matter in hand, which was, I think, the question of landlords.

There is, as I have suggested, a good deal to be said for landlordism in principle, from the point of view of those who like the hills as they are. The logical conclusion of the opposite idea would be mountain-railways and huts where you could buy lemonade (*ausblick* advertised) in improbable and, one would have hoped, impossible places ; and the diminution of the area under deer might very well mean a corresponding increase of the area under orange-peel. There is also a personal side to the matter ; and whatever general views about the rights and wrongs of the case we may hold, there seems to me no reason on earth why, so long as the present economic system (or absence of system) is maintained generally, the owners of this particular form of capital, not in any case a very profitable form nowadays, should be not only regarded as the proper objects, but treated as the natural victims of public resentment, any more than the owners of shares in cigarette-factories or mines or joint-stock banks—which are in many ways just as iniquitous as deer-forests, if not more so, and do not atone for their moral deficiencies by any aesthetic advantages. Certainly I for one would endorse the existence of a great deal of wickedness in high places, or low either, in order to keep the sound of the bells of St. Clement's from penetrating to the moors of Scotland.

There are after all opportunities enough, or nearly

enough, for access to the Scottish hills, which do not in-
volve any harm or interference with the legal rights of
their owners. The old type of landlord with his dog-like
instincts is on the way to becoming an interesting survival,
and except in the shooting season (and for grouse-moors,
which matter less to the walker, the nesting season) there
are few places where you cannot obtain leave to go. In
the Rothiemurchus forest there are actually notices of the
politest kind giving the public leave to walk through it
except during the shooting; and I observe that even
camping in Glen Derry has lately been permitted. There
are also rights-of-way, which I am making no regular
attempt in this book to indicate specifically to the reader,
as I consider that if he expects any consideration beyond
his bare rights, which will not carry him very far, he
should always be willing to waive them in the interests of a
stalk, if he is asked to do so. I have more than once been
held up for an hour or two in this way. Perhaps however
this is the appropriate moment for a warning that much of
the ground covered in this book is not open to the public.
I have visited it either with permission, or without permission, but in the latter case only at such times and
places as I knew made the intrusion harmless. If there
are exceptions to this generalisation, I can honestly say
that they are few.

Be that as it may, it is thanks to the landlords that
Braemar has not by any means been spoilt by its popu-
larity. It has a few eye-sores of recent date : the war
memorial, a tin shop, and a streak of red tennis-courts
across the green floor of the Cluny, which is to blame for
the addition to the summer population of a suburban
element long kept at bay by the absence of opportunities
for standardised amusement. But it has not a single ' de-

sirable residence ', and despite its sudden accessibility since cars have become general, is vexed with a mechanical fever only for an hour or two of each summer afternoon. There is plenty of hospitality—I would not call it ' accommodation '—to be had in the cottages ; the two hotels are dear but good value for the money if you have it ; and the village is within range, but not easy range, of nearly every significant top in the northern half of the Grampians.

A good point at last to make up my mind to attempt some sort of a definition of my subject, and to enquire how far this book is going to take us. For ' the Grampians ' really cover a quite unspecified area. Are all the Highland hills south-east of Glen More Grampians ? Really I don't know ; but if so, this will have to be volume one of quite a large collection. The scattered and cross-connected ranges and groups which fill this area will not, try as you will, fit into any definite subsections. Geologically I believe they are considered to be the scarred remains of one continuous plateau, or, in more technical language, ' peneplain '. In the edge of that plateau we have at least something definite for the eye ; for the rim of the Highlands can be seen standing up like a wall right across Scotland, more particularly from the section of the lowland frontier-road between Stirling and Perth. The spine of the present range is harder to trace. It appears however to run north-east and south-west roughly parallel to the beginning of the lowland plain, broader and higher at the ends (the Cairngorms and the Lochnagar group at the one corresponding, very roughly, to the masses around Beinn Nevis and Glen Coe and that round the head of Glen Lyon at the other) and narrower and lower towards the central watershed at the pass of Drumochter. But on both

D

sides of this main chain (if such it be) there are outlying masses, ridges or single hills, more or less attached to it, and without more immediate family ties amongst themselves.

I believe therefore that the great castles of Argyle and Lochaber are a true part of the Grampian range, but the influence of the neighbouring Atlantic has certainly given to them a personality distinct from the rest. Nor could anyone miss the great sculptural differences not only in surface but in main features ; for this area and that of the Cairngorms, the two regions in all Scotland within which a general level of great height is most equally maintained, contrast vividly in that the one is broken up into many more individual peaks and the other characteristically presents long extensions of level summit. Of course there are exceptions in both cases. There is also a certain natural break in the continuity of the range, which is emphasised on the map by the line of the West Highland railway, running from Crianlarich on to the huge desert of the Moor of Rannoch, and past Loch Treig (where the break is most artificial) into Glen Spean. There is therefore much to be said in favour of leaving the west coast to take care of its own and treating only the part of the Highlands north-east of this line as the Grampians proper for the purposes of this book.

If it be thought that this is only to make virtue of necessity, which is partly true, let it be said at once, that, by this perhaps arbitrary limitation, which excludes, I admit, some of the best country, as well as what is actually the highest summit, in Scotland, we shall not deprive ourselves of a yet almost infinite variety of mountain-characters. Indeed the programme still errs on the ambitious side. It is true that the west has a more romantic appeal—

50

the very word sounds romantic—and it is perhaps a natural error to disparage the eastern Highlands by comparison. But in reality this will be found to be quite unjustified, and for the walker at least I for one am of the firm opinion that the best parts of all the Highlands are those upon which this book will touch. The western, or rather the anti-eastern, heresy is accepted all too commonly ; but I am sorry to find that it has spread beyond the vulgar to the author of *Return to Scotland*, whose picture of Queen Victoria comfortably settled in the Cairngorms is however a delicate sarcasm. I would not for the world brush the dust from its wings by any clumsy reference to facts which can be learnt in a moment from the map.

Having now discovered, or invented, a local habitation for the name, I have also just realised that if the process be to cover as much of the Grampians as possible, starting from the north (which now seems to me the best plan, as I have no principle of selection to diminish the field for me by the omission of inessentials), the Muse of true science has apparently inspired me, though all unconscious of her guiding hand, to start, as I did, with Beinn A'an and Lochnagar, which are the two final prongs of this end of the chain. So that if we now come to the main Cairngorm group, as my inclination had intended, we shall also be following the just order of events.

But it is without self-confidence that I approach the crowning glory of the eastern Highlands ; the more especially as to write of the Cairngorms challenges comparison with the ampler knowledge and experience of Seton Gordon, whose books about them are well-known, and in point of detail can add very little which will be useful for the walker to what is given in the Scottish

Mountaineering Club's official guide. I cannot hope to be as interesting as the one or as serviceable as the other, but only that the enthusiasm of an amateur may speak to amateurs with an equal and sympathetic voice. To be expert one should live amongst the hills at all times and seasons, which few of us are able to do, or perhaps in the end would care to, for the life of pleasure should have its alternations—town and country, the joys of health and dissipation, each depending on the other like the two buckets in a well. But very few are free to realise even the half, and I shall console myself with the thought that most of my readers, like myself, must be content with rare holiday visits to the hills, and may therefore forgive me if I walk with them as a mere companion and only here and there as an instructor.

I must then depend upon the Muse once more to come to my rescue ; or if she will not condescend below things unattempted yet, if Muichdhui and Braeriach are so much less worthy than Oreb and Sinai and th' Aonian mount, of one of her important appearances (which I strenuously deny) then, since some invocation I must have, let me descend from the sublime to the ridiculous, and at least make free with Thomson's

' O DODINGTON ! attend my rural song '

(But not, O Dodington ! Thomson's numerous but trite or inappropriate epithets !).

CHAPTER V

LAIRIG GHRU

THE British Islands contain no solid block of mountain-country to compare with the Cairngorms, not only in character but in extent. Although there is a single point which actually exceeds the highest of them by a hundred and ten feet, in average level this region surpasses any other of comparable size. The distances from the habittable valleys to the tops are also proportionately greater, so that the ascent of any single top is work for a day, and to accomplish anything really worth while requires a long day. The number of separate summits contained in an area, into which half the Lake District would fit, is comparatively small, but there is an infinite field for exploration of crag and corrie, and sustained adventures in the regions of wind and cloud, without recourse to the shelter of any glen, are possible. In a word, the composition is one of mass rather than of line.

Nor let it be thought that these hills which are approached from valleys already at a high level above the sea (in the case of Deeside more than a thousand feet), are for that reason no more impressive than hills a thousand feet lower rising directly from sea-level. Proportion is much ; but not all. The extra height of the whole may not affect the spatial relations of the glens and summits within the system, but it does alter their superficial character and

53

determine the characteristic animal and plant types. A phrase of music sounded in the treble and the same phrase in the bass have the same internal relation but the emotional qualities of the two may be quite different.

The most accurate idea of the arrangement of these hills can be obtained from the north-west. To this quarter they face squarely and from their base the wide forest of Rothiemurchus stretches to the Spey ; a forest in the old sense of the word, for it is the largest surviving fragment of the vast forests of a thousand years ago, since gradually destroyed—not more for timber than for the purpose of extirpating wolves. But the Cairngorms are after all only a major incident in the course of Strathspey, and send but tributaries, Feshie, Druie and Nethy into its great river. They are the very source of the converging streams which go to form the Dee upon the opposite side ; and upon this side they have a frontal screen of foothills worthy of their dignity, through which they can only be approached with a proper respect, or be seen from a distance but in partial glimpses. Their imperial glamour gains from these preliminaries, which also protect them from the profane proprietary glances of the casual tourist ' in search of Scotland '. Yet even if you have seen them only from the railway or main road through Aviemore, you may well doubt if the majesty of those blue fastnesses, which fill the sky southward, can stand in need of the least imaginative addition.

To understand the difference in the two aspects, we may imagine that the original block of granite out of which they were carved was tilted upwards a little at the north-western edge, so that the longer lines of drainage would be in the reverse direction. In fact very little of what may be called the internal drainage finds its way to the Spey, and even less must have done so in former times ; for it is recognised that the Eidart, which is the branch-head-stream of the present River Feshie on the Cairngorm side, at one time flowed into the Geldie and so to the Dee. It is true that the Avon, the largest single stream which flows out of the Cairngorms, does come eventually into the Spey by devious routes : but this also looks like an accident, if it is right to suppose that the Avon, instead of turning south at a right angle at Inchrory, used to flow straight on into the present river Don, which rises within less than a mile of the bend and continues the line taken by the course of the Avon up to that point. The cause of the divergence would be found in the existence of a band of softer lime-stone, running from Loch Bulig to Tomintoul, in which the Avon (helped by the waters of the Bulig, pressing southward at this point) has gradually worn for itself a new bed.

Apart from Beinn A'an and Beinn a Bourd, which really belong to them, but are outliers and lend themselves most naturally to treatment as a separate group, the Cairngorms fall into two parts on either side of the famous Lairig Ghru, each consisting of a main ridge of four thousand foot level and a number of subsidiary hills and ridges, each with one deep-hidden loch of some size, and each with at least one Lochan Uaine—the name is so much dissemi-nated as to be useless for particularising. At either edge these masses are carried on into the lower parts of the chain, which branches north-eastward from the main Grampian ridge, and of which they form the main bulk for a distance of some twenty miles. Through the Lairig from Braemar to Aviemore is over thirty.

This route will be a good introduction to the Cairn-gorms as a whole. To do justice to the occasion, it shall be a perfect cloudless day, too fine indeed, for by eleven o'clock the haze will be gathering to obscure the distances. But this shall not matter this time—there will be chances enough for looking at the view, and to better advantage, from the tops. From the low note of Dodington let me now leap the scale to the highest, and let Homer and Mr. Pope conjure for us the golden air which can be breathed on such a day amongst the Cairngorms, in which, I hope, such details as shall fill the picture up may be seen shimmering and with the eye of youth :—

> ' The Cloud-compelling God her Suit approv'd,
> And smil'd superior on his Best-belov'd.
> Then called his Coursers, and his Chariot took ;
> The stedfast Firmament beneath them shook :
> Rapt by th' Æthereal Steeds the Chariot roll'd ;
> Brass were their Hoofs, their curling Manes of Gold.
> Of Heav'ns undrossy Gold the God's Array
> Refulgent, flash'd intolerable Day.
> High on the Throne he shines : His Coursers fly,
> Between th' extended Earth and starry Sky.
> But when to *Ida's* topmost Height he came,
> (Fair Nurse of Fountains, and of Savage Game)
> Where o'er her pointed Summits proudly rais'd,
> His Fane breath'd Odours, and his Altar blaz'd ;
> There, from his radiant Car, the sacred Sire
> Of Gods and Men releas'd the Steeds of Fire :
> Blue ambient Mists th' immortal Steeds embrac'd ;
> High on the cloudy Point his Seat he plac'd.
> Thence his broad Eye the subject World surveys,
> The Town, the Tents, and navigable Seas.'

(Art should mourn polytheism as a lost mode. Critics complain that the classics say little of Nature. But the art appropriate to Nature is the art of animating inanimate

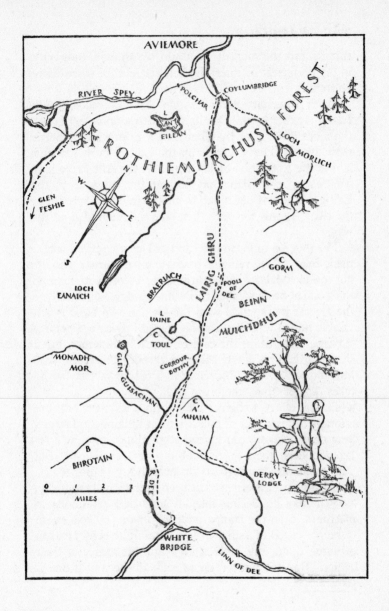

AVIEMORE

RIVER SPEY

POLCHAR

COYLUMBRIDGE

ROTHIEMURCHUS FOREST

L AN T EILEAN

LOCH MORLICH

GLEN FESHIE

N
W   E
S

LOCH EANAICH

BRAERIACH

LAIRIG GHRU

POOLS OF DEE

C GORM

BEINN

MUICHDHUI

L UAINE

C TOUL

CORROUR BOTHY

MONADH MOR

GLEN GUISACHAN

C A' MHAIM

B BHROTAIN

0   1   2   3
MILES

R. DEE

DERRY LODGE

WHITE BRIDGE

LINN OF DEE

things, and the ancient poets do so, though indirectly, in the perfectest manner, by their accounts of these divine episodes.)

From Braemar there are two ways of reaching the Lairig : either by the Dee itself, which sounds, but is not, the more direct ; or by Glen Derry, from which a better path turns at Derry Lodge up the Luibeg burn and cuts across the watershed of its tributary, the Allt Preas nam Meirleach, into Glen Dee, just at the entrance to the Lairig. There is not much to choose in distance between the two. Let us for once then take the main glen all the way.

The first six miles to the Linn of Dee are served with a made road, which remains passable for motorists who are not too particular for the three more before you come to the wooden bridge, called the White Bridge, which crosses the Dee at its junction with the Geldie. So far it is advisable not to walk if it can be helped. Even a bicycle is extremely useful, in the case of return to Braemar, but I should advise no one to take this through the Lairig with him for preference. Bicycling as a matter of fact hardly takes longer than motoring along this road, and the additional effort is slight. This form of exercise requires a totally different set of muscles from walking, and after a long day's walking can indeed seem almost more of a relaxation even than the immobility of a cushioned seat. The main disadvantage is the probability of punctures, unless my own experience has been exceptionally unlucky; as well may be, seeing that all sorts and conditions of machines, even the comparatively guileless bicycle, seem to be possessed of sufficient low cunning to sense, and to presume upon, my more than virgin innocence of their habits. But it is not too far to walk all the way if one is making straight for Aviemore, so for once let us assume that we do so.

We leave Braemar at an early hour of dews and silence, let us say seven o'clock, but suppose it is midsummer and the sun already in the glen : one of those mornings when the birch-and-pine smoke goes up from each cottage, in hardly wavering pillars upon which the light air seems to be supported, and what we breathe is like a fragment of the pure aether caught within its vault. Yet an anxious moment, for the crumbling of that invisible dome may mean a wind from the east and three remorseless days of rain and mist. This time at least—for to-day every promise is to be as surely fulfilled as it is born to be in the emotional paradises of Los Angeles—our anxiety shall be blown into the sea by a light breath coming into our faces from the west : the smile of Jove and the first seal of the day's good fortune.

The road first leads through birches, which open out on the right hand after half-a-mile, to show the purple side of Carn na Drochaide and the pool where the Dee is divided by an island of stones, by which the eye can judge the level of the water and decide whether or not the ford at the first milestone is passable. At two miles we come opposite the delta of the Quoich over which the eastern Cairngorms, Beinn a Bourd with its white horseshoe nearest at hand, come for the first time into view. A mile further on the road crosses the falls of Corriemulzie at the foot of the glen of that name. It is worth stopping to look at them if there is plenty of water at the moment, but not otherwise. Then down a steep hill past old Mar Lodge, where there are well-grown larches, to the ugly Victoria Bridge, a private bridge leading to the present house, by which, on the left, all that remains of the fir-tree used in old days as

59

a gallows for sheep-stealers and the like, now, very properly, itself hangs in chains ; then into a level clearing which contains the clachan of Inverey.

There is a better way to walk—it is not exactly a short cut—as far as Corriemulzie. This is, to go up the road in Braemar known as Chapel Brae, and across the very beautiful moor which forms a sort of wing on this side of Morrone. There are several paths of sorts across this moor. It is best *not* to take the first on the right at the top of the hill, but to go on higher than the farm of Tomintoul almost to the only cottage above it (the croft of Muickan, formerly the Downies'), where, at the fence, an old road leads off to the right, just below the steep side of Morrone. It cannot very well be missed, or lost once you are on it.

It is also well to know, that, with reasonable luck, quarters can be found at Inverey ; more particularly, try Miss Gruer of Thistle Cottage, who can at least always provide a most substantial tea. This halting-place will of course be of most use to those coming from the other side, but may also be considered as a means of shortening the journey to the Cairngorms by some five miles for those who are unprovided with any form of transport but their legs.

You can hardly be excused for not visiting the Linn of Dee, which is a mile beyond Inverey. This monument of erosion, with its sinister, slow whirlpools, is at all times and seasons worth seeing out of more than mere curiosity. At the right time of year you may happen also to see a salmon or two taking the falls above the bridge. It is however sad to record that in the last few years the Linn has become too easy a goal for the tripper, with the usual results. I wish you at least have the good luck to see it when it is not in its worst state of disorder.

Above the bridge the Dee flows in much diminished glory through a treeless and somewhat dreary glen, bordered by low hills, which would not lead the stranger to suspect the towering heights at their back, both north and south. Nor does the apparent head of the glen, which is not the path of the Dee but that of the Geldie (leading without even a perceptible watershed into the head of Glen Feshie and on to Speyside), present any summit upon which the eye will settle. But this low relief is but designed to add to the effectiveness of the immense height and bulk that is in store after the Dee's sharp turn at the White Bridge. Here we leave the road (to follow the Geldie for another mile) by a path leading fairly close to the left or eastern bank. There is another path marked as leaving the road a mile or two back, which I do not remember, but would not, I think, save any appreciable distance.

It is a few years since I went this way in this direction, and I cannot therefore describe this part of the route as I should like. It would however be impossible to forget how, a short way from the White Bridge, the Devil's Point, with the mass of Cairn Toul looming behind, shoots up ahead like a peak of steel—an inaccessible pyramid of black shining slabs. This frontal view of the most striking group in the whole Cairngorms, framed between the declivities of Beinn Bhrotain in the foreground and the gentler hillside upon the edge of which you stand, is the reward of taking the harder path by Glen Dee. As you go on, Cairn Toul opens out more and more, its summit and that of the Devil's Point that thousand feet apart which seems to be just the right distance to add, by means of a mutual contrast and interrelation of line, to the one yet greater height, and to the other depth.

61

You pass close to the Chest, or ' Kist ' of Dee, one of that kind of rock-bath—the Linn of Avon and some pools in the Eidart are others like it—which with me call up almost a Panic impulse to plunge in. It may be noticed by the way that these and other types of linns and falls are nearly always to be found just before the junction of the one river with another ; there is no doubt a simple geological explanation. Beinn Bhrotain, on the other side, is the first of the big Cairngorms upon our way. From this direction it appears merely huge and spreading ; its sternest side is turned northwards. It is redeemed from shapelessness by the little cone of Carn Cloch-mhuilinn (' the Millstone ') jutting from it to the south. The recesses and gullies which the intervening space contains have a more friendly and sympathetic air than the other Cairngorms anywhere seem to admit ; they are also full of good deer-pasture.

As you pass the corner of Beinn Bhrotain, where its real crags begin, you come, in about an hour and a half's walking, opposite Glen Guisachan, a rather gloomy valley lying in a rectangle of almost continuous precipice with a green flat marshy bottom through which the burn coils slowly. It is the deer-sanctuary of the Mar Forest, and therefore I have only once been inside it and that by mistake, but it is unpleasant to walk in and you will lose nothing by treating it with the same delicacy. The cliffs at the end of Glen Guisachan are those along the edge of Monadh Mor, the flattest hill in the Cairngorms, which forms a highway from Beinn Bhrotain part way to Cairn Toul. Behind it extends the upland moss which recedes as far as to the last ridge of the Cairngorms to the west ; but no part of this can of course be seen from the Lairig path. On the right hand side above you runs the path from Derry Lodge, which joins yours a mile or two farther on.

Just beyond the junction of the paths, on the other side of the Dee, is the stone bothy, called the Corrour, from Coire Odhar, by which it is overlooked. This stands beside the burn which comes down from the col between the Devil's Point and Cairn Toul, and marks the point where the easiest ascent of either should begin. Originally built in this strategic position for a watcher, amongst whose duties it was to preserve the approach to that most sacred mountain—the only one of the four highest tops which is wholly in Aberdeenshire and wholly in the Mar Forest—it has, after an interval of disuse, now strangely altered in character, and been converted to the very opposite purpose. For it is actually the property of the Cairngorm Club, and may be used as a shelter for the night by anyone who needs it, upon the moral condition of replenishing supplies of fuel for the next-comers to use. (There is plenty of bog-fir in the wet ground by the Dee, at least near the mouth of Glen Guisachan, and of course peat and heather.) I believe it is largely used, and has been made to accommodate twenty or thirty people at a time ; which is very likely seeing that the Lairig has become a regular thoroughfare, rather too much of a regular thoroughfare since the opening of Youth Hostels at Ballater and Aviemore. This applies of course only to the full summer season. It is therefore better if possible to go this way, especially if you wish to stay at this hut, either earlier or later in the year.

The channelled ridge on the right is Carn a' Mhaim, a spur of Beinn Muichdhui, which seems for some reason peculiarly liable to attract cloud-bursts. The watcher at the bothy was once nearly carried away by one ; and I was once caught on Carn a' Mhaim in a storm which amounted to something of the kind. But to-day such things be far from us. It is now midday ; Jove now sits on Ida and surveys, and the blue mists hide his golden horses somewhere south by Beinn a' Ghlo. Nearer at hand the flakes of mica sparkle out of the granite in path and burn ; the trout may be seen darting in the crystalline pools ; and perhaps high up in a grassy corrie a herd of deer may be feeding, or an eagle send the few grouse cowering across the heather.

At this point, close to the flat crumpled boulder called Clach nan Taillear—the translation is obvious—lunch may be tempting. But it is always well to go on pacing your appetite a little longer after it has caught you up, so let us go say that mile further to the burn which takes its name from the Tailor's Stone. Here we are immediately below the peak of Cairn Toul, which raises its barren stones, amongst which there is hardly a trace of any vegetation, in sombre tones against even the bluest sky. Probably even the relief of a lingering snow-field is absent, for snow in summer requires a better foothold than those steep sides offer.

We are now in the very middle of the Lairig (for the length of the pass proper is almost wholly upon this side of the watershed) and can easily judge of the reasons of its fame as the finest and the longest hill-pass in the British Isles. This must particularly strike anyone who has started with the impression that he is out for an easy stroll, and is not accustomed to the hills ; for although the steepest part is to come, this route has far more of the nature of a hill-climb than of a pass-walk, and must be treated quite as seriously as, say, the ascent of Beinn Muichdhui. For some of the way the walking is very

Alex. Beattie

IV.

LOCH AN EILEIN

rough by any standard, and for miles there is no shelter, so that in bad weather, and especially in winter, the journey may often be impossible. A good many travellers have at one time or another been caught and overwhelmed by storms on their way through the Lairig. Proper equipment for feet and body, as well as provisions, are therefore essential. Shorts and a thin shirt, without extra clothes in case of need, are quite definitely not the thing, any more than for any other expedition into the wild places of the Scottish hills, where the weather changes so rapidly and can be so unexpectedly severe. All of which remarks must seem already obvious to anyone who knows anything of the country, and are required only because the hills have lately been so much opened up to numbers of people who have no experience whatever of the conditions to be expected, or often even of the distances involved. I have come across strangers starting to walk through the Lairig who probably would not dream of undertaking more than a walk across the local golf-course at home, and no better prepared ; and had once to argue quite firmly, and perhaps impertinently, with an old lady and gentleman from the south of England, who were, at two o'clock in the afternoon, proceeding along the path from Derry Lodge at a quiet two and a half miles an hour, and that on a bad day, before they could be persuaded that they were extremely unlikely to get to Aviemore that night, if at all. Of course for anyone who knows what he is doing the Lairig presents no difficulty. But all will admit its grandeur.

Perhaps many will also interest themselves in the curiosity of its full name, Lairig Ghru, which apparently no one can interpret. Sometimes it is shown, but, it seems, without authority, as Lairig Ghruamach, which would mean 'Dreadful Pass '. But to me the word ' ghru '

E

conveys a sensation of terror more indefinitely definite. Seton Gordon mentions a theory held by a Rothiemurchus stalker, that the original form of the name was Lairig Cruidh, ' Pass of the Cattle ', to make a pair with the other name, Lairig an Laoigh, ' Pass of the Calves ' which belongs to the milder route on the other side of the Beinn Muichdhui group. As the cautious minister replied when asked if he thought he would ever be a bishop : ' It is pawssible, but not prawbable '. The student of textual criticism will perceive the unlikeliness of the corruption ; and prefer ' Ghru ' to ' Cruidh ', as the walker will prefer Ghru to Laoigh, and for the same reason—*quia difficilius*. In the end, it is appropriate that the name of this pass should remain thus wrapped in darkness, and a name of power.

In the distance of a little over a mile between Allt Clach nan Taillear and Allt a' Choire Mhoir, the great Garbh Coire, which lies between Cairn Toul and Braeriach, opens out to view. The word ' corrie ' has too much thrust upon it ; it has to do duty for anything from a grassy hollow or cutting in the hillside to this vast pot-hole, roughly a mile wide and nearly two miles in length, surrounded by its four thousand foot wall upon every side except the one through which issues one half of the Dee ; and has also to serve for the several great mouthfuls out of its rocky circumference, through which descend the tributary streams. The finest and most precipitous of these is Coire Bhrochain, immediately beneath the summit of Braeriach, which has for some time been in sight. But the next to it, further into the Garbh Coire, has the distinction of being in the direct lineal ascent of the Dee, which falls into it from the summit-plateau almost in one reckless dive of a thousand feet. This however is practically hidden from the Lairig by the projecting crags. The highest of the inner corries is that below Cairn Toul, in which one of the Lochan Uaines hangs precariously. It gives its name to the highest point visible on the edge of the cliffs between Braeriach and Cairn Toul.

The Dee has two sources, and perhaps there is no great river which has any that could make it so proud. They are quite different, and each a marvel of its kind, one springing from that high granite plateau of Braeriach at a height at which one would have thought enough rain could not have collected to form this already considerable torrent, which launches itself out into the world with a far more than infant energy and determination ; the other from a chain of pools, lying amongst the rocks at the head of the steepest and narrowest mountain-pass in Britain, which are connected only by some secret channels of their own, and, it is said, never freeze even in the most relentless winter. So blended, these waters of Dee by which we have passed, perfectly transparent as they are, though flashing superficially in the bright sun, seem to have their ideal counterpart in a perfect union of the divine courage and an infinite and imperturbable wisdom.

On past the Pools the Lairig path now leads us, but they are still some way ahead. The Allt a' Choire Mhoir is rather curiously named, because it comes straight down from very close to the summit of Beinn Muichdhui at a point where there is hardly a corrie at all, except a slight hollow in which the springs of the burn rise. At its junction with the Dee the path crosses and continues on the Braeriach side underneath the shallow Coire Ruadh, where the zigzags of a track which leads to the top of Braeriach can be made out. The ascent begins to be steeper as the glen narrows to vanishing point, and before the

Pools are reached the path as such has disappeared and it is necessary to pick one's way carefully amongst masses of loose rocks tumbled from the heights on either side, beneath which the water flows concealed for some distance. This rough going lasts for perhaps a mile and a half, right across the summit of the pass. The best way, where the path now buried in this debris used to run, can be traced by the marks of other people's nails on the stones and a helpful series of small cairns.

The summit of the pass is very little higher than the Pools of Dee. It will take about an hour to reach it from the Allt Clach nan Taillear, this being the most severe part, making perhaps four hours altogether from the White Bridge, allowing for halts. Here the Allt na Ciche, usually known as the March Burn—for just beyond it you step out of Aberdeen into Inverness—falls in a long cascade from the middle of the chain which connects Beinn Muichdhui with Cairn Gorm. It is matched by a burn which comes down from Sron na Lairige just across the boundary and on the other side of the glen. Below spreads far and wide the forest of Rothiemurchus, and beyond it, still some three and a half hours distant, flows the Spey. The Moray Firth shows on the horizon. But for two miles more the prospect is narrowed by the walls of the long spurs of Braeriach and Cairn Gorm on either side. They are Sron na Lairige and Creag an Leth-choin, that is, the Crag of the Lurcher or 'Half-dog'—someone's favourite, which was killed, one day long since gone by, upon its lowering cliff. The most impressive point is at about a mile below the watershed.

This northern reach of the Lairig is unlike the rest, for hitherto the actual sides of the pass, however steep, have never been precipitous. But the defile is short, for

68

through it, at the end of the very stony ground, the path drops rapidly. Below the last of the crags upon the right, it crosses a mile or two of soft peaty ground, threading its way through moraine-mounds, amongst which a large stream is quickly collected. The name of this is the Allt Dhru—surely the same word as Ghru, for phonetically *dh* and *gh* are almost interchangeable in Gaelic. It is not long before the first trees are reached, at a level to which we have not fallen since leaving the White Bridge, and thereafter we follow the course of the river, soon flowing in a deep channel far below us, for many miles.

There are many branching tracks leading here and there deviously through this fragrant and enchanted forest, in which, with leisure, one could idle long days away, but no directions as to these can be so useful as the map, and besides, the Cairngorm Club has set up a number of sign-posts at points of difficulty : except that a warning may be useful as to one detail—not to cross the first foot-bridge you come to (this leads into a green but deserted clearing in the forest, and apparently to nowhere else in particular) but to go on till you get to the Cairngorm Club's bridge, which bears a suitable inscription to identify it. This spans the Dhru shortly after it has been joined by the Beanaidh, the river which flows out of Loch Eanaich on the other side of Braeriach. From here there are two paths to Aviemore. One goes by Loch an Eilein and the Polchar ; the other soon leads you out of the virgin forest across a stretch of open moor and then past the first farms, in clearings which have not been abandoned, into Coylum-bridge. These outlying homesteads have a pleasant and friendly air of welcome, even on a fine evening, as behind them the sun falls lower, irradiating the now dim outlines of the great hills and the tops of the majestic trees ; still

69

more so the last time I came through the Lairig, for although it was full summer, conditions were very different from these.

For once, we had covered the full distance from Braemar, and it was after five o'clock before we reached the summit of the Lairig, as we had not made a very early start ; in fact the day was so unpromising that it was with hesitation that we started at all. Clouds hung on all the hills, and there was sometimes rain, so that we were rather wet before we got to the Pools of Dee. But no sooner had we crossed the watershed than we met the full force of a heavy storm. There was no thunder, but the rain came down in blinding and drenching torrents on our chests and faces, and continued without intermission all the way to Coylumbridge. It was so heavy that it seemed impossible that it should last more than a few minutes. But the waters of the Atlantic were spending themselves in a direct assault upon the rampart of the high Cairngorms. By the time we reached Aviemore we were chilled inwardly by the continual streams of water down our bodies, and quite exhausted by the very weight of it in our clothes. The things in our rucksacks were almost as wet as what we had on. Even my compass was filled with water, so that the needle was deranged and useless, and that though it is kept in my sporan, which is of stout leather and will generally keep the things inside it dry through the very worst of rain.

Coylumbridge is a pretty village, and its air is rich with the pines and the blue smoke of the pinewood burning. I should strongly advise you to find quarters there if you possibly can. There is certainly one private hotel nearby of a luxurious order, but I understand that cottages may also be prepared to give the tired and humble walker their simpler and more worthy entertainment. At Aviemore there are hotels, the cheapest, which is tolerable in its way, being the Temperance Hotel, the first you come to from Coylumbridge, but on the other side of the railway from the road. There is also of course the Youth Hostel. But Aviemore is a wretched place, with a splendid and yet appropriate name—which appears to represent the words *aghaidh mor*, meaning 'the great hill-face', referring of course to the wall of hills facing towards it. The village consists of a mere line of petrol-pumps and tin shops planted at the side of the Great North road, with a huge station where 'trains all night groan on the rail', the most effective of all sounds to dispel the self-sufficiency of health and strength which comes of having given yourself to the wilds and allowed yourself to forget the dismalities of organised society. You may not be so easily affected in this way, but there is another good practical reason for remaining at Coylumbridge which only supermen will despise ; and that is to be found in the extra two miles of road which must be covered to reach Aviemore, only to be retraced if you are returning to the Cairngorms.

CHAPTER VI

CAIRN GORM

FROM Strathspey there are two other passes to choose from for a return to Deeside. One is the Lairig Laoigh, the Calves' Pass, which leads most directly from Abernethy, farther down the Spey, but can be joined from Aviemore without any extra distance by a path continuing the road to Loch Morlich through the miniature pass of Rebhoan, which is at the very north of the last northward spur of Cairn Gorm. This is easier but somewhat longer than the Lairig Ghru, and much less interesting. The other is from the head of the glen of the Feshie, a river which joins the Spey about six miles higher up than Aviemore. There is a road most of the way up this glen, so that the distance is short if you can be driven the first part of the way, especially since from the foot of Glen Geldie on the other side there is also a road into Braemar—the same road by which we came from Braemar as far as the White Bridge.

Glen Feshie is fine enough in itself, and it has the unique, if dubious, distinction of containing an original work by Landseer, who used often to paint there. But except possibly for convenience the pass has not very much to recommend it ; it is almost flat and rather boggy, and gives no view. So easy is the passage of the hills at this place, that for some time, indeed ever since the time of

72

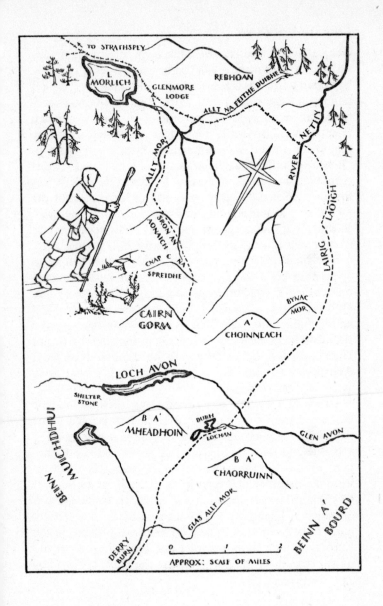

TO STRATHSPEY

L. MORLICH

GLENMORE LODGE

REBHOAN

ALLT NA FEITHE DUIBHE

RIVER NETHY

ALLT MOR

SRON AN AONAICH

CNAP C NA SPREIDHE

CAIRN GORM

A' CHOINNEACH

BYNAC MOR

LAIRIG LAOIGH

LOCH AVON

SHELTER STONE

BEINN MUICHDHUI

B A' MHEADHOIN

DUBH LOCHAN

GLEN AVON

B A' CHAORRUINN

GLAS ALLT MOR

DERRY BURN

BEINN A' BOURD

0   1   2

APPROX: SCALE OF MILES

General Wade himself, there has been talk of taking advantage of it to make a road right across. One can only hope that what two centuries have left undone will be left undone by the third; but since a million-pound racetrack has been made from Bridge of Orchy through Glencoe it is impossible not to fear the worst. It is true that there are no such immediate beauties as those of Glencoe to suffer, but the existence of a main road at this point would do much to destroy the remoteness of the remotest part of the Cairngorms, and to leave them at the mercy of the undeserving and unappreciative motorist. But of these routes enough has been said elsewhere, and from now on I shall keep rather to the hills themselves.

The range of the Cairngorms which comes nearest to civilisation upon the Inverness-shire side is the westernmost, which runs from Mullach Clach a' Bhlair to Sgoran Dubh alongside Glen Feshie, whence it can be approached without difficulty. To Braeriach, the way is along the Beanaidh and then up from Loch Eanaich by Coire Dhondail. But the easiest way to four thousand feet from Aviemore is to climb Cairn Gorm, especially if you drive as far as Loch Morlich.

I took this route a day or two later than the stormy passage of the Lairig mentioned in the last chapter. The day was not a good one for walking, though the morning was fine and still, for the air was heavy and the Cairngorms hidden in mist—we hoped a lifting mist; but we were disappointed. A road leads through the forest past Coylumbridge and on to Loch Morlich, at the farther end of which is Glenmore Lodge, at a distance of about six miles from Aviemore. The road follows the course of the Luineag, which flows out of Loch Morlich, joining the united streams of the Beanaidh and the Dhru at Coylum-

74

bridge. It passes two or three once celebrated wells, one at least of which has mineral properties.

Loch Morlich, which takes all the drainage of this side of the Cairn Gorm range, is a loch of fair size, roughly square in shape and of a breadth sufficient to place the whole view in just the right perspective—a view familiar to anyone who (as all should) has provided himself with the special one inch ordnance survey map of the Cairngorms, upon the outside cover of which it is represented. This picture gives a fair shorthand notion of the scene. Actually of course the whole extent of the Cairn Gorm ridge can be seen, from the summit to Creag an Lethchoin, with the corries enclosed between, but the picture has by no means exaggerated the effect of towering height which the Cairngorms possess when looked at from the north as from no other quarter, especially if a cap of snow places the accent correctly. It is also quite right to stress the yellow sands at the east end of the loch, which so catch the eye, calling up the most idyllic fancies, in reality. Indeed there is a charm, even something voluptuous, in the whole neighbourhood. Any place in it might easily be labelled 'another part of the wood', the scene for who knows what romantic episode—

> ' Love's gentleness and lies
> in the velvet forest '.

Fortunately this part of the wood now belongs to the Forestry Commissioners and should thus be properly preserved whatever happens to the rest : for it must be admitted that the landlords of deer-forests are not kind to their trees (which the deer prevent from seeding) so that the very word 'forest' no longer even suggests their presence to anyone familiar with the Highlands.

75

At Loch Morlich the real ascent begins. Just before the lodge the path turns to the right past the end of the loch. It twice crosses the main stream of the system, which here forms a salient, and then follows its right bank as far as the edge of the trees—that is, to a distance of about two miles from the lodge. Here it climbs on to the long shoulder called Sron an Aonaich and follows this to the top of Cairn Gorm. The track which leads straight on past the lodge is the one leading through the pass of Rebhoan into the Lairig Laoigh.

Once on the Sron, you are at a height of about a thousand feet above Loch Morlich, and although there are still two thousand more to climb, the stiffest part of the ascent is now behind. The water of the Allt Mor seems far below, running through the wood in a deeply-worn bed, like that of the Dhru descending from the Lairig. (The depth of these channels, which is not characteristic of granite, so far as I can judge, must be due to the greater depth of superficial deposits of soft material, consisting partly of decayed vegetation and partly of fragments washed down from the high tops, which has accumulated on the unusually broad strip of more or less level country between the foot of the hills and the bed of the Spey. To the conservation of these deposits the existence of the forest must also contribute.) On the Sron you may expect to be received by a breath of wind and a taste of the higher air. But on the day of which I am speaking we were less fortunate, and found the long climb very hot and tiresome. It is not an interesting one in any case. The long shoulder ascends in a series of steps, with intermediate levels or pockets which present very little variety. We found ourselves in mist at three thousand feet, but the way is clearly marked with cairns and cannot be lost. The regular slope of the hill would be sufficient guidance, and simply by going on climbing you must inevitably arrive at the top. The only possibility of mistake would be to go too far to the left and on to the point called Cnap Coire na Spreidhe, but this is hardly out of the way and would not mean losing any height. (Why this point is so named is rather puzzling, for so far as I know there is no Coire na Spreidhe, ' Cattle Corrie '.) However, it would not be possible to mistake it for the top of Cairn Gorm, because of the large cairn which marks the real summit.

On this side of Cairn Gorm a fair growth of vegetation, consisting of blaeberries and similar plants, reaches almost to the top and reminds one of the milder Perthshire hills, which, even when almost as high, are less stark of feature than most of the Cairngorms. This is the more surprising since it occurs on the most exposed face. Speaking from memory, I have the impression that the north side of Beinn a Bourd is another example of the same kind. One would naturally suppose that it has something to do with a difference in the composition of the soil ; but I was interested to come across the following passage, commenting on the same phenomenon in more general terms, in an essay upon the structure of the Highlands by the Glasgow geographer, Mr. Stevens :

' Contrasts of vegetation occur at many places in the Highlands without any explanation being obvious. In Glen Roy, for example, the south-east aspect is strikingly brown and forbidding in contrast with the green and apparently less favourable north-west ; and this is a contrast which is repeated frequently in the west-central Highlands, and emphasises the physiographic uniformity of the composition of the region '.

To this circumstance it may be that Cairn Gorm owes

its name; for the word *gorm* appears to mean, ' green '
rather than ' blue,' as it is often translated. In Gaelic,
however, as in other primitive languages, colour-terms lack
that precision which we expect from them in the speech of
peoples amongst whom the visual arts have been perfected.
They seem to denote general differences of light and shade
rather than varieties of tone and actual pigmentation—
what one might call the quantitative rather than the quali-
tative values of colour. (That colour has this quantitative
value, though it may not be so termed, and that the effects
of perspective can be assisted by the use of colour so understood, is claimed as a technical rediscovery of modern
painters, which can, it appears, be proved by physical
experiment.) The name of Cairn Gorm, enlarged into a
general designation of the surrounding hills, has usurped
an older title, which also describes them in terms of colour.
This was ' Monadh Ruadh ', ' the Red Hills '—in contra-
distinction to the ' Monadh Liath ' or ' the Grey Hills ' on
the opposite side of the Spey. The redness is primarily no
doubt that of the rosy-tinted granite which sometimes
shows in the bare gravelly slopes of the high tops ; but
I am inclined to think that here again the reference is
also to a certain clarity of lighting that often does distinguish the Cairngorms as compared with the neighbouring hills. The Monadh Liath, for example, have
no such naked edges of rock to catch and sharpen any
passing radiance.

The summit of Cairn Gorm aspires little more than the
other hills of the region to conical form ; but it is more
definite than that of Beinn Muichdhui. From that direction
it has the appearance of a flattened breast with a single
incrustation of rock, rising perceptibly but not self-
assertively from the great plateau which unites the two

mountains and forms the main eastern ridge of the Monadh Ruadh. Naturally it is the best point of all for the northerly view, which must extend for immense distances; unfortunately it is so long since I have seen it in good conditions that I can say nothing of it more than we can all equally imagine. In the other direction the broad masses of Beinn Muichdhui close the outlook. Between these two main summits, but rather farther to the east, is Beinn a' Mheadhoin, 'the Hill in the Middle', whose almost sheer sides, with those of Cairn Gorm, which are even steeper, enclose the deep-hidden waters of Loch Avon. To the east, beyond the lower Beinn Bynac, which is all but part of Cairn Gorm, Beinn a Bourd shows its least impressive side.

We reached here at a little after one o'clock, that is three hours and a quarter after leaving Aviemore, and near the cairn met two stout fellows on their way to spend the night at the Shelter Stone. There is always a certain strangeness about these meetings in a thick mist and we wished them well, without envying them. The night in fact turned out very wet, and they must have found it an unpleasant one. I have never slept at the Stone myself, so I cannot specify its exact degree of comfort. As free accommodation goes, it is probably just good enough in fine weather ; and undoubtedly a useful refuge in an emergency. It is the largest of the boulders which lie strewn near the west end of Loch Avon beneath a huge flat-topped mass of rock on the Muichdhui side which is called after it, and so is wonderfully placed for access to all the best places in the Cairngorms. Its position is worth noting in case you should ever care to chance its hospitality.

We had our lunch, like every one else who climbs Cairn Gorm, by the convenient and excellent spring called the

79

Marquis' Well (it is supposed after a certain sixteenth-century Marquis of Huntly). It lies quite close to the path, about a hundred feet below the top. Then we started the descent towards Loch Avon. This is the only part which needed real care in the mist, as there is only one way open through the crags on this side of the hill, between ' the Chimneys ', above the head of the Nethy, and Stac an Fharaidh, from which the precipices fall to Loch Avon. I must say the opening is several hundred yards across, but it is desirable to keep as near as possible to Stac an Fharaidh, a projecting fragment of rock which loomed through the mist as we approached, and then to drop first to the bealach called the Saddle between Cairn Gorm and A' Choinneach, and thence to the east end of Loch Avon, both very steep gradients. At the Saddle we came to the edge of the mist again and looked down upon the water almost immediately below. Loch Avon has a colour of its own, a deep greenish purple turning at the edge, where the sandy shallows appear through it, to a paler greeny-blue. To-day in the dim light, which gave it a deeper and more lifeless tone, it looked more than ever like the splash of ink in Stephens' advertisements. Above the mist the top of Beinn a' Mheadhoin just showed, taking from the bank of grey vapour which so nearly concealed it altogether a savage blackness and an almost awe-inspiring height. This effect is increased because at the Saddle you stand so near in horizontal distance ; for the two slopes on either side of Loch Avon are as steep and as close to each other as the opposite walls of the Lairig.

The Avon is a large stream. It is most easily crossed either at the point where it leaves the loch, or at the ford which serves the Lairig Laoigh path a mile farther down its course. It will not be out of place to warn you that at

V.   THE CARR BRIDGE

times when the water is high it may be unfordable, and this should be taken into account by anyone who wishes to cross the Cairngorms on this side. In this event the easiest route from Cairn Gorm to Braemar would be by way of Beinn Muichdhui : it need hardly be said that this is also the finest. On this occasion, we were able to cross at some point intermediate between the loch and the ford and made our way round the shoulder of Beinn a' Mhead-hoin to join the Lairig Laoigh path just beyond the Dubh Lochan. There is no good route for this part of the way and the going is very rough, as a mass of moraine material fills the glen below Loch Avon. At the Dubh Lochan it was so warm and still, though the sky was heavily over-clouded, that we thought of bathing ; but we decided against it, and went on our way to the head of the pass, from which the track drops into Glen Derry and joins the right-of-way up Coire Etchachan to Beinn Muichdhui. Here the southern march of Banffshire is crossed, and it is possible to boast that you have traversed the breadth of a county since the top of Cairn Gorm.

From the junction of the paths it is little more than an hour's walk down Glen Derry to Derry Lodge. We found that to this side of the hills the south-east wind was now bringing heavy rain, and when we reached the lodge at about half-past five, we were very wet ; and not without pity in our hearts for the inhabitants of a number of tents which we passed—nor without surprise either, for camping would never have been allowed in this perfect place until a year or two ago. Of this last part of the route I shall have more to say in another chapter since it is the main highway into the Cairngorms from the south side, not excepting even the Lairig.

Our day made only eight and a half hours in all, the last

part taken in very gentle stages, and would have been a very easy one had weather conditions been pleasanter. To walk on to Braemar would of course have taken another three hours ; or perhaps an hour and a half to Inverey. But even with this addition it can be seen that this way of crossing the Cairngorms is not an impossible day's walking. It takes hardly any longer to include Beinn Muichdhui, and in good weather this is infinitely to be preferred. But as this is the most accessible of the four highest tops from Braemar, let us now approach it, as it will normally be approached.

CHAPTER VII

THE BEINN MUICHDHUI GROUP

To reach Derry Lodge from Braemar, you must take the other road from the Linn of Dee, that is, start to follow the river downstream on the side away from the main road after crossing the bridge, and turn off to the left up Glen Lui. I should warn motorists that there is now a gate across the Glen Lui road. Make inquiries in Braemar as to how to obtain a key for this : by being too communicative I might perhaps defeat the good object of having the gate, which is to restrict the number of family parties who make their way disrespectfully to the foot of the Cairngorms merely to picnic. The walker from Braemar however will be better advised to cross the Dee and follow the by-road on the north side instead of the main road ; or even to go up Glen Quoich and cut across behind wooded Creag Bhalg, by the cleft of Clais Fhearnaig, of which we shall have more to say in a later chapter.

Glen Lui has greater attractions than Glen Dee. The lower part of it as far as the Black Bridge, where the road crosses the river, is wooded and heathery, and throughout this stretch the Lui runs in a series of pretty falls and linns, some of which make good bathing places ; all the better since there is a plantation between the road and the water. There is also a footpath close to the bank, starting just beyond the gate. Near the Black Bridge the Alpine cone of Derry Cairngorm, the most graceful of all the Monadh

Ruadh, shows temptingly ahead. Thence to the lodge, which stands out of sight at the back of a plantation, the glen is green and flat, with the ruins of former clachans visible. The road fords a burn called a' Mhadaidh Allaidh which might be translated ' the big bad wolf '—supposed the last of his kind in this part of Scotland. The rugged and shapely hill which heads the glen westwards is Carn a' Mhaim, bearing little resemblance from this direction to its other side, the ridge which borders the Lairig opposite Cairn Toul. At Derry Lodge, the top of Cairngorm of Derry can now no longer be seen, being obscured by the nearer point of Carn Crom which is its southward continuation.

The lodge is now hardly ever in use, but a little beyond it there is a stalker's cottage, the home of a succession of giants, well-known to all who have walked regularly through their hills. Amongst them was Sandy Mac-Donald, I think the finest man I ever saw, whose sharp-pointed beard and flashing eye (which got him the nickname of ' *An Brochdach*', or ' the Badger ') might be thought to go a trifle strangely with the tuneful voice and his courtesy as a friend. The main path into the Lairig Ghru leads past the cottage ; while Glen Derry, with its right of way to the Lairig Laoigh, forks to the right, due north, just at the back of the plantation. Both these paths take you to Beinn Muichdhui, and are the two main routes—one on either side of Derry Cairngorm, which is the central of the three main outposts of that huge mountain ; the others, to south and north, being Cairn a' Mhaim and Beinn a' Mheadhoin. The normal and easier route is by Glen Derry and Coire Etchachan, the way by the Luibeg being somewhat shorter and steeper, and also, I think, less interesting.

84

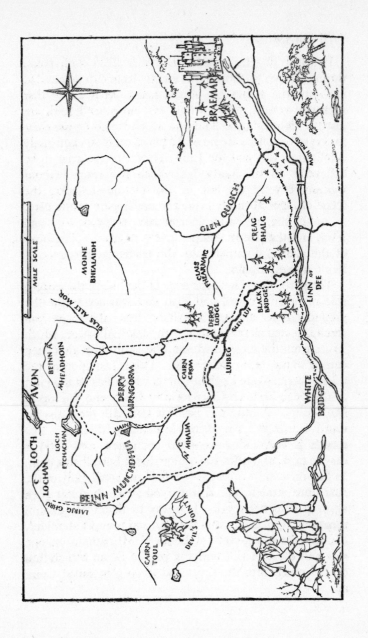

For just two miles Glen Derry is filled with trees, through which the burn flows swiftly from cup to jewelled cup—for the stones are almost gems—as if aware that such gay vessels, which would suit no other liquid, are just the right thing to hold one which would be too clear for crystal. There are no other burns quite so exquisitely coloured as this and the Lui. They must be seen to be believed. At the footbridge, which you reach without warning beyond the last of the moraine-hillocks, the scene changes abruptly : for the upper part of the glen, no doubt the bed of an ancient lake, is green, bare and level, and the stream comparatively stagnant. The head of the glen is dominated by the triangular precipice of Beinn a' Mheadhoin.

The path keeps along the edge of the hill on the eastern side for a mile or so, and then goes out across the flat ground. After an hour's walking from the lodge you reach the considerable burn of the Glas Allt Mor, which issues from the moss of Moine Bhealaidh through a deep cutting in the outline of the hill. This is just opposite the raised corrie, Coire Lochan Uaine, which lies on the joint of the ridge between Cairngorm of Derry and the top of Muichdhui. A little way past the Glas Allt the paths for Cairn Gorm and for Beinn Muichdhui diverge. The former is very indistinct—it is not much used—and is easy to miss, as it often looks more like a burn than a path. In fact the easiest course is to follow the small gully of the *next* burn straight uphill until you strike the clear path again at a higher level. The way to Beinn Muichdhui turns out to the left across the glen and round a shoulder, beneath the black cliffs of Beinn a' Mheadhoin on one side and those of this outlying part of Beinn Muichdhui on the other, into the short and steep glen called Coire

Etchachan. This is a severe hour's climb, or say an hour and a quarter from the Glas Allt Mor. At the top of the corrie you find yourself standing by Loch Etchachan, the highest real loch in Britain and I believe the highest water in which there are known to be trout. Now for the first time the whole superstructure, if not the actual top, of Beinn Muichdhui comes into sight on the left, the summit of Cairn Gorm across the gulf of Loch Avon to the right, and some parts of their connecting plateau. Hitherto you have not had so much as a glimpse of the real goal, but here, at over three thousand feet up, you find yourself all at once in that upland region of the high tops, which is a world sensibly distinct in character from all outside its borders—borders in this direction well defined.

I well remember one cold day in September when we reached the top of Coire Etchachan, a party of five, after struggling up its slope against a fierce wind, only to meet a storm of hail and icy rain, blown with such a double fury across the shelterless spaces around the loch as made further progress impossible, and forced us back the way we had come. Even in the best shelter we could find at the foot of the corrie our fingers were too chilled to hold a sandwich, and we preferred to come straight home without eating our lunch. It is true that even in the lower valley conditions were none of the mildest, but judging by them one could have had no conception of the quality of the storm in these exposed places where the high tops begin.

Towards Cairn Gorm, to the west of Beinn a' Mheadhoin, which is close at hand, there is a gap through which Loch Avon can be reached. The ground is level at first, so level that with very little inducement the waters of Loch Etchachan would flow that way, through the tarn

which is its lesser namesake, instead of into Glen Derry ;
and then there is a short and breakneck descent, once no
doubt an ' ice-fall '. After many years I well remember
being here on a wet and gloomy day, which seemed the
more so because we were camping in the heart of the
Cairngorms at the time. In mist we rose from our tent, in
mist climbed Beinn Muichdhui ; and late in the day
reached Loch Avon by this route. The crags of Loch
Avon are perhaps the most imposing in the whole Cairngorms. That evening, with the wet mist on the black
shining tops impending over us and a drizzle of rain below,
the effect was oppressive and overwhelming : and, with
the prospect of anything but good cheer in store at the end
of the day, we could almost feel the weight of the hills.

> ' Taciti, soli e senza compagnia
>   n'andavam, l'un dinanzi e l'altro dopo,
>   come fratri minor vanno per via.'

And indeed as we passed under Coire Domhain and Coire
Raibert by the north bank of the loch, its waters reflecting
the mournful sky with an added touch of melancholy, we
might quite well have fancied ourselves to have strayed in
Dante's footsteps into one of the deep pouches of the
circle in hell next above the bottomless pit, of which he
speaks in the lines just quoted.

Loch Avon with its precipices is gloomy even on a fine
day. But at Loch Etchachan the sunshine can be direct
and free as upon the very tops. For the immediate slopes,
though bare and stony, are gentle, except that the farther
or western side of the loch lies close against the flank of
that long northward-projecting buttress of Muichdhui
which comes to a full stop above Loch Avon in Cairn
Etchachan and the massive buttress known as Shelter

Stone Crag. Once or twice I have been here in such perfect conditions. The best day of all was one for whose supremacy my sister, who was with me, can also vouch : a day early in September, the first of a fine spell after a period of bad weather, so that the visibility was momentarily perfect also—even by the day following, this had altered much for the worse.

The path from Loch Etchachan to the top of Muichdhui is a gradual one and every step can be enjoyed. This part of the climb may take about an hour, more or less ; this time less, although we had part of our lunch half-way at the only burn which the path crosses. At the head of this burn is a small tarn ; you pass between this and the edge of a sheer cliff falling to Coire Sputain Dearg on the south side, and across this gulf you look towards the slope of Cairngorm of Derry and down to another Lochan Uaine, which, although the highest of all the Lochan Uaines is yet nearly a thousand feet below the rim of the precipice. I cannot remember whether it can actually be seen from this point as it can from farther along the corrie southward. Just beyond this corner is the frontier of the four thousand foot territory, and the acres of piled boulders which form the summit-plateau begin. Before the summit itself is reached you come to the remains of a bothy, now in ruins, but still at least useful as a shelter in a strong wind, which was for a summer the home of the surveyors who mapped the district. In all directions there are lines of cairns which converge on the top, and may be useful in mist ; for the rise is gradual and often interrupted, and the chief cairn is not easily found in such conditions, although it is large enough for a dozen. The bothy is a better landmark from this side, and the cairn is only three or four hundred yards beyond.

From Beinn Muichdhui, which it must be remembered is the second highest point in Scotland and was for long, in less scientific days, thought to be the highest of all, almost the whole of the Highlands can be seen ; for its central position adds to the advantage of height. ' It has not been proved ', Seton Gordon remarks, ' that the Coolin Hills of Skye can be seen from here '. This may be so, but upon this perfect day we certainly thought we saw them distinctly, as blue needles on the farthest western horizon. Of the more certain landmarks in the various directions we made out also Beinn Nevis, Tarbet Ness and the Sutherland Beinn More. Braeriach and Cairn Toul, just across the Lairig, are always impressive from Beinn Muichdhui : their sides look almost sheer ; and Cairn Toul at least creates the illusion of being loftier than Muichdhui itself. In fact I remember hearing from an Irish clergyman, a great old sportsman who later became better acquainted with the country, that when he first came to it and climbed Muichdhui, in their innocence (seeing Cairn Toul ahead and, it seemed, well above them) he and his companion made up their minds that they had somehow come to the top of the wrong hill ; and proceeded, gallantly enough, to descend into the Lairig and climb Cairn Toul as well—and by a very severe route too. He was so stiff afterwards, he said, that for a fortnight he could hardly bear to kneel down in church ! We smiled the smile of the superior fiend, because, as it happened, this conversation took place on the very day after we had done the tour of all the four big tops, a feat of which we were at the moment unduly vain. But we had not the heart to mention this to him at such a moment. (As a matter of fact, granted that he was probably not in any sort of training at the time, in point of effort he had done quite as much as we had ; so that except for not being so stiff, or anyhow not having to go to church, we had no reason to boast.)

To the top of Cairn Gorm is a walk of about an hour and a half. Though the connecting plateau is stony in parts, especially at the Beinn Muichdhui end, it is easy walking on the whole, and for sheer enjoyment and exhilaration cannot be excelled. The county boundary of Banff runs along it, the marching county for the first two miles being Aberdeen, and thence Inverness. A little before the point where the three meet is a little tarn called Lochan Buidhe or na Ciche, which is the highest in the British Isles, and just to the west of this the March Burn rises. All the burns on the east side flow to Loch Avon. As far as the Lochan and beyond it the plateau is over a mile broad, so that they have quite long courses before plunging over the crags. The Cairn Gorm portion of the ridge is much narrower. It falls away rapidly in the Loch Avon direction, but only the lower parts of the corries on this side are precipitous ; whereas the main northern corries, Coire an Lochain and Coire an t-Sneachda, drop straight from the summit to the edge of their tiny lochans, and they are so much the headier from above. The highest point between the two main summits of the range is Cairn Lochain, only seventeen feet less than the four thousand. This stands right over the cliffs of the corrie from which it takes its name. It is very little out of the way and should certainly be climbed if time allows.

Apart from the changing views in all directions which the plateau offers, the very substance of the ground is delightful to tread. It may be slightly more sheltered than the summit-plateaus of Braeriach and Beinn a Bourd, and perhaps for this reason bears a good growth of turf and mountain-grasses, varied with clusters of cushion-pink and many different kinds of Alpine moss. These grow for the most part round the springs or on patches from which the snow has lately cleared, and shine out against the neutral background with a strange insistence. No painter has used more striking colours than El Greco : and perhaps I can give some idea of the extraordinary vividness of these mosses, which seem to feed only upon light, by saying that they might have been the palette for the best of his flesh-tints, saffrons, sanguines and viridians. But his pictures, in which the individual quality of each tone has been so deliberately sharpened and pointed, would not by themselves convey the impression that the same tones in their own setting are also capable of natural harmonies.

But on the day of which I am now speaking, Margaret and I were not, as it happened, bound for Cairn Gorm. Our first thought after the climb was to look for a drink at the head of the Allt a' Choire Mhoir, which rises among banks of fine granite-sand just west of the notch in Muichdhui's summit. One of its pools in particular is my favourite drinking-place : a clean-cut bowl as big as a child's head into which the water wells from below, and which, at about 4150 ft., must be the highest spring in Scotland. But sometimes after a long spell of fine weather this is dried up, and you must go quite a long way down the burn to find water. Below us was a herd of perhaps a hundred deer ; but warned by scouts posted far off on Cairn Lochain they all moved out of sight. After lunch we recrossed the top and went down into the north-western corrie, the one to the west of Sron na Daimh. This I call the Snowy Corrie, for there is generally snow lying in it all the year round ; and so there was to-day, one large and several small patches, almost black with age and decay. Lower down the corrie there are also several small tarns. These seem naturally to drain to Loch Etchachan, but the Cairn Etchachan spur just catches the water and diverts it northward to Loch Avon. We went over this spur and down the declivity under Sron na Daimh to Loch Etchachan, where we bathed in the biggest burn (for even on such a day the loch seemed far too cold) and then slowly made our way home by the usual thoroughfare.

Two years later, a few days before the end of the same month, September, was another lovely day on Muichdhui. This time the morning was clear and frosty, with a light north-west wind. Yet the distant view, though good except to the north-east, was less perfect. We saw an eagle in the distance over Cairn Gorm and what we thought was a raven over Coire Sputain Dearg; but this may have been a mistake, as they are very rare in the Monadh Ruadh. As we came down Coire Etchachan, the Glas Allt Mor across the glen was framed in a magnificent double rainbow, close and perfectly clear, the sign of a heavy shower, which was the only one of the day, although the edge of the clouds had occasionally touched the high hills.

Winter seemed at hand by every sign. Once we heard an early stag roar out across the Moine Bhealaidh; and at the summit we came in for a slight sprinkling of snow. This lay all over Lochnagar and the southern hills from the previous day. But of old snow I have never seen so little; after a fine warm summer there was not a sign of it even in the Snowy Corrie. But the year seemed destined to make a sudden end. This did not seem to deter two men whom we met on the return journey. They were on their way to camp the night upon the top, I think under the impression that the bothy there could still give them

93

some shelter. I hardly believe they can have done so in the end, as at this height at night the cold must have been intense.

A normal time for the ascent of Beinn Muichdhui from Derry Lodge by the Loch Etchachan route is about three and a quarter hours. By the Luibeg it can be done in about a quarter of an hour less, but with more effort. This is not a right-of-way. It is distinctly the less interesting ascent, and I prefer it rather as a quick way down.

For this route, from Derry Lodge take the Lairig path, which is clearly marked and unmistakable, till, after two miles, beyond a flat piece of ground covered with deep heather, you come to a bridge across the Luibeg burn, which comes down from Beinn Muichdhui at a right angle. Here there is a mighty view framed in the narrow glen, where as far as to the very top (concealed from all the other neighbouring points which cannot rival it in height) or at least to the cornice of Coire Sputain Dearg, Beinn Muichdhui reveals its stature in a single sweep. The way up, along the sharp forward shoulder, is plain to see. There is a path (not marked on the map) which strikes off to the right up the glen a little way before you come to the bridge, leading to the foot of this shoulder, Sron Riach, which starts abruptly and is fairly steep all the way. The last part of the route, before the four-thousand-foot level is reached, follows the edge of the cliffs immediately above Lochan Uaine ; you then cross the upper part of Coire Clach nan Taillear, and so come directly to the summit.

It may also be found a pleasant change to descend by way of the Derry Coire Lochan Uaine. For this you should take the Loch Etchachan track only as far as the tarn, and then follow the edge of Coire Sputain Dearg north-east until it becomes possible to strike at right angles south-west, that is towards the top of Cairngorm of Derry. This line brings you nearly across the unnamed peak (3629 ft.) which I have christened ' the Aitionnach Cairn ', after Loch Etchachan (a name supposed to be a corruption of the word *aiteal* or *aitionn*, meaning ' juniper '). Take care not to go down the first dip on the left past the Aitionnach Cairn, which would bring you to the foot of Coire Etchachan : you must traverse this and cross a slight intervening rise. This brings you to the edge of Coire Lochan Uaine ; there is a steep but quite practicable staircase down, on the right bank of the burn which falls into the lochan.

Coire Lochan Uaine seems always to be full of deer. Hinds and fawns were bleating at each other there when last I came down it one early July day, and I nearly stepped on one late fawn as I jumped off a rock into the heather. It is the perfect type of what is meant by a corrie, to which all others which pass under that name are approximations. This was realised by another before me, the famous poet, Uilleam Ruidhe-noamh, who was, however, more of a poacher by profession, and a redoubtable one. He built a bothy in the corrie, where he lived for a long time, and wrote its praises in a well-known Gaelic song. Jock Stewart and I were unaware of following in his distinguished footsteps, when we chose it as a discreet and convenient place to camp in a good many years ago : during which, if I have declined in manly virtue, I think I can claim to have grown in wisdom—for I would never do it again. We found it a great task to carry up the supplies and accoutrements necessary, and then for five days the corrie was never free from a soaking mist, so that only shame kept us from returning home incontinently. To hear the deer and the ptarmigan moving in their hundreds around us at early dawn was not enough to console us for the discomforts of the situation, and on the sixth day we had determined upon an honourable retreat. The morning was bright and fair at last ; for the first time we saw the creamy waterfall descend into the lochan, and the blue sky encircled by the green lip of the corrie ; and then, to crown all, an eagle sailed over in the painted air. We were not seduced to remain ; but before we went home, having packed up and built a small cairn of remembrance, we went up Beinn a' Mheadhoin, upon a day of bright sunshine that might have come from a newly created world.

You could also return from Muichdhui by way of Cairngorm of Derry, which is immediately over the southern corner of Coire Lochan Uaine, and, though it is rough for the most part, can be descended without meeting crags in any direction. But of this hill, as well as of Beinn a' Mheadhoin and Carn a' Mhaim, I shall tell you more by describing a rather interesting tour of them which I made with Patrick Monkhouse one day in July some years ago.

We left Derry Lodge at twenty past ten on a fine morning and reached the Banffshire march on the Lairig Laoigh path a little before midday for the ascent of Beinn a' Mheadhoin. There is no recognised route up this hill, which is steep on all sides (least so to the north-west), but this is the most direct and obvious way from Braemar, and is one which I have taken on many occasions, because of all the steep climbs I know it is the pleasantest, especially on a hot day. For the best route to the more gentle slopes of the upper part of the hill is by the tumbling burn which falls down to the top of the pass, and then flows, more or less by accident, to the Banffshire side, and for part of the

96

VI.   LOCH AVON AND BEINN MUICHDHUI

way the easiest thing is to scramble up the very bed of the
burn with the water splashing over one in a light cool
spray. It is called Allt an t-Seallaidh, 'Prospect Burn ',
because of the open view in both directions which it
commands. At rather over 3250 ft. it ends in a broad
grassy hollow between the two southern tops of the hill.
Beyond the point on the left the precipices visible from
Glen Derry fall suddenly, while north of that on the
right there is a mile of undulating plateau, which ends at
the actual summit (3883 ft.). This hollow makes a sheltered upland pasture which is a favourite haunt of deer in
fine weather, and since by climbing the burn you land
upon it without warning, granted a north-west wind there
is a good chance of surprising a fine herd here at very close
quarters.

There is nowhere from which a more comprehensive
view of the whole structure of the Cairn Gorm-Muichdhui
range can be obtained than Beinn a' Mheadhoin, which,
as has previously been noticed, means ' the Hill in the
Middle '. The spelling of the name which I have used
(this or ' Mheadhon ') is the only one which I have anywhere seen in print, and according to the ordinary rules of
Gaelic phonetics this should be pronounced ' a' Vane '.
But it should be mentioned that I have always heard the
hill referred to as if it were ' Ben-a-Mane '.

In cases where a phonetic spelling is current and
accepted in ordinary usage, my rule has been to adopt it,
even if it is incorrect from the point of view of the meaning
in Gaelic ; for instance in the case of Beinn a' Bourd—
which should really be ' Beinn a' Bhuird ', but if so spelt
would have to be pronounced as if it began with a V ;
Bulig, which is more correctly ' Builg ' or ' Bhuilg ' (being of the same root *bolg*, meaning ' bag ' or ' pocket ',

G

which occurs in all Aryan languages) ; and many more. Such names as Cairn Gorm, Cairn Toul, Braeriach and Beinn Muichdhui, are of course thoroughly Anglicised, and are so well known in those forms that it would really be pedantic to resort to a Gaelic spelling, especially since in their current forms they represent the Gaelic with fair accuracy.

There is another variant of ' Muichdhui ' in common use, which is ' Macdhui ' ; the first meaning ' the Hill of the Black Sow ' and the second ' the Hill of Macduff '. The second is obviously incorrect, if it be taken to refer to the present family of Duff, who have become owners of the Mar Forest only in recent times ; but it is more plausible in the light of records which prove the existence of a former laird of the name in these parts, though whether his domains extended so far as to include the mountain I am not certain. The first spelling, which I have used, however, upon several grounds seems to me distinctly to be preferred. In the first place, it is more in keeping with the generally descriptive nature of names in this part of the country ; although I should hesitate to be dogmatic as to which aspect has been supposed to resemble a black sow : possibly the broad swelling back of it as seen from across the Lairig to the west—there is a conspicuous mountain in Donegal called Muckish which from one quarter presents a somewhat similar appearance. Again, something beginning with ' mac ' is such a likely corruption of a Highland name in English that it would indeed have been almost too much to expect that such a name as Muichdhui could have escaped relapsing into that form ; whereas it is just as hard to see how ' Macdhui ' could ever have burgeoned into the stranger one I have adopted. English tourists are not only less inclined to see fanciful resemblances to black sows than the natives, but wholly ignorant of the Gaelic to describe them. In fact it would have required an elaborate and quite motiveless fraud to impose the name Muichdhui upon an unsuspecting public, if it were not the right one.

Beinn a' Mheadhoin, then, has borne the brunt of this discussion because it is the best-placed of all the Cairngorms to choose for meditation upon the rest. Its summit also offers a fine though restricted view northward, to the west of Cairn Gorm, down Strath Nethy and across Beinn Bynac, where the coastline can be seen as far as the Dornoch Firth; and a breathless drop into the inky waters of Loch Avon fifteen hundred feet below. The plateau is fairly smooth, but there are one or two enormous hanging boulders which are a peculiar feature of the hill, and it would be worth while to climb it in order to look at them if for no other reason. The largest of all, a square block as big as a cottage, stands on the very summit. I was once nearly blown off the flat top of it by a violent south-west wind; but to-day we sat there very pleasantly for some minutes, the rest being all the more welcome as we cannot have taken much over half an hour to climb from the foot of Allt an t-Seallaidh. I do not know whether these stacks of granite, clearly normal glacial deposits, though remarkable for size and position, are of the same type geologically as the outcrops on Beinn A'an, which are quite different in general appearance and give the impression of having been forced through the surface-material from below. It might be interesting to compare both groups systematically with that on Beinn Bynac, known as the Barns of Bynac, which I have not inspected. I have also a doubtful recollection of a smaller such outcrop upon Beinn a' Chaoruinn.

At a quarter to one o'clock we went down at an angle across the very stony slopes and screes of the western face to Loch Etchachan, seeing an eagle upon the way. He flew out from the great crags of Coire Etchachan, passed close above our heads, and disappeared round the Loch Avon shoulder of Beinn a' Mheadhoin. From Loch Etchachan we went on to Cairngorm of Derry, which we reached at five minutes past two, having lunched on the way at the headsprings of the Caochan Cothaiche, just under the Aitionnach Cairn, looking into the edge of the Sputain Dearg precipices. Of these, and into the Muich-dhui Lochan Uaine, there is a direct view from Derry Cairngorm. This hill is a huge natural cairn, and the ground upon every side is some of the stoniest to be found anywhere, so that the going is not of the best. We then retraced our steps part of the way and made for Beinn Muichdhui.

Muichdhui to-day appeared to be the scene of unusual human activity, for we met several parties of people upon their way down, and found out from one of them what the reason was : the Cairngorm Club was erecting the indi-cator which now stands at the top ; and, sure enough, there we found them in force, with men, with women, with ponies and paraphernalia, almost with massed bands —a surprising sight after a day spent in the usual empti-ness of the hills. Now I believe that a certain degree of unsociability in these conditions is as familiar to those who think it their duty to love mankind at large as to myself ; but apart from this altogether, I had at that time a some-what unreasonable objection to the existence of such things as indicators, which I looked on as a sort of dese-cration ; for the unformed *eros* normally insists upon some notion of sanctity in its object. It may therefore be imagined that we responded without cordiality when we were received as belated admirers of the deed of darkness which had just been performed. We explained that we merely happened to be passing that way, which was the case, and in order to keep up the right casual appearance proceeded, after only a few minutes' delay and without sitting down upon the top of Beinn Muichdhui, in the direction of Carn a' Mhaim. It must be admitted that this eagerness was partly the result of our having observed the signs of a gathering storm; for the air was now darkened by a thick haze which disappointed us of any view and was no doubt a symptom of the divine displeasure.

We left the top at half-past three, going at first south-east as if making for the Sron Riach descent but turning instead down the ridge on the east side of Coire Clach nan Taillear, where there is a long and very stony descent which brought us in forty minutes to the col between Beinn Muichdhui and Carn a' Mhaim at a level of only 2650 ft., the lowest we had touched since climbing Beinn a' Mheadhoin. An edge nearly two miles in length, the narrowest I think in all the Monadh Ruadh, on both sides steep but nowhere precipitous, leads to the top of Carn a' Mhaim (3329 ft.). For some time thunder had been heard and was now alarmingly close, and not wishing to be caught right in the centre of the storm upon the top, we made haste to leave it, choosing for the purpose a grassy hollow facing north-east towards the foot of Sron Riach. A more direct and probably an easier route would have been south-east by the edge of Coire na Poit right to the bridge on the main path. However we made up for this by speedy going once we joined the Luibeg path, covering the distance to the Derry in forty minutes, which made only an hour and a quarter from the top of Carn a' Mhaim.

By this time we were fairly drenched and were yet worse off before we had bicycled home, not without mechanical misadventures.

The storm rumbled on all evening, till just before sunset the sky cleared and a tall flaunting rainbow arched the glen of the Dee from Carn na Drochaide to Morrone. We spent the last hour of twilight at ducks and drakes in one of the still pools, turning at intervals to catch the faint piercing incense distilled out of the birches as they dried after the rain.

CHAPTER VIII

BRAERIACH AND CAIRN TOUL

THE Cairn Gorm-Muichdhui plateau is perhaps more varied, but to Braeriach and Cairn Toul across the Lairig belongs what is probably the most tremendous single feature. In both cases, as in the Cairngorms generally, the north-eastern faces of the hills, being those upon which it may be presumed that the glaciers held out longest, are the most indented with grand and precipitous corries; but whereas in the eastern group these are separated from the area of highest level by the general slope, and the sheer drop is proportionately less, the gigantic cliffs of Braeriach and Cairn Toul fall directly from their summits. To compare with them we may no doubt cite Lochnagar and Beinn a Bourd as examples, but the considerable difference in the summit-levels must be borne in mind; for Braeriach (4248 ft.) is only forty-eight feet lower than Beinn Muichdhui, and Cairn Toul falls short of it again by no more than seven feet. This is roughly four hundred feet higher than the average for Lochnagar and Beinn a Bourd.

The western half of the Cairngorms is also the most extensive continuous plateau. Between its boundaries, east the Braeriach-Cairn Toul ridge, as continued southward by Monadh Mor and Beinn Bhrotain, and west the more regular line of hills at something over three thousand foot level which runs from Sgoran Dubh to Mullach Clach a' Bhlair, this plateau consists of a shallow depression centring at Lochan nan Cnapan (about 2850 ft.) and covers an area of some forty square miles. On the whole it is most accessible from Speyside, especially from Glen Feshie, which lies immediately beneath the western ridge. To this ridge it is a very long day's expedition from Deeside, but on the other hand the Beinn Bhrotain group makes a comparatively short day from this direction : while Braeriach and Cairn Toul, taken jointly, are more or less equidistant from either valley. This country, except the rocky fringes, is not however suitable for exploration except in fine dry weather, as it consists in the main of large expanses of peat-hags and moss which much rain makes very difficult, though there is no bog of such an extreme type as not to become good firm ground in the right conditions.

This tract of upland bears the name of Moine Mor, the Great Moss. To its edge two deep glens, Glen Guisachan and Glen Eanaich, penetrate through the bulwarks of the high rocky hills from east and north. From the latter, past the bothy which stands just short of the loch, leads a track which forms the most direct route to the plateau from the north, climbing steeply on to it through the crags of Coire Dhondail ; to Glen Guisachan we have already been introduced. But most of the water which falls in this catchment flows southward, down the less sharply defined glen of the Eidart, into the Feshie, which itself rises not in the Cairngorms but on the edge of Athole forest to the south.

From the Lairig the great outer ridge of the plateau is accessible at few points. The northernmost is by Coire Ruadh (also known as Coire na Lairige and not to be

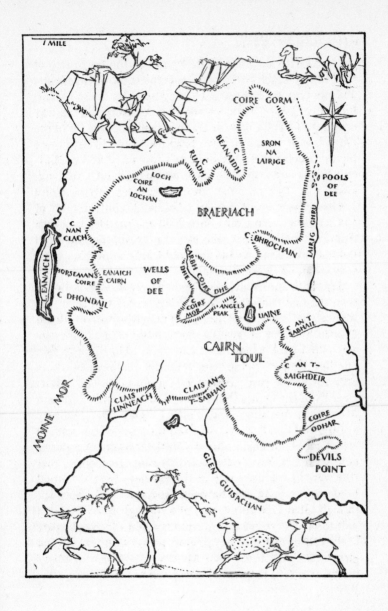

1 MILE

COIRE GORM

C BEANAIDH

C RUADH

SRON NA LAIRIGE

POOLS OF DEE

LOCH COIRE AN LOCHAN

BRAERIACH

LAIRIG GHRU

C NAN CLACH

C BHROCHAIN

HORSEMAN'S COIRE

EANAICH CAIRN

WELLS OF DEE

GARBH COIRE DHÉ

C DHONDAIL

COIRE MOR

ANGEL'S PEAK

L UAINE

C AN T SABHAIL

CAIRN TOUL

C AN T- SAIGHDEIR

L. EANAICH

MOINE MOR

CLAIS LINNEACH

CLAIS AN T-SABHAIL

COIRE ODHAR

DEVILS POINT

GLEN GUISACHAN

confused with a greater Coire Ruadh on the north face of the hill), by which an old path leads to the top of Braeriach ; and the only other reasonable way up is by Coire Odhar, for Cairn Toul. Between the two summits, all the way round the Garbh Coire (or Pit an Deamhain, ' the Pit of the Devil ', as it is said to have been called in old days more picturesquely) there are only two just feasible, but difficult routes : the east face of the actual peak of Cairn Toul, along the edge of either of the flanking corries, Coire Lochan Uaine and Coire an t-Sabhail ; and the bluff of Braeriach between Coire Bhrochain and the Dee as it falls from the Wells. Braeriach can also be approached from the north by Sron na Lairige, and Cairn Toul from Glen Guisachan or Beinn Bhrotain.

The path into the Lairig from Derry Lodge is better than the one from the White Bridge. For two miles the way is the same as to the Sron Riach ascent of Beinn Muichdhui, but it crosses the Luibeg and climbs the watershed by Lochan Feith nan Sgor. On the way that one fine view of Beinn Muichdhui is obtained, but lasts only for a few yards before it is again concealed. It is clear from the names Preas nam Meirleach and Clais nam Meirleach, meaning ' the Thicket ' and ' the Hollow ' ' of the Robbers ', as well as from the story of the solitary tree, Craobh an Oir, under which the treasure of a pot of gold was once hastily concealed by some freebooter, that this was the regular route in the old days for the mutual predatory expeditions between Speyside and Deeside : though Glen Dee also is part of a through route by Glen Tilt to places farther south, and no doubt the greater part of the cattle went that way in more peaceful times. So the glen of the Allt Preas nam Meirleach is a glen of many forays, which in the animal world, here as elsewhere, con-

106

tinue to this day. Last time I came through it, just above Craobh an Oir, a young eagle was being mobbed and hustled miserably, low above the heather, by a hawk not a tenth of its own size, until it was allowed to make off discomfited round the flank of Cairn Crom. This happened not far from the very rocks which by a strange coincidence are called ' the Hawk's Crags ', so the name is still, apparently, an appropriate one. By this way it takes about an hour and a half to reach the Corrour bothy, from which either to climb Cairn Toul directly or to go on up the Lairig to climb Braeriach at Coire Ruadh.

To the top of this corrie is a climb of about a thousand feet from the Dee. You then stand upon a neck, the narrowest part of the ridge, on the other side of which are the crags of Coire Beanaidh, in the north face, while on the one hand the ground rises to Sron na Lairige and on the other to Braeriach, the top of which is another five hundred feet above. It can be reached in an average time of four and a half hours from the Derry—about an hour and a quarter from the crossing of the Dee at the Allt a' Choire Mhoir.

This last part of the ascent of Braeriach is straightforward enough in good weather but requires very great care in mist, owing to the peculiar conformation of the hill. The ridge is attenuated and on the southern side curiously scalloped : the fairly steep gradient from the north stops without finding level and breaks away into the abyss of Coire Bhrochain, so that it would be by no means difficult to walk over its edge, and this is the more dangerous because there are one or two promontories jutting from the cliff-face which may be mistaken for the line of the summit ; but if there is any wind it is always possible to recognise the presence of such crags by sound (and the warning is often a useful one). On the other hand, coming from Coire Ruadh, you must be careful not to allow yourself to start going downhill at any stage : if you do this it means either that you have surmounted the ridge just as the crags begin to thrust out from it, to the east of Coire Bhrochain, and are dropping towards the Garbh Coire, or else that you have turned right-handed across its slope and are making for the edge of the northern corries. The route is about south-west at first and then due west to the first of the two cairns which mark the top ; the second is a few yards south-east again. They both stand on the very edge of the precipice, and neither is very large.

I once went up Braeriach in a very thick mist. We reached the top safely enough, although once we were rather alarmed to discover that we had walked on to one of the slight projections in the cliff instead of along its edge (and had of course to come back). But we decided not to go on to Cairn Toul as we had intended. On the way down, at a certain point, we had a long and truly a serious argument as to whether we should go to the right or to the left ! I cannot remember the precise circumstances but the confusion must have been caused by the fact that the wind, though really from the north-east, had been swirling up the gullies of Coire Bhrochain from the south and we had got used to it coming from that quarter. Fortunately the opinion which led us to face into it, that is to the left, prevailed ; but we were not both equally confident that each step we took might not be our last—for a turn in the wrong direction would have taken us straight over the cliffs—until we found ourselves safely back at Coire Ruadh.

It is well worth while to go out of your way in the ascent of Braeriach on to Sron na Lairige (3839 ft.), or to climb it directly just above the Pools of Dee, as Bernard Cook and I did one perfect early September day. For one thing, during the ascent the eye commands the northern defile of the Lairig looking across to the Lurcher's Crag close at hand, with the March Burn dancing very prettily down the opposite hillside. But more especially I am thinking of the magnificent view westward to the black knob of rock beyond Loch Eanaich, which is Sgoran Dubh, raking the northern corries of Braeriach *en enfilade*. The nearest at hand of these are the twin corries, Coire Beanaidh and the other Coire Ruadh, and beyond them the more lofty Coire an Lochain (not to be confused with the corrie of the same name beyond the Lurcher's Crag). The loch which lies in it is just out of sight. All these are rock-bound corries of a similar type to those north of the Cairn Gorm ridge, running far back between long separating spurs of jagged cliff.

Coire Bhrochain on the other hand is of a shallower semicircular kind, and merges at the sides into the steep slopes of the hill. It means ' the Corrie of the Porridge '; I have no doubt because it can be imagined to be something of the shape of a porridge-pot, and also because the mist often hangs there when it has cleared off the hills, steaming slowly out of it up the chimneys in the cliff-face and away over the lip of Braeriach, into thin air. There are other but less acceptable explanations, one depending upon a story that some cattle which were being herded through the Lairig somehow managed to escape their drovers and, wandering up to the top of Braeriach, plunged over into the corrie, where they were crushed by the headlong fall into the semblance of porridge; another upon a yet more absurd legend which I have for the moment forgotten as it deserves.

On Braeriach we joined my sister, who had made the direct ascent, and all went on for lunch at the Wells of Dee. We had started early and were in no hurry to leave this lovely place and its refreshing waters. A powerful west wind battered our heads and spun the Dee over the edge of the precipice in clouds of spray. It quickened even the natural champagne-quality of the air, which, perhaps because it was the first day we had been in the hills that year, had quite astonishing effects. For we spent an hour and a half there laughing and talking irresponsibly, and anyone who had chanced to come along might well have imagined that we had chosen this dangerously unsuitable place to hold a cocktail party. I had noticed the same pleasant but silly effect in Switzerland on first going out, but never before in Scotland in anything like the same degree.

The last of the Wells of Dee to the south is just under the point called the Eanaich Cairn, from which you can look down to Loch Eanaich and across it into the crags and screes of the Sgoran Dubh ridge, with their screen of flying-buttresses and fallen boulders. Between Braeriach and the Cairn is the broadest section of the ridge, the only part which amounts to anything that can be described as a plateau. Elsewhere, all the way to Cairn Toul and on to the Devil's Point, the ground falls rapidly away from the edge of the corries of Pit an Deamhain, which accounts for the somewhat curious fact that the Dee is the only stream which flows over the precipice : thus maintaining its royal distinction. Over the higher ground south of the Eanaich Cairn, and another small rise, the walking is fairly rough, but not barbarous, and soon brings you to the col at the head of Clais Linneach, from which perhaps the finest view of the corrie immediately below, the Garbh

Coire Mor, properly so called, and of the Garbh Coire Dhé, is to be obtained. The wall of Sgor an Lochain Uaine stretches outwards immediately above you. From here to the top of Cairn Toul is what must be the roughest stretch of high ground to be found in Britain, for every foot of the way must be picked across masses of loose boulders of considerable size. They can only be covered by stepping or jumping from one to the other, hardly once touching the not more solid but more stable earth, so that without some agility only very slow progress is possible.

Sgor an Lochain Uaine which rises to a height very nearly equal to that of Braeriach and Cairn Toul (4200 ft.), takes its name from the lochan which hangs in such an adventurous position in the corrie between it and the latter. It is a fine point, precipitous on both sides, yet it can be climbed en route for Cairn Toul with very little additional trouble, although the most natural course is to round it at a convenient level. It is also called the Angel's Peak, a name given to it with the excellent intention of ' keeping the Devil in his place ' on the other side of Cairn Toul, which has ' stuck ' perhaps because in shape it does look rather like the shoulder of an angel's or an eagle's folded wing, with that suggestion of a tall keen-eyed figure standing motionless above the world in menace or in guardianship. But it would never do to turn it into Gaelic, as the Gaelic name for the Devil's Point, which is Bod an Diabhail, has been done into English, or the angel would look very like a fallen one, and the Devil as usual get the last laugh.

Having spent so long at lunch-time we did not reach the top of Cairn Toul till five o'clock, and though this is a delectable place to sit for a while, listening to the magnified whisper of the Dee as it is borne up from the Lairig, and gazing round the horizon, which is open in all directions—for Cairn Toul is the most pointed of the Monadh Ruadh—we spent little time there. There was an ominous darkening in the sky which might have meant bad weather, although in fact the squall passed over harmlessly. We had a friendly encounter with a strange visitor to such a barren place, a bumble-bee, which had perhaps been blown by the strong west wind, now somewhat fallen, from his distant honey-pastures in Glen Feshie or Strathspey, and now seemed to be resting exhausted in the shelter of the cairn. We tried to refresh him with a drop of an excellent whisky which has saved many lives before now, and whether restored by this treatment or in such a repugnance—though I should not like to think that such a pleasant creature was a voluntary teetotaller—he soon took off for his solitary flight towards Carn a' Mhaim.

The summit of Cairn Toul consists of a tiny level platform, lying north and south, at either end of which there is a modest cairn. Each way there are mighty corries : Coire Lochan Uaine and Coire an t-Saighdeir, 'the Archer Corrie', separated by the less strong-featured Coire an t-Sabhail, which takes its name from the hill (for the Gaelic spelling of Cairn Toul is Carn an t-Sabhail, meaning 'the Cairn of the Barn'). Between these corries, at each corner of the top, there is a possible but arduous way up from the glen. Westward the slope is almost equally steep down to the four thousand foot level, but thereafter eases off to some extent, the gentlest gradient being along the highest part of the ground which runs out south-west towards the head of Glen Guisachan. But for a long way the boulders are still the main obstacle to a rapid descent. For the normal way down one should bear from the four thousand foot line first south and then south-east round Coire an t-Saighdeir in the direction of Bod an Diabhail, and so down Coire Odhar to the Corrour bothy. This time however we inadvertently kept too far to the west, and thus it came about that we decided for once to seek variety and Glen Guisachan.

For this descent one has to be careful to get to the west of the line of crags which extends continuously from the Devil's Point in this direction for not much less than two miles, that is to say well to the west of the burn next before the actual headstream of the Guisachan (which rises close beneath the summit in the hollow of Clais an t-Sabhail)—and even then there are seven or eight hundred feet which should very nearly be marked ' not negotiable '. As a matter of fact we did not ourselves go quite far enough to the west, and Bernard had quite a nasty fall down a long slab of rock and nearly got hurt. Sliding in this way was certainly the most natural means of progression and the incident nearly wrung from me the admission that even a kilt has its disadvantages.

A propos, as I am in all probability the only Englishman who habitually wears a kilt (though mine is not of any proprietary tartan, and I wear it only upon active service in the hills, for which God or man so well devised it—least of all at exhibitions of Scottish national self-consciousness) I may be pardoned a digression in which to expound its virtues.

Let us take for text the classic remark made about it by a high French military authority : ' Pour la guerre ce n'est pas bon, mais pour l'amour c'est magnifique '. The latter assertion may give a clue to the reason why so many true Highlanders now show a deplorable shyness about wearing it, but unfortunately if the wide spaces of Scot-land have a fault, it is that they give so few opportunities of testing its truth.

One can well understand however that the kilt is not the best of all possible garments for floundering in French mud, although upon the right ground it has served the Highlanders well in many battles against troops in more orthodox equipment. But the walker is going neither to war nor to love—he has at his disposal the exhilaration of both without the expense—and for him it is nearly per-fection. It gives the greatest possible freedom for climbing, yet protects against piercing winds and enables him to sit comfortably on the wettest ground. Most im-portant of all, it keeps the central heating system of the body working in times of exposure, and thus does more to preserve the vital powers than any other kind of garment. Only in very hot weather is it uncomfortable. For this and other reasons it would not be suitable for any hills outside Scotland, especially those of a Mediterranean type, such as the hills of Corsica ; which are in many ways very like the Cairngorms, but with this great difference, that instead of low heather you have there the deep and prickly *maquis* which makes a covering for the knees absolutely necessary. But after all is it not true that what exactly suits one set of circumstances, and one only, best satisfies the aesthetic ideal of function ? The kilt is both cheap, for it can hardly wear out, and eminently graceful; and its swing helps you along when you are tired. A good leather sporan, which is its proper appendage, is also much more serviceable and safer than pockets ; it holds more and keeps matches and tobacco dry to the last, barring complete immersions and the very worst of storms. The white horsehair beards which gentlemen hang round their waists at dances are a nasty perversion of this useful article.

But kilt or no kilt, we were soon all safely down in Glen Guisachan, which, as has already been noticed, is a deer-sanctuary. It has plenty of grass for them but is very flat and wet, for all the water from the high hills which frown upon it from every side soaks into the ground before it finds its way into the meandering burn. The name means ' the Glen of the Fir-trees ', but the only traces of these which now remain are the numerous half-carbonised stumps and fragments of wood which lie about buried or half-buried in the peat. We went straight down through the glen, taking bog and burn as they came, to the Dee, which we waded, being by this time too wet for that to make any difference. But we should have had to do so in any case, as by this stage the lusty young stream by which we had lunched, so near to the sky, was already swollen to a substantial belt of water. Then, crossing the broken stretch of ground called Clais a' Mhadaidh, the Wolf's Hollow, we reached the Derry path again, and there made a last halt, being now near enough to home to permit ourselves the luxury of emptying the flask, as a fillip before starting on a forced march to cover the last stage of the journey; for darkness was gathering, and it had fallen before we reached Derry Lodge at a quarter past nine.

A magnificent day of fifteen hours in the open, including the time taken to drive to Derry Lodge and back. But this is not to serve as an example to anyone for whom time is an object.

CHAPTER IX

BEINN BHROTAIN AND SGORAN DUBH

An account of another expedition in the same neighbourhood will give a better idea of the normal ascent of Cairn Toul, and introduce also the southernmost mass of the Cairngorms, which consists of Monadh Mor and Beinn Bhrotain. This was undertaken in very different conditions of weather, which gave little temptation to linger idly on the way.

This time we started from the White Bridge in Glen Dee, and so took about two hours to reach the Corrour bothy—from the Derry this takes something like half an hour less. The early morning was sunny, but this is generally a bad sign ; worse still the wind was in the east ; and by the time we had started to climb, or before, the sky was overclouded. Up Coire Odhar to the col between Cairn Toul and the Devil's Point is a fairly stiff climb, but it need not take long, if you make up your mind to it. There is the ghost of a path *en lacets*. But we kept straight up, and in another forty minutes, by a quarter of an hour after midday, we had reached the col, and from there added the further three hundred feet to the Devil's Point.

Bod an Diabhail, except on the east side, does not seem so steep and forbidding from the top as it does from below ; nor is it high enough for any very considerable view, except that it commands the whole length of the Lairig

116

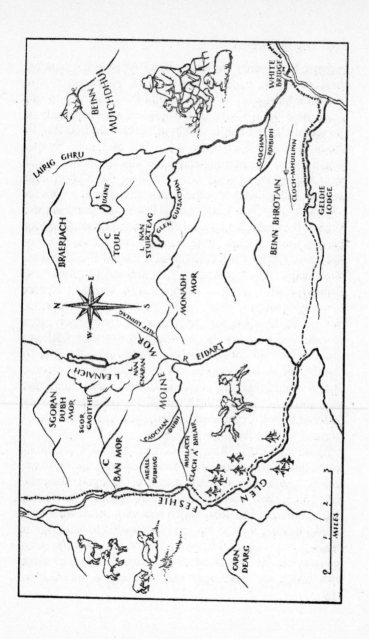

perhaps better than any other hill. After a few minutes there, we went back to the col and thence across the stretch of hill-meadow called A'Bhuidheannaich up to and along the edge of Coire an t-Saighdeir, and eventually to the top of Cairn Toul, in all about twelve hundred feet, in about an hour. We left the top at half past one. By this time mist was threatening and there was some rain, which grew heavier as we made our way along the high ground west of the headwaters of the Guisachan, between Clais an t-Sabhail and Clais Linneach, to Loch nan Stuirteag, the Loch of the Gulls, which lies below the three thousand foot level on the very edge of the Moine Mor, and has its overflow eastward into the Guisachan. This is also called on some maps ' Lochan Suarach ', which would mean ' the Contemptible Loch ', a curious name which is almost certainly incorrect, being the more probable corruption. It is apt all the same, for the lochan is a dreary little patch of water lying among the peat-hags in this untypical and almost unvisited corner of the Cairngorms ; for it is so close to the march between two counties and two forests, that, I should imagine, even the stalkers rarely come this way, and it lies on a bealach which is a thoroughfare only between a great expanse of wilderness and the most desolate and unfriendly of glens.

As we lunched in the rain beside its burn a heavy cloud was rolling down upon us. We stayed only ten minutes, and at 2.40 went on to the ascent of Monadh Mor, the hill which rises beyond the lochan towards the south. Before entering the mist, which was very thick, we took a careful bearing for the top, and followed it so well that in three-quarters of an hour we arrived precisely at the cairn (3651 ft.) at the north end of the ridge : a piece of work with which we were very well pleased, as we had no clearly defined lie of the ground to help us, and the cairn is a small one which in the mist was only visible for a few yards. Thence, along the level top to the second cairn, rather less than a mile to the south, and on to the col below, the way was very much easier to follow. We covered the distance in perhaps half an hour.

It was a great piece of good fortune that at the col the mist lifted a little above us, for the wind was blowing up from the rough corrie at the south-west corner of Glen Guisachan which bears the romantic name of Coire Cath nam Fionn, ' the Battle-Corrie of the Fingalians '—who are also recalled by other names in the Cairngorms, such as that given to the ford of the Avon on the Lairig Laoigh path, and indeed, according to one legend, by the name of the Avon itself. The rocky buttresses of Beinn Bhrotain thrust outwards through the mist with a very fine effect, much exceeding in grandeur any which better weather, with all its compensations, could have shown. We were soon into the bank of cloud again, but it was only a quarter of an hour before we found ourselves above it at the top of Beinn Bhrotain, and thereafter to our surprise we were in sunshine for the rest of the day.

Beinn Bhrotain (3795 ft.) is the highest and the largest of the lesser Cairngorms, and in any other company would rank as a first-class mountain. Its summit, upon a smaller scale, is of the same indefinite but not quite level type as that of Beinn Muichdhui and is divided into two parts by a slight dip in a somewhat similar fashion. The best of the view is to the south, and along Glen Dee, and the Devil's Point looks well across the chasm of Glen Guisachan. Monadh Mor blocks the outlook over the plateau westward. There are several ways down, amongst which I have tried the bluff south of Caochan Roibidh, which leads directly eastward to the Dee, the course of the Allt Garbh, and a way across the top of Carn Cloch-mhuilinn (3087 ft.). The best is by the Allt Garbh : the upper part consists of long grassy terraces which you can easily run down for a long way without meeting an obstacle, and the lower part, just before the burn falls into the Dee, is in a steepish and very attractive gully, fringed with long heather and a few rowans. But this evening, leaving the top at half-past four, we kept to the west of Carn Cloch-mhuilinn and then went straight across Carn Geldie to the White Bridge, which we reached just after six. There is some point in taking this route, because it is sometimes difficult to cross the Dee above the White Bridge, and at any time there are few places where it is possible to do so without getting wet. Then we rested for some time on the smooth river bank, and were mightily pleased with the welcoming geniality of the warm July sun after the changes and chances of the day.

And now one more day's journey, though a long one, remains to be told, and we shall have completed our explorations in the western Monadh Ruadh. It is one for which good training is necessary, so we left it for the last of a season already rich in good walks. For there had been a fortnight of continuous sunshine, which upheld September's reputation as on the whole one of the two best months of the year in Scotland, although for long-distance expeditions the shortness of the days is beginning to be something of a disadvantage. Our objective on this occasion being Sgoran Dubh, the farthest of all the high Cairngorms from the Braemar side, we were so uncertain that we should be off the hill again before dark that we thought it as well to include an electric torch in the equipment.

VII.

BRAERIACH FROM THE NORTH

The party consisted of Robin Gerard, Bernard and myself. We left Braemar at about seven o'clock to motor to
the White Bridge, where, at quarter to eight, we left the
car. (It is possible to take one a mile farther to the foot-
bridge over the Geldie, but our intention was to return by
Glen Dee.) The sun was not yet in the glen, and there
must have been several degrees of frost in the air, for we
were uncomfortably cold until we had walked as much as
a couple of miles. Up the left bank of the Geldie a broad
shooting-track runs for about three miles to the now dis-
used Geldie Lodge, which lies on the other side of the
river, and then a path of sorts leads on, still on the left
bank, into Glen Feshie, crossing the Eidart where it joins
the Feshie three miles farther on. So far it is an uninteresting walk through low peaty country, and over the formless watershed the path is not altogether easy to follow, so
indeterminate are the landmarks ; for the Feshie, which
now flows north-east for the first part of its course and just
before it is joined by the Eidart makes a hairpin-bend to
continue due west, used at one time to go straight on in the
line of the upper part of its course into the Geldie, from
which it is still scarcely separated ; so that probably in
time of spate some of its water still goes that way, and its
direction might at any time be changed anew by some
exceptional flood.

At the county march we turned across the edge of the
low hill on our right into Glen Eidart, where there is no
perceptible path, at least on this side of the river, so that
the going is fairly heavy. By now it was also very hot, in
contrast to the morning, and so continued all day. The
Eidart is a magnificent stream flowing for the lower part
of its course in a shallow crevasse. It descends rapidly
across many slabs and ledges of rock through a series of

tempting pools, which to-day were as clear as any in the Cairngorms; though I should suppose that normally these waters would be discoloured by the peat of the Moine Mor with that rich brown tinge characteristic of most Scottish burns outside this particular area. The glen too is less gloomy and less fenced in with crags than many in the Cairngorms, and is no doubt the more cheerful for its southern aspect. But it is headed with no mean bastions of rock, the formation of those on the left around the north-east-facing Coire Mharconaich, which are the biggest, reminding me rather of the very rough crinkled types of rock which give such picturesque irregularity for instance to the hills of upper Strathearn, than of the stern and uncompromising cliffs which we generally find in this part of the country (though there is perhaps some accidental likeness to be found in Carn a' Mhaim). This is no doubt due to an intrusion of a different type of rock upon the otherwise uniform Cairngorm granite.

Four miles up, north of Coire Mharconaich, the glen comes to a sudden end against a steep 500 ft. wall which is a vertical section of the Moine Mor plateau. Here the Eidart divides into two main streams, one, the Allt Luineag, coming from the centre of the plateau generally and the Cairn Toul ridge in particular on the right, and the other, which has a shorter course, coming down from the left from the broad ridge between Carn Ban Mor and Mullach Clach a' Bhlair. The latter flows in a succession of little waterfalls down a very curiously shaped rift—I do not know whether it would better be described as a corrie or a gully—perhaps the word ' ghyll ' most suggests it— which winds its way far into the hill, and is not very like anything I have noticed elsewhere. The sides of this are so smooth and grassy, and the scene seemed so peaceful, with the warmth of the sunshine on us and the cheerful modulations of the burn in our ears, that it would have been easy to fancy oneself perhaps in some ' heugh ' in the sheep-country of the Borders rather than so many miles from anywhere in the very heart of the Monadh Ruadh. The burn is called the Caochan Dubh, the pretty word *caochan* being an old Gaelic word for ' burn ' which is rather less common in this part of the country than in the west. In the Cairngorms there are also Caochan Roibidh on Beinn Bhrotain and Caochans Cothaiche and na Spolda on Cairngorm of Derry, but not many more. It seems here to be associated mainly with a type of burn which flows steeply in a deep channel, but this does not apply elsewhere.

The short but steep climb out of the Caochan on to the edge of the plateau did not take long, and there suddenly in every direction the big hills, of which hitherto we had not even caught sight all day, sprang into view with a tremendous, almost a theatrical, effect. Here, at midday, we sat down for our first rest, feeling it to be well deserved by our efforts and these well rewarded. As we looked round at each familiar summit seen in this new aspect, our eyes rested in particular upon one long flat-topped mountain to the north-east, and for a few moments we were puzzled as to what it could possibly be. Almost at once of course we realised that it was Cairn Toul, but so changed in appearance by this angle of vision as to be at first unrecognisable. What is of still more interest, I at least understood for the first time why it is called ' the Hill of the Barn ', for from this point the resemblance to a barn is carried out most realistically, the summit forming the flat upper edge of the roof, broader from this side than one would have imagined it, with the Archer Corrie forming a

123

complete gable at one end and the corner of Coire Lochan Uaine just showing to suggest the corresponding one at the other.

Now we went off into the heart of the Moine Mor. A derelict waste of peat-hags this now seems to be, silent and rather weird even in the sunshine ; perhaps the more so because so many relics of former summer-shielings are to be seen scattered about its surface. Right across it from east to west traces of an ancient track can be made out by means of the chain of cairns which still mark the line, and no doubt in wet weather this would be the only practicable route across the moss. But to-day after the long dry spell it was quite firm, though tiring, walking.

For a time our ways parted, Robin and Bernard making straight on a line north-north-west towards Sgor Gaoithe above Loch Eanaich, and I wishing first to explore the western ridge. Within a minute or two we had completely lost sight of each other amongst the rolling waves of peat. A heat-haze was by this time dancing over the ground and after a quarter of an hour by myself I began to feel the queer stillness of the place more insistently. I saw nothing living, except once or twice a stag and once a single ptarmigan, but there were constant appearances of life, and several times the glass was turned on what had seemed to be a moving object, but revealed nothing. ' De non apparentibus et non existentibus eadem est ratio ' —so, there is the same *unreason* in the face of any discrepancy between sensible appearance and reality. I was carried in this confusion of mind so far that when for a moment only I caught sight of an eagle in the direction of Loch Eanaich, I had quite convinced myself that it was but the wraith of an eagle until I heard later from the others that they had seen it also.

124

But I have no doubts in my mind as to the black intransigence of the deep Coire Garbhlach, which eats into the western edge of the plateau below Meall Dubbag (3268 ft.). It is the only rocky corrie upon this side, and in shape, for it is a precipitous Caochan Dubh, is quite individual. Nor shall I forget the sensation of finding myself looking down unawares upon the domesticated-looking farmsteads of Glen Feshie, lying so close below that I could have been in their midst in less than half an hour.

I crossed Carn Ban Mor (3443 ft.), where the walking starts to improve, and indeed becomes perfect as the general level of the ridge rises slightly towards Sgoran Dubh ; and on Sgor Gaoithe (3658 ft.) at half-past one, I came up again with Robin and Bernard. I was glad to stop for a few minutes and eat something, after seven hours without food during which, except for the drive from Braemar, we had been going hard across rough country with only one rest. From here it is only a mile to Sgoran Dubh (3635 ft.), which was our turning-point, and we were back on Sgor Gaoithe by half-past two. We then went on for a twenty minutes halt and lunch proper to the first spring southward on the edge of the moss, above the corner of Coire Odhar known as Coire Odhar nan Each. This well is appropriately named Fuaran Diotach or ' the-Spring-where-a-Meal-is-Taken '.

Sgoran Dubh, which is rather to the north of the lower end of Loch Eanaich, stands at the head of a three-mile chain running gradually down into the Rothiemurchus forest near Loch an Eilein. The Sgoran Dubh-Sgor Gaoithe ridge falls all but perpendicularly into Loch Eanaich in a precipice which consists of an alternating series of chimneys and sharply projecting edges of rock, with a wealth—if wealth is not altogether the wrong term—of suspended pinnacles and flying-buttresses. The best view of it is to be obtained from farther to the east round Coire Odhar, which heads Glen Eanaich. This and the other side of the loch, which descends of course from Braeriach, are also rocky and almost equally steep, so that the loch is all but completely surrounded with an escarpment of rock. Since it lies at only a little over sixteen hundred feet above the sea, the total height from Sgoran Dubh to the water level exceeds by about five hundred feet even the drop from the top of Beinn a' Mheadhoin into Loch Avon. The loch is somewhat broader than Loch Avon; but apart from this factor, which somewhat reduces the effect of height, and its comparative accessibility at the lower end, it would have a good claim to be thought the more impressive of the two. Sgor Gaoithe, justly called ' the Peak of the Winds ' is the highest of the towering blades of rock of which the ridge is made up. I can think of only one other place from which one can thus look down two thousand feet of uninterrupted precipice, and that is from the top of an astonishing mountain called Slieve League on the edge of the cliffs of south-west Donegal.

After our late lunch we walked round Coire Odhar for some distance, and then turned south once more to Loch nan Cnapan, which may be said to lie in the very centre of the moss. Between this and Monadh Mor, which was our next objective (simply as being the easiest route home), the Allt Luineag flows in a moat-like channel, rich in hill-flowers at the right time of year, which is pleasant to visit but makes rather a tiresome obstacle. This name means ' the Burn of Songs '. It is also called Allt Linneach or ' the Burn of Pools ', which characterises it perhaps rather better, for in the flatter upper part of its course, where it would have been rather easier to cross, it flows somewhat sluggishly from pool to pool amongst the hags ; but both are charming names and you can take your choice. We then worked across the flank of Monadh Mor, which is very stony going, to its south top, stopping on the way to look for Cairngorm stones. These are most likely to be found where a vein of quartz can be detected, at the point where it disappears into the ground, but are not very easy for the inexpert eye to recognise. Robin, who knows the look of them, had the good luck to find some likely crystals. We were on Monadh Mor by ten minutes past five and on Beinn Bhrotain by six.

Although this was the highest point we had touched in the course of the day, I am afraid we treated it with the indifference proper to a mere incident in the return journey ; for now we were almost on our own doorstep. We came rapidly down the excellent grassy stair-way of the upper Allt Garbh, and at its foot Bernard and I succeeded in crossing the Dee dryshod, more by luck than by good management, whilst Robin waded. Back at last upon the path, we found great satisfaction in lighting our pipes and proceeding slowly to the White Bridge in an atmosphere of comfortable meditation. We reached there at quarter to eight after just twelve hours on the hill, of which at the very most one hour was spent in halts. We thought this very good time. If one were trying to break records, I do not imagine that this tour could be accomplished in less than eleven and a half hours, and in unfavourable conditions it would certainly take very much longer than twelve.

CHAPTER X

GOOD-BYE TO THE CAIRNGORMS

Before leaving the Cairngorms it may possibly be of sufficient interest to resurvey them rapidly by devoting a short chapter to an account of our one-day ascent of the four high tops. This is not a remarkable achievement, although the length of the day certainly is well above the average. It is recorded as having been done upon several occasions, and has since been quite eclipsed by a walk including Beinn a' Bourd and Beinn A'an which has been performed two or three times in the past few years. But this requires special transport-arrangements at either end, and the like, and so to my mind takes on rather too professional and organised an appearance to win wholehearted approval. The four tops ascent was however a very interesting tour for other reasons, and I have definite knowledge of only one other occasion upon which it has been done from the Braemar side. This was by Downie when he was a young man.

But there is one small section of the Cairngorms as yet untouched, for it does not fall in naturally with any of the more important groups, of which it would be suitable to say a few words first. This is the small range consisting of Beinn a' Chaoruinn (3553 ft.), which stands between the Lairig Laoigh (opposite Beinn a' Mheadhoin) and Beinn a' Bourd ; and its southward extension to Beinn Bhreac

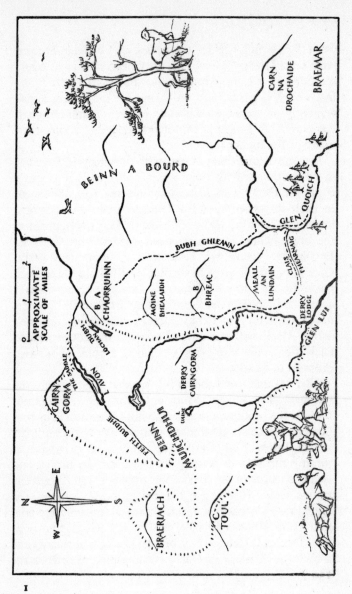

(3051 ft.), which divides the upper part of Glen Quoich from Glen Derry. These hills are perhaps the most rarely ascended of all the Monadh Ruadh—even Downie, for instance, had never been on them—for they cannot conveniently be combined with any other hill, and although comparatively low are yet not any easier of access than many of the higher ranges.

My only expedition to them, with the village of Braemar as its starting and finishing point, took nearly ten hours. From the Derry it could be done in much less. We went in each direction by Glen Quoich, upon the outward journey following its course for nearly four miles, as far as the angle where it swings north-east behind Carn na Drochaide. Here we branched off along the Dubh Gleann on to the edge of the Moine Bhealaidh, and then made for the top of Beinn a' Chaoruinn, north-west across the plateau, and back along its western border, near Glen Derry, to Beinn Bhreac ; whence we returned across Meall an Lundain and through the cutting called Clais Fhearnaig into Glen Quoich at a point about two miles from its foot.

Glen Quoich is a beautiful wooded glen which the serious walker is likely to miss altogether, since it does not provide the best route to any high hill. The linn at its foot however attracts a good many visitors, although, until the bridge below Mar Castle was built, the necessity of fording the Dee or wading it, as we did on the way to Beinn a' Chaoruinn, made the outing a mildly adventurous one. Just above the bridge which crosses the Quoich at a place where it rushes through a narrow channel in the rocks, like a mill-race, may be seen what is known as the ' Devil's Punchbowl ', a boiling pot-hole at the edge of a broad slab, *cuach* in Gaelic, from which the glen takes its name. There is a bothy at the foot of the Dubh Gleann, from which, or just short of it, there is a possible (but the least interesting) way up Beinn a' Bourd, over the spur called An Diollaid; and so far there is a good path on the right bank of the stream. But from there on and for the rest of the day until the return into Glen Quoich the going was very heavy.

The Moine Bhealaidh, which we approached by way of the Allt an Aghaidh Mhilis, 'the Burn on the Sweet Hill-face', from the head of the Dubh Gleann, is an extensive peat moss similar in type only to the Moine Mor within the Cairngorm region. It runs for over two miles in a broad level stretch between the tops of Beinn a' Chaoruinn and Beinn Bhreac, and in a more broken form eastwards to the sloping side of Beinn a' Bourd, in much the same fashion as the Moine Mor connects with the Cairn Toul ridge. It is a favourite place for the deer, of which we saw large numbers at close quarters, and there were also some ptarmigan with their young broods, although these are birds which generally prefer the very highest levels and the most barren and stony summits, even to nest. They are rarely seen below 3000 feet.

In Glen Quoich, at not more than a few yards range, we had the unusual spectacle of a fox trying to climb a tree! When at last he caught sight of us, and of course made off as fast as he could, we came up to investigate, and discovered that his temptation was a dead rabbit, suspended there apparently as a bait of some kind, but hardly one would suppose for a fox; which, although it should be admitted that Aesop is the best scientific authority my memory can produce in support of this item of natural history, is presumably not by any means an arboreal creature.

The summit of Beinn a' Chaoruinn is a presentable cone which falls steeply towards the Dubh Lochan on its west side, and also towards a good north-eastern corrie, Coire nan Clach, which faces the upper Avon. But the view is severely restricted, and Beinn Bhreac, though five hundred feet lower, seemed to me to offer a much better prospect. The edge of the plateau is however the best possible place from which to form a general idea of the construction of the Beinn Muichdhui massif, upon which, in this first week of July, there was still a great deal of snow. Near Beinn Bhreac we came across a rain-gauge, for which I believe the keeper at Derry is responsible, its readings forming a part of the data upon which the weather statistics of this part of the country are based. But perhaps the most interesting physical feature of the range is the narrow and unexpected defile of Clais Fhearnaig, a dry gully cutting sharply across the back of the hill between Meall an Lundain (2550 ft.), the hill immediately above the Derry Lodge, and Creag Bhalg (2190 ft.) above the Linn of Quoich. In it there are one or two lonely trees of a kind not often found except in the lower glens ; the name means ' the Cleft of the Alders ', and I think one of them is an alder in point of fact. Upon the authority of the Scottish Mountaineering Club Guidebook, I may add, as a matter of some interest, that this rather curious formation is supposed to be due to a glacial overflow-channel.

So much for Beinn a' Chaoruinn. Of the four tops ascent, as we shall now be upon well-known ground, I shall give little more than an outline.

Conditions were not encouraging when we left the Derry entrance at 8.30. There was a good deal of mist about, which rather delayed us in the climb to Cairn Gorm from the Saddle and on the way to Beinn Muichdhui ; in fact it was not until the early afternoon that we finally made up our minds to carry our programme through. We passed Coire Lochan Uaine at 9.30, crossed the Banff march at 10, reached Loch Avon by 11.15 and the top of Cairn Gorm by 12.20. We saw an eagle beating the heather below Cairngorm of Derry, and near the Dubh Lochan a fox and many coveys of grouse—perhaps keeping away up here on purpose to be at a safe distance from the guns farther down Glen Avon, for the day, as it happened, was ' the Twelfth '.

On Cairn Gorm we started to lunch, but the mist suddenly lifted and showed the top of Beinn a' Mheadhoin, on which we made out a considerable herd of deer. It is a good weather-sign for deer to be feeding at this height, and suitably encouraged by the general improvement in conditions, we set out again at once. The clouds still hung round us most of the way to Beinn Muichdhui, but once they parted for a few moments to frame a long vista coloured in successive blues and greens far across Strathspey and the northern hills, upon which the sunshine was falling here and there : a glimpse infinitely more moving than the perfect ' bird's eye ', because it gave no time for the brain to come into action ; ' simple and faithless ' as one of those commonplace gestures, a raised arm or head inclined, which once in a way your eye may light on—and capture if you happen to be a Renoir or a John.

We cut low across the rocks of the Feith Buidhe—the corries on this side looking very fine—and reached the summit of Beinn Muichdhui at 1.55. We left ten minutes later and went down into the Lairig by the steep side of the Allt a' Choire Mhoir, to reach the foot of the Braeriach track at three o'clock. The mist hung like a smoke-barrage in an even horizontal line as far down as the lip of Coire na Lairige (Coire Ruadh), but as we climbed it rose before us like a slowly lifted curtain, till when we reached the Braeriach cairn at 4.15 all was clear except for 'the steaming of the porridge' in Coire Bhrochain.

When at last we reached Cairn Toul at 5.45, there was not a sign of either mist or haze in any direction. All the virtue of the day, which had been fine below the mist, seemed to have saved itself up for us as a final reward, and we lingered on our throne to taste to the full the sweet beginnings of the still, perfect evening. We then made an unpleasantly steep descent into Coire an t-Saighdeir, down a chimney of polished grass and scree leading from the south-east ridge ; and I must say that, coming as it did at the end of the day, my knees felt this imposition a good deal. The bottom of the corrie is one mass of fallen boulders, beneath which the burn entirely disappears, until it issues on the hillside below ; and the effect of enormous ruin upon every side is increased by the striking absence of water.

We waded the Dee, and made a last halt there, till 7.10, and then by very fast walking reached the Derry at 8.40, in just over twelve hours since we left it that morning. But once more the roads gave us more trouble than the hills, and we did not get back to Braemar until after ten o'clock.

. . . .

It is fitting to take leave of the Cairngorms with the crumbling desolation of the Archer's Corrie as last impression. For after days of sunshine, days of colour, days of gloom and storm, enjoyed amongst them in as many various moods, the summary of our thoughts of them, more than of other hills, is inevitably serious, and even sad.

134

Only a stranger from lands farther from the sky can think of ' the eternal hills ' as so much less mortal than ourselves ; but most of them have found ways to hide that they too are slowly dying. When we look at the scarred sides of Loch Avon, or at Braeriach, which in the piling up of centuries has worn to so thin a shell that each successive vertical section of granite, as it falls, must now steal something also from the height, they seem almost to be in suffering ; and the venerable thought is again borne in upon us that nothing is imperishable—not even time itself, of whose power their condition is the vast evidence. We may be tempted to imagine their story told, and no sooner told than reduced to insignificance by some celestial Gibbon, in a passage to compare with that (speaking of those ' sixty phantoms of kings, which have passed before our eyes and faintly dwell on our remembrance ') with which his forty-eighth chapter closes—or, I suppose, a period yet more tremendous, if that could be conceived.

But of all the vanities, time alone needs, and will endure, no monument.

CHAPTER XI

PERTHSHIRE

PERTHSHIRE is one of the five large Highland counties, but unlike the others it is not wholly Highland. There is a south-eastern strip of the fairest type of Lowland country, consisting of the Vale of Allan and the lower valleys of the Earn and Tay. These form a continuous fertile carse, which Strathmore prolongs into Angus, filling the space between the Ochils and Sidlaws towards the sea and the long wall of the lower Grampians, which sweeps through Callander, Crieff, Dunkeld and Blairgowrie, right across the county. In that line of blue hills ever in sight its perfection lies, and thence the fresh winds blow their intimation of glories yet ahead.

The centre of this district and the chief taking-off place for all the routes by rail or road, which will bring you within striking distance of the hills, is ' the Fair City ' of Perth ; and a fair city it still is too, as modern cities go, though those who live in it do not think so, and have been known to abuse it (regardless of punctuation) as ' a low, lying place '.

Within the bounds of Perthshire the transformation of Lowland scenery into Highland therefore takes place in a fully representative number of many possible forms, and these possess at once a common character and marked individual differences. The main near-side valley of the

136

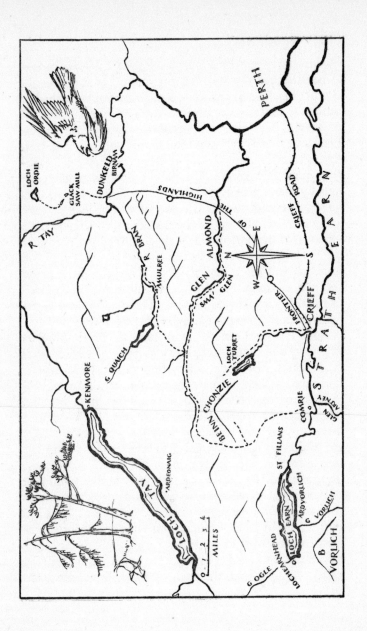

Grampian range, which mere volume of water has caused to be miscalled the Tay, is structurally a continuation of Glen Garry, and so springs from the central watershed of Scotland, halfway to Inverness. The normal laws of geography thus dictate the gradual stages by which this leads into scenery of a more and more Highland character. By contrast, on one side, the waters of narrow Loch Lubnaig burst turbulently through the horizon of the high hills by the Pass of Leny, and, on the other, the Isla cuts its way through the solid rock below Craighall; while agricultural Strathearn (unlike the others, apparently not a transverse but a longitudinal valley, and the southernmost of the almost parallel series continued in Loch Tay, Loch Rannoch and Loch Ericht), leads peacefully in its broad bed almost along the edge of the hills as far as the loch from which it takes its source. There at last the Highlands enclose it round and make it their own.

But Perthshire can do more than this to establish its title to unquestioned superiority in point of variety to all other shires. Its Highland portion also falls into several fairly well defined sections with characters distinct.

In the extreme south-western corner are the Trossachs. They need no fresh advertisement, and for that among other reasons least enlist my personal sympathies. They are based on Glasgow rather than on Perth, and so in any case fall rather outside the orbit of this book. Next to the Trossachs and first upon our path there is a strip of lower hill-country, where there is woodland in plenty, moors deep in heather, and many small and good trout-lochs and burns. From Loch Lubnaig this runs still from southwest to north-east in accordance with the general Highland trend, and reaches as far as the upper part of the Tay valley (before it joins the main Tummel-Garry glen), and

138

beyond the lower Tay across to Strathardle and lower Glenshee. In this area what is not pastoral is all preserved for game, mainly, of course, grouse, but the close country abounds also in black game, pheasants, roe and caper-cailzies. There is no deer-forest, except Glenartney, and no hill of first rank except Beinn Vorlich. This may therefore be regarded as a transitional section. North-west again, across Loch Tay, thence north to Loch Ran-noch and west right to the head of Glen Lyon on the Argyle march, lies the main mass of the Perthshire hills, the highest of all, but perhaps not in all ways the most interesting. However, this is excellent open country for the walker. It is for the most part under sheep. Still to the north, but farther east, filling the whole northern segment of the county, the Athole forests roll away in wave upon wave of heath and rounded hill towards the main Grampian chain, which forms the county boundary in this direction. The extreme west of Perthshire con-tains the beginnings of yet another, a very different style of country—the Moor of Rannoch and the superlatively wild places of Badenoch, where Scotland's east meets west.

In the south-eastern Highland belt there is little of first-rate interest to the walker, and I do not intend to treat it systematically. Not that by any other standard but that of the Highlands this country is not lovely enough, and my own affections are so deeply involved in it that before we get once more to serious business, I cannot forbear to idle there upon the way. There are so many places in which I have spent not days but weeks of what, it seems in retrospect, must have been continual enchantment, so many houses which are so much more than houses, so many friends.

139

The old song, *The Earl of Athole's Wooing*, will be familiar to many :

> ' Blair in Athole's mine, Jeannie,
> Fair Dunkeld is mine, Jeannie,
> St. Johnstoun's Bower
> And Huntingtower,
> And all that's mine is thine, Jeannie.'

The ironical may smile, the much-abused cynic—who is nothing more than the most amiable of us in one of his dyspeptic moods, for people who are not nice haven't enough power of feeling to be cynical—may even sneer at this severely practical method of courtship. But there is such a thing as a romantic form of bribery, and a young woman to whom a handsome financial settlement would make little or no appeal—and again, there are many such young women—might without inconsistency in character yield to the spell cast by these names.

It is not difficult to understand the extreme reluctance of Scottish lairds to part with estates, the possession of which can sustain them spiritually long after becoming almost a material liability, and this not merely in their pride and prejudice (so that they can go on having themselves announced in terms of territorial dignity) but in their sensibility, and even sense. I sometimes think that it might be an enlightened act of injustice to ease the burden of death-duties a little—for Scotland only—out of mere respect for human personality. The proper experts at the Treasury could be trusted to hunt up a better Parliamentary reason. But perhaps we might attach a condition or two for the benefit of walkers. I don't think it would be the least bit sillier than many of the suggestions made by more serious reformers for reconciling these supposedly inveterate hostile tribes, and at least somebody would be pleased.

Dunkeld, about fifteen miles away, is the nearest place to Perth which lies really within the Highlands. You may reach it very easily—it is one of the first places on the main road or railway-line to Inverness—and arrive there through the portals of the little pass formed between Birnam and Newtyle Hills.

This Birnam is, almost incredibly, the Birnam of Macbeth ; and since Dunsinane Hill is one of the Sidlaws and a good thirteen miles to the north-east, the armies had the whole width of Strathmore at its widest point between them. All invaders of Scotland north of Perth, from Agricola onwards, must of necessity have made their way past the Sidlaws on one side or the other, either through Strathmore or by the Carse of Gowrie, though the latter would be a risky passage for troops without naval support. The stronghold of Dunsinane (where traces of fortifications are still visible) seems therefore to have been well chosen as Macbeth's headquarters, for it would command both these routes as effectively as possible. In marching on Dunkeld, Malcolm may perhaps at first have had the intention of trying to slip past Macbeth, who obviously controlled the left bank of the Tay, by taking the route along the edge of the hills through Blairgowrie and Alyth. Encouraged no doubt by the strength of his English reinforcements, we may suppose, however, that he changed his mind, and decided to make the direct assault on Dunsinane ; and the happy thought of taking Birnam Wood with him as what would now be called ' camouflage ' enabled him to make this strategy effective. It is curious, by the way, that Holinshed places Dunsinane in Fife. If this is a mere inaccuracy, it yet does not

141

discredit his account very much, for the tradition of the battle can be traced back into the fourteenth century, earlier than his version; but it is quite possible that the ancient ' Kingdom of Fife ' extended beyond the bounds of the present county.

Dunkeld is a place at the junction of several roads and rivers, where, for that reason, more history than the tragedy of Macbeth has been made, and it still bears the stamp of an almost vanished importance. But the Tay is the making of it. Having just taken a fast corner through a narrow wooded pass a little to the west, the river sweeps round the ruins of the cathedral, like a late-Victorian duchess cutting her husband's friends, with a swish of her broad train. The fine beeches improve on the effect. Above Dunkeld, as far as Ballinluig, where the Tay enters it from the west, the main valley opens out into a broad flat, once apparently the bed of a glacial lake. In this are Dalguise and Guay, sidings for the timber traffic. At Guay during the war there was a place where they used to launch whole trunks down a kind of shoot in the side of the hill, to end their career against a buffer of earth built at the foot, with seismic echoes. It was a fascinating process to watch. Here also is the farm of Inchmagranachain.

I have not much to say about the walking from Dunkeld. On either side of the Tay valley there are pretty stretches of high moorland, but no real hill-ranges. I did, however, spend three weeks there by myself, or, to be more precise, at Birnam, which is Dunkeld's modern suburb, in the early spring of 1925. The date I remember and mention, because it was at this time that the search-parties were out so long on the hills far to the west upon the marches of Argyle, looking for the body of the lost mountaineer Henderson. This made more of a stir in Scotland at the time than perhaps such things do nowadays. I was rather tempted to join them, but could not spare the time just then, as I was there to work ; nor did I do any full day's walking, for the same reason. For short days I found the little wooded hills very pleasant. Here spring comes earlier than to the high hills, and there was no snow ; so far from it, that I sun-bathed on several afternoons in a little clearing above the face of rocky Craig Vinean—even in this time of the *giovinetto anno*, when the sun still ' his locks subdued '.

Only one of these walks, the longest, is worth mentioning particularly. This was by the wood-paths past Glack sawmill to Loch Ordie, one of several lochs which lie strewn over the face of the moors between Strathtay and Strathardle. It would be more interesting, if one did not wish to return to Dunkeld, to continue the walk to Kirkmichael in Strathardle, past the two Lochan Oisinneach, another three or four miles to the north. This would make a comfortable full day well worth while doing, though in the shooting-season there would be strong objections to it. There are paths all the way, and a hotel at Kirkmichael, which looks nice from outside, but I know nothing of it from within. There are also shorter ways of communication between Strathtay and Strathardle, the most direct being to cross north-east from near Ballinluig by Loch Broom. So far as I remember there is a tolerable path by this route, certainly on the Strathardle side of it, and Loch Broom itself lies in about the pleasantest and for the view the most open part of the moor. On the other side, I should think a good enough day which would take you to Aberfeldy could be devised, but I don't know this bit.

In connection with the walk to Loch Ordie only one incident now comes into my head. On the way home, I happened to be lying still and rather sleepily in an overgrown roadman's hollow beside the cart-track which leads above the glen along the west side of Craigie Barns, and thus it was I had the chance of observing a hawk at closer quarters than I had ever done. As she hovered not far away from me, I kept as quiet as possible with my eyes nearly shut. She came nearer and yet nearer to investigate, and eventually floated at the very edge of the hollow, so close that I could have touched her with my long stick—only she would hardly have waited for that ! In the country idleness has also its rewards.

This is not the right vein of sententiousness for a book about walking ; but then, as we said, Dunkeld is not really the place for the severer kind. With a car or a bicycle it could, however, be made as good a centre for the exploration of the sub-Highland belt of Perthshire as any except Crieff or elsewhere in Strathearn. But the Amulree hotel, which lies about halfway between them, would be better than either. The way to this is by the Bran, a tumbling boisterous river which comes into Strathtay from the west between steep Craig Vinean and the gentler side of Birnam Hill.

Amulree is close to the wide area of hills, known as the Blue Crags, reaching from the edge of the Lowlands to Loch Tay, of which the highest, Beinn Chonzie, touches the three thousand-foot level. It is within easy reach of several roads, one up Glen Almond, the central, and much the finest, glen of this mass, another up Glen Quaich over to Kenmore, and another, more of a thorough-fare, to Aberfeldy. The road south to Crieff passes through the pretty and celebrated Sma' Glen, which has

Ossianic associations, and is much featured in the guide-books. It is, as a matter of fact, a small section of Glen Almond. This, if you measure it from the junction of the Almond with the Tay not far above Perth, must be one of the longest true glens in Scotland. Glen Lyon, which has the reputation of being the longest, is about twenty-seven miles long, and Glen Almond is only about four or five miles less.

Glen Almond has also the indisputable distinction of containing Trinity College, the only public school in the Highlands. It is impossible not to feel that education there must owe as much of its success to the happy circumstance of position, as it does at Winchester or Oxford to the very different atmospheric influence of their venerable stones and gardens ; that is, much more than to the best of masters and systems. It is a school which is bound to the clerical tradition of management. Ten years ago one would have assumed this to be a very severe handicap ; but the avowed obscurantists of the last generation of headmasters were after all many of them personalities of a high order, and one begins to wonder how they will compare with the agreeable young men who, in the general confusion, are now popular with governing bodies anxious to seem up to date. The ecclesiastical mind, at its best, does perhaps preserve the relics of a spirit which is still capable of educational consequences.

In its time the church has at least done what it could to discountenance the trivialities, now known as the wonders, of science. It is a pathetic symptom of intellectual decline and craving for applause that some of its leaders have stooped to claim science as the latest support for theology —as if the examination of matter could possibly lead to metaphysical, and not merely to useful or more often

K

dangerous, conclusions ; while for different reasons, if any, most schoolmasters have also offered it their now secular blessing.

> ' " The common Soul, of Heaven's more frugal make,
>   Serves but to keep fools pert, and knaves awake :
>   A drowsy Watchman, that just gives a knock,
>   And breaks our rest, to tell us what's o'clock.
>   Yet by some object ev'ry brain is stirr'd ;
>   The dull may waken to a humming-bird ;
>   The most recluse, discreetly open'd, find
>   Congenial matter in the Cockle-kind ;
>   The mind, in Metaphysics at a loss,
>   May wander in a wilderness of Moss ;
>   The head that turns at superlunar things,
>   Poiz'd with a tail, may steer on Wilkins' wings.
>   ' O ! would the Sons of Men once think their Eyes
>   And Reason giv'n them but to study *Flies* !
>   See Nature in some partial narrow shape,
>   And let the Author of the Whole escape :
>   Learn but to trifle ; or, who most observe,
>   To wonder at their Maker, not to serve ! ' " '

Could I but quote the whole to show with what un-erring and disarming satire Pope caught the process in its early beginnings !

We come now to Strathearn. Crieff, its chief town, is a modern place of some size with little to recommend it to walkers, at least nothing worth coming back to, though you might find it a handy place to start, say, for a walk over the Blue Crags into Glen Almond, and on to Amulree, or, longer, to Ardtalanaig on Loch Tay. There is a shorter route to Loch Tay from Comrie, six miles farther up the valley. This leads through Glen Lednock, partly by road, to Ardeonaig, where there is a hotel. It is a recognised route and, I think, an old right-of-way. The highest and best convenient objective from either of these places is, however, Beinn Chonzie (pronounced Ben-y-Hone), a hill which can be reached either by Glen Turret, Glen Lednock or Glen Almond, and from the nearest point on the road in each case should not take more than about two hours to climb.

Strange as it may seem, I am never quite sure whether I have climbed Beinn Chonzie. When I was at school at Crieff there was once some kind of a whole-day expedition to Loch Turret, during which another boy and myself slipped off for some time, and went up what seemed to be the highest hill in sight. The scale of things alters so much since one was eleven or twelve years old that it is hard to be sure, but I think we must have reached the first point on the ridge short of the top. It cannot have been merely Carn Chois, as we were, so far as I remember, well above the head of the loch to the north.

We often used to get fairly far afield at other points on the Blue Crags, up the Barvick, the Keltie and the Shaggie burns, certainly much farther than we were supposed to go, thanks to an admirable system by which we were allowed to spend the whole day, on Saturdays in the summer, on excursion into the hills in twos or threes, climbing, fighting, building dams in the burns, or sometimes fly-fishing or " guddling " for trout. These days to me were heaven in academe ; and I remember with some shame my hypocritical enthusiasm for a whole day's cricket—a game I have always actively detested, though the feeling has somewhat weakened with disuse—when it was not fine enough for an ' exeat ', and yet was so inconsiderate as to clear up at about eleven o'clock.

There are one or two special memories. All time spent in idleness is in the gospel according to schools time wasted, and in this sense I say, sometimes we would waste half the day, before we were well started, in a particular wood which happened to be unusually well furnished with wild strawberries. Much of the pleasure was no doubt induced by a sense of being ' out of bounds ', as on another occasion, when in point of emotional thrill we might as well have discovered King Solomon's mines—when at the edge of a pine-wood, sudden as magic, a great cliff of red porphyry appeared below us, and beyond it an unknown stretch of open moor, and a burn where afterwards we used often to bathe. The particular form of bathing which we found appropriate here was to slide on our bottoms down some weedy rock-channels, which made good natural water-shoots.

South of Comrie is the curiously isolated deer-forest of Glenartney, whose name at least Scott has made generally familiar. There is no other regular forest for many miles in any direction, I suppose none nearer than Rannoch and the Black Mount ; so Glenartney must depend greatly upon fencing, and there are places, notably upon the steep east face of Beinn Vorlich, where it is next to impossible to maintain the fences against the winter snows and storms. For this reason the deer must often escape into free territory. The main stream of Glenartney is called the Ruchill, and by this, nearly passing that fine old house, Aberuchill Castle, there is a sixteen-mile walk through the forest to Callander and the Trossachs. The little hills round Comrie are also exceptionally picturesque and rocky. The other circumstance for which it is remarkable is its liability to earthquake shocks. This need cause no alarm, for their violence is only comparative ; that is to say, few or none of them are detectible except by the seismograph.

Loch Earn is pretty, and at the far end begins to be fine.

Being fairly broad, it is less impressive than Loch Lubnaig; it is better than Loch Tay, but a bad second to Loch Rannoch. St. Fillans at the east end, five miles or so from Comrie, is only good enough for the children's holidays, but Lochearnhead at the west is greatly superior and would not be at all a bad walking-centre, being within immediate reach of Beinn Vorlich and the Braes of Balquhidder, and, with the assistance of train and car, of a much wider range of the high hills to the north.

If I am ever there again and want an afternoon's walk, I shall certainly try the hill immediately north of Balquhidder, which from the map I notice is called Meall an t-Seallaidh, the Hill of the View. The name is obviously an appropriate one, since the hill must command three lochs in three directions, Loch Earn, Loch Voil and Loch Lubnaig, and a fine prospect northward as well. Very likely you could also see Loch Tay. I only wish I had realised its potentialities before, and I hope someone else will prove them for me.

But Beinn Vorlich is the pride and glory of Loch Earn. True, it stands so far back at the head of an enclosed glen, that only from directly opposite can it be seen at all ; but then it is a sight for the gods. It has been called ' a lesser Matterhorn ', a description which I give for what it is worth, having no acquaintance with the Matterhorn. It is certainly one of the most shapely hills in Scotland. A steep continuous forward shoulder leads to a peaked summit, and the special effect is due to the fact that this shoulder has a definite curve towards the west and back again, which picks out the north-eastern corrie in a deep contrasting shade. The hill also looks magnificent when seen from much farther to the north, across a foreground of the lower hills between Loch Earn and Loch Tay, which

149

exaggerate its apparent height. Thus from every aspect the dispositions of nature have been so contrived, as to make only 3224 ft. serve for the construction of what is, in all essential features, a giant among mountains.

The natural, and probably the best, way to Beinn Vorlich is by Glen Vorlich, the foot of which is rather nearer to Lochearnhead than to St. Fillans. Permission should certainly be asked, as the path starts very close to Ardvorlich House. I cannot pass Ardvorlich without a tribute to the memory of seven winters spent within its hospitable walls, not to mention visits at other times of the year. But it will be of more interest to the world at large to know that it is the Darlinvaroch of Scott's *Legend of Montrose*, a book which I must admit I have never brought myself to read.

The main path up this particularly lovely little glen leads over the Bealach Dearg, under the black precipices east of the ben, to Callander, joining the Glenartney track on the far side. It is supposed to be haunted by a ghostly piper. When the wind screams through the pass it is easy to get such notions. Even on rather still days, when alone on the moors, I have often been unable to decide without a great effort of attention, whether what seemed to my ear to be a strain, a very distant strain, of pipe-music, is fact or fiction—and always pipe-music, the music which I think has grown naturally from the natural sounds of the hills (and perhaps for that reason appeals so little to those who are not familiar and at ease with those sounds), never the notes of any more explicit instrument. But in this case there is also a ' Piper's Grave ' to give the ghost more substance. The walk to Callander is in itself well worth doing : the distance is only ten or eleven miles, and the route is a direct one, if you keep almost due north all the way, and avoid following the headwaters of the Ruchill down into Glenartney. This glen must be crossed at right angles. The record for this course is probably held by a black collie which belonged to Jock Stewart. When we were about to motor back from Callander to Ardvorlich along the main road, which would be about sixteen miles, we found that he had disappeared ; but he was home before us, having obviously taken the path across the hill and raced the car all the way.

For Beinn Vorlich, however, you must leave this path quite early and follow the main shoulder to the top. The way is unmistakable, but it is a fairly stiff, steady climb. There are steep and rocky corries on either side of the ridge, and indeed all round the summit, though there are ways between them. But the east face is inaccessible.

Behind Beinn Vorlich and connected with it by the Bealach an Dubh Choirein, to which there is a drop of nearly a thousand feet, is the long knife-edge of Stuc a' Chroin, almost equal in height to Beinn Vorlich itself, but more or less concealed from the north aspect. It is, however, the more conspicuous part of the range from the west. Once more the eastern side of the ridge, which is the higher, is precipitous for the greater part of its length. This addition to the walk should not be undertaken in mist, as the corries are intricate and dangerous, and in such conditions the only safe course is to return from Beinn Vorlich as you have come. On the other hand, in clear conditions it would be a pity not to include this fine hill in the expedition.

From the Stuc a descent can be made into Glen Ample, either north-west by the Allt Chroisg, or by returning almost to the Bealach an Dubh Choirein and then down the bluff above the Allt a' Choire Fhuadaraich. Here I see there is a path marked on the half-inch map, for which

Messrs. Bartholomew, not I, must answer at the Day of Judgment—without prejudice to the nice question whether limited companies and bodies corporate, not having souls, possess the requisite theological status. You could then, according to taste and destination, either follow Glen Ample to near Lochearnhead; or cross its low watershed, and so drop almost at once to beside Loch Lubnaig; or else pursue Messrs. Bartholomew's path, or the line of it, over the hills westward to Balquhidder Station. From either Beinn Vorlich or Stuc a' Chroin there is also a direct south-east descent on to the Callander path.

With the account of but one more incident, I must leave the neighbourhood of Beinn Vorlich and fly back across Scotland to the very north of Perthshire again—though most reluctantly, for personal attachments would keep me here for ever if I had my way. It is a trifling and rather foolish anecdote, but it has a moral; and worse morals have been the excuse for worse stories.

It was nearly two in the afternoon of a fine New Year's Day, when three of us, then young and innocent as the driven snow which lay deep over all the hills, took it into our heads that it would be a great adventure to try to get to the top of the ben in these conditions. And so it was. The snow became deeper and deeper, but more and more crusty on the surface, as we climbed the shoulder. At times we plunged into it waist-high, and it was only by greater and greater exertions that we made our way so far as the point about seven hundred feet below the top where the gradient becomes noticeably more severe. Here we stopped to draw breath, and looked round at a very fine, but not altogether reassuring, scene. The upper slopes were almost icy and were freezing harder minute by minute; the daylight, though prolonged artificially by the

152

Robert M. Adam

VIII.

GLEN LOCHAY

height, was at its ebb ; and the brightness of the snow was fast growing dim.

There can be no doubt that to have gone any farther would have been the end of us one way or the other. To slip—and how we could have failed to slip, if not in going up, then certainly in coming down, I don't know—would have meant a fall into one or other of the ice-bound corries on either side of the ridge. If, however, we had by any chance reached the top safely, it would by that time have been quite dark, and we should have had to sit and freeze to death. Yet such heroism burned in the majority of our hearts (not mine) that we (still speaking collectively) were fain despite all odds not to relinquish the enterprise which we had already made such strenuous efforts to accomplish. We had brought with us a flask containing the precious remnant of a convivial Hogmanay, and my companions, who were older than I was and had just reached years of indiscretion, thought that this would come in very use-fully to hearten us for the assault. I have always thought better of my own judgment than of my courage, and there was a far-off time when I would no more have tasted whisky in any circumstances than I hope, in those par-ticular circumstances, either I or they now would dream of doing so. So, in their cups, I began to think more seriously of the position. As a result, I swore that I would not go another step, and maintained this unmanly attitude so uncompromisingly, that at last they too were con-strained, if not persuaded, to yield my point.

As it was we found going down much harder than coming up had been, and rolled, tumbled and stumbled the greater part of the way. But we enjoyed this so much that we got back feeling almost as pleased with ourselves as if we had really been to the top.

CHAPTER XII

THE CAIRNWELL TO GLEN TILT

THE tinkers, as the gypsies of Scotland are called, are to be seen everywhere in the Highlands during the summer months, even in the loneliest places, where they seem to exist without any visible means of support. It is this mystery of their livelihood, as if they could feed themselves merely on spells and incantations, or, like Anacreon's crickets, on a few drops of dew—for they have a reputation for honesty and seem to drink all they can ever earn or beg—which gives gypsies their strange interest for the domesticated man, not less than the rather obvious picturesqueness of their outfit; or even than their essential cosmopolitanism, a characteristic always a little bit intimidating to provincial minds. Some atmosphere surrounds them, which has the virtue that, whether we come across their bivouacs on the moors or downs, beside the stunted hawthorns at the bend of an Irish turf-road, or on a patch of waste land by the back-streets of an industrial town, the spot becomes, as it were, ' fixed ' on the memory, as, through some medium or other, what are called ' spirit-photographs ' appear on negatives exposed to rays which to the eye revealed nothing immaterial.

So, when through the padded silence of the hill-mist there fell on my ears a tinkling, at first unrecognisable, sound, and coming out of the edge of the cloud a minute later I found myself looking down on a party of tinkers making their way in single file along the edge of a broad shiny road—a band with more than the usual paraphernalia of brass rails and gilt-edged insecurity, having two or three piebalds and, I think, a monkey, for all the world like an eastern caravan crossing the Khyber Pass rather than a mere troupe of Scottish tinkers, probably with no pretensions to true Romany blood—the slight incident discovered for me for the first time the full loneliness and romance of the road through the Cairnwell Pass, as a mere means of travelling so long familiar. Yet it is one of the most important tourist-routes in Scotland.

This pass, the summit of which is 2199 ft. above sea level, is the highest in the British Isles, and carries the only road across ' the Mounth ', the main Grampian chain, between the much lower crossings thirty miles on either side, at Drumochter, on the way from Perth to Inverness, and at the Cairn o' Mounth, between Banchory and Laurencekirk. Throughout the winter snow generally makes it impassable, and there is no house for several miles on either side of the summit. In quite recent years a tramp perished in the attempt to force his way through sometime in the winter, and was not missed or found until the road was cleared by the highway-authorities in May. The once dangerous double corner known as the Devil's Elbow, just below the summit on the south side, made the pass the terror of travellers in the days of the old stage-coach in which my mother paid her first visit to Braemar. But they used to get fresh horses at the Spital of Glenshee to bring them over the hill, and so contrived to enter the village in the grand manner, with much pretty blowing and trumpeting. The length and steepness of the climb still makes it difficult even for the proud owners of high-powered

155

cars altogether to ignore the unfamiliar wildness of the place, although there is not a remarkable view in either direction, while the humbler type of motorist usually must stop for some time to cool his engine, whether he will or no.

The hills to the east side of the pass are the Braes of Angus, which we have already explored, and the long stony ridge running along that side towards the south is Creag Leacach, one of the closest connections of the Glas Maol. To the west the Grampian chain is traceable through its irregularities as a continuous entity for ten miles (as the crow flies) as far as the rift of Glen Tilt, which cleaves it like an arrow. Here, to the south, is the separated massif of Beinn a' Ghlo. Beyond Glen Tilt the chain loses itself in the wilderness of the Western Athole and Gaick forests, whose eccentricities are impossible to reduce to any definite plan.

It is with the part of the range between the Cairnwell Pass and Glen Tilt—the Cairnwell, Cairn Aosda, the Socachs, Carn nan Sac, Carn a' Gheoidh, Carn Bhinnein, the Beinn Iutharns, Carn Bhac, Glas Tulaichean and Carn an Righ—that this chapter will be concerned.

The best base for these hills is the Spital of Glenshee, upon which converge the three main glens draining the range ; upper Glen Shee itself (also called Glen Beag), Glen Taitneach and Glen Lochsie. Of these three my preference is for Glen Taitneach, ' Pleasant Glen '. Glen Lochsie has the doubtful distinction of containing the only private railway in the British Isles. The owner made it to get to his shooting. If it had been a road instead, it would have been more useful to you and me—and perhaps that is why it is not.

The ' Spital ', fifteen miles south of Braemar and thirty-five north of Perth, is the old ' hospital—or ' hospice ', as

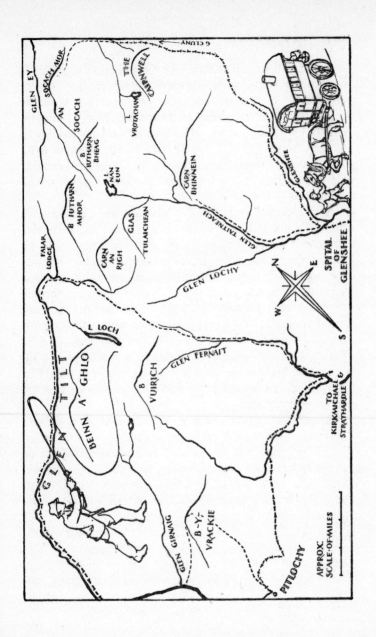

it would still be called abroad—of the mountain road. I
have never stayed at the present inn there, but should
imagine it to be good and not too expensive as these
things go. It is to be suspected that nowadays it survives
chiefly by selling petrol. The land around is ' smiling ',
as they were fond of saying two hundred years ago,
but not particularly fertile except in Fingalian legends.
Of these there is, exceptionally, some topographical
evidence.

The approach from Perth is pleasant and gradual, and
there is a public motor-service in summer. But there are
two roads for the Lowland part of the journey, as far as
Blairgowrie, and the coach-route unfortunately follows
the one which misses the most interesting sight, the deservedly famous beech-hedge of Meikleour—a real hedge
of full-grown beech-trees, lining the road for several
hundred yards. This vegetable Babylon, with its continuous smooth wall of green or copper finish, has a
beauty which is unique. It must be a troublesome and
expensive business to keep it in order, but it is none the
less quite well looked after, and continues to be pruned
about every second year.

Above Blairgowrie, where you cross the Highland
limes, the glen is wooded as far as Bridge of Cally, after
which it opens out into a long pretty valley, which is
sweet rather than exciting until you come to the Spital.
One more inn is passed, at Persie, but both this and that
at Bridge of Cally are primarily fishing inns and are not so
situated as to be of much use to walkers.

An Socach, which is to the north of the main watershed, at the beginning of the long ridge running along the
left bank of the Cluny into Braemar, is rather out of the
way, but the rest of the range, which runs along the

Perthshire-Aberdeenshire march west of the Cairnwell, or most of it (not including Carn Bhac, which again lies rather far to the north) could be managed in one day from the Spital, certainly in two. It might be difficult to include Carn an Righ, which is isolated and the farthest to the west. But the arrangement of these hills is very conveniently adapted to one's powers, whatever they may be, or the inclination of the moment, and the plan I should recommend would be to start with the Cairnwell, or, if you like, Carn Aosda, which is next to the north of the Cairnwell, and to walk over just as many of them as you feel fit for. You would always be within two hours' walk from home whenever you chose to come down, provided you did not go farther north than Beinn Iutharn Mhor, or so far west as Carn an Righ. The going is easy; with a lift to the summit of the Cairnwell Pass, which is easily secured, the initial climb would be slight; and the only considerable drop to break a long high-level walk is that between Carn Bhinnein and the Beinn Iutharn group. Glas Tulaichean, which is the highest of the range and has the best corries, should not be missed; and as it lies south of the county march well into Perthshire, its inclusion should easily be managed.

The following is a reckoning, roughly worked out, of what would be reasonable times for a day taking in the whole round from the Spital of Glenshee and back :

To top of Cairnwell Pass (2199 ft.), a climb of 1000 ft.	1½ hrs.
To top of Cairnwell (3059 ft.) - - - -	¾ hr.
To top of Cairn Aosda (3003 ft.), with a drop to 2550 ft. - - - - - - -	½ hr.
Back to main ridge at Carn nan Sac (3000 ft.) -	½ hr.
Over Carn a' Gheoidh (3194 ft.) to Carn Bhinnein (3006 ft.) - - - - - - - -	1 hr.

Down to Glen Taitneach (about 2000 ft.) and over
    Carn a' Chlarsaich (2845 ft.) to Beinn Iutharn
    Bheag (3121 ft.) - - - - - - 1½ hrs.
Over Mam nan Carr (3224 ft.) to Beinn Iutharn
    Mhor (3424 ft.) - - - - - - 1 hr.
Back by Mam nan Carr to Carn an Righ (3377 ft.),
    with drop to below 2500 ft. - - - - 1½ hrs.
Glas Tulaichean (3445 ft.), with drop to about
    2500 ft. - - - - - - - 1¼ hrs.
Back to the Spital, descending either into Glen Tait-
    neach or Glen Lochsie - - - - - 2 hrs.
Add for rests, refreshments and contingencies - 1 hr.
                                     ———
                 Total time, about 12½ hrs.

Perhaps these times are rather on the optimistic side, for checking them as a total by Naismith's formula, I work it out at half an hour more.

I should explain that Naismith's formula is a means of calculating the time to allow for a day's walking based on the two factors of distance and height. It allows one hour for every three miles plus an additional half hour for every thousand feet climbed. If one is fairly generous over the distance-measurements, I have found that it works out with remarkable accuracy. Its application to the present case is as follows :

           28 miles = 9½ hrs.
           7000 ft. = 3½ hrs.
                 ———
              13 hrs.

It is supposed to allow for reasonable halts, a moderate load, and normally good conditions. For refinements, and an alternative formula of his own, consult Monkhouse in *On Foot in North Wales*. I don't think, however, that for practical purposes Naismith's can be improved on ; the margin of error is not fine enough. The normal speed of active walkers varies surprisingly little, though their powers of endurance do very much, but any special factor such as very bad weather, long stretches of stony or broken ground, or bog, may of course throw out the formula to an incalculable extent. I have rather the impression that weight carried makes less difference to speed, except in making descents, especially steep ones, than it does to endurance and after-fatigue.

These calculations are at any rate sufficient to prove that this round could be accomplished in one day, though it would certainly be an abnormally long day, and would be still well on the long side even if the first few miles along the road were done by car. As is usual on level summits at round about the three thousand-foot level, the going is excellent, except on Carn an Righ, which is rough. The eastern tops are chiefly light springy moss over gravel, and the Beinn Iutharn group is similar but more grassy, especially Glas Tulaichean. It is a noticeable fact that as a general rule in the Grampians the best walking is at a height of between 3000 and 3500 feet. Lower than this the hills are generally too heathery for really comfortable progress, and higher they become more rocky and desolate. It need hardly be said that the moment I have pronounced this generalisation, I start to think of so many exceptions that I am almost tempted to take it back. None the less I think it is pretty true on the average.

My own experience of these hills was gained on expeditions made, for the eastern of them, from the north, and for the western, from Strathardle by way of Glen Fernait.

From Glen Shee I have not gone farther afield than

Carn a' Gheoidh and the Cairnwell. I remember this occasion very well, because on the way up the first glen below the Devil's Elbow, I found myself running into a grouse-shoot. It is fortunate that those were days in which, being still at school, I was inclined to be in tolerable training, for in much anxiety and humiliation I made my escape by running up the side of the hill westward as hard as I could, and disappearing (if I had been seen at all) over the sky-line and into the next glen, Glen Coolah, —a name which sounds like something in the ' Prophetic Books '. Thence I quickly climbed to Carn nan Sac, and on to Carn a' Gheoidh, ' the Hill of the Hollow Stones '. The next blow to my conscience was that on the way to Carn Bhinnein, I suddenly caught sight of a man with a pony immediately in my path, a few hundred yards ahead. What he can have been doing there I do not know, as it was surely too early in the year for stalking to have begun. But not stopping to speculate or caring to enquire, I turned tail, and followed the ridge back to Cairnwell. Probably my times for this short and swift excursion would have made history, and it is a pity that I did not think of keeping them to put on record.

As these hills have practically no rock and, besides, almost any way down from the ridge must lead back more or less quickly to civilisation, they are a good safe field for experimenting with the technique of mists. We had an interesting day of this kind amongst them one July day when the south wind was bringing up the rain-clouds, which sometimes pile up slowly against this long barrier, like reinforcements massing for an offensive, before the weather breaks upon the Braemar side.

Climbing from the north near Glen Cluny Lodge, we reached the edge of the mist halfway up Carn Aosda at

about 2200 ft. So far the gradient is comfortable and unbroken, but even so we took it slowly because of the damp
heaviness of the day. We were in some difficulty in finding
the top, because we had only the half-inch map, with contours 250 feet apart ; a scale which is useless and indeed
dangerous for mist-work upon the severer types of hill. It
is in a case like this that an aneroid comes in useful, but we
had not one with us. There are two false tops, which we
scaled in turn, and, not content with that, we went on
downhill, north towards the Cairnwell, for some distance
without having been on the real top at all, and did not
discover the mistake till we caught sight of the loch called
Loch Vrotachan, which lies just to the west of the col.
Returning on our tracks, what with one diversion and
another we only found the summit-cairn at twenty minutes
past eleven. However we had no difficulty in finding our
way to the top of the Cairnwell, and thence along the ridge,
which has no further snares and delusions, to the top of
Carn Bhinnein. The time was then twenty past one.
Here at last we encountered a wind strong enough to blow
the mist into shreds and tatters around us, and had something of a view.

Carn Bhinnein is a shapely little hill. Its summit is like
the boss at the end of too many banisters, a rounded cone
terminating a southward bend of the ridge. The green
sides drop steeply into Glen Taitneach, which extends for
half a mile past it northward to the county march, where it
all but joins the headwaters of the Baddoch Burn upon the
other side. The hillside immediately opposite is also steep
and rocky, but just to the north is a low broken stretch of
bad going, which would have to be crossed in order to
reach the Beinn Iutharns. The west branch of the Taitneach, however, leads right to Loch nan Eun, at the foot

163

of Beinn Iutharn Bheag, and this would be a better route for anyone coming not over the Carn a' Gheoidh range, but up Glen Taitneach directly from the Spital.

We stopped for part of our lunch on Carn Bhinnein and for the rest in the glen below, and left the head of the Baddoch Glen for An Socach to the north at half past two. The climb took us about an hour. The going was heathery and very rough, and a heavy storm of rain came on, so that this part of the day was not altogether pleasant ; and on the ridge of An Socach, which is a long flat hill rising very slightly to just over the three thousand-foot level at the ends, we were once more in thick mist. We spent a long time exploring this plateau in every direction at the western end, without ever being quite sure whether we had hit on the highest ground or not, and then followed the ridge eastwards and down to the Baddoch burn. We crossed the long shoulder of Carn Aosda, by which we had ascended at the outset, in order to get back to the main road at the place where we had left our bicycles, and were there by a quarter to six.

A walk very well worth doing on a fine day would be to follow the range of An Socach over several low tops, the last of which is Morrone, right into Braemar. This would take about three to three and a half hours. It would make an original and striking approach from the south, especially for anyone who had never been in this part of the country before. The approach by the main road unfortunately gives little idea of the full magnificence of the region, because the hills on either side of Glen Cluny are high enough to cut off all view of the Cairngorms or Lochnagar.

Two roads join the main road up Glen Shee from the left-hand side, one at the north end of the Bridge of Cally and the other about five miles farther on. Both lead into the unassuming valley of Strathardle, of which Kirkmichael is the metropolis. From Kirkmichael the public road makes a semicircle to the head of the glen and over the shoulder of Ben-y-Vrackie to Pitlochry : but at the top of the bend a private road strikes off to the north, up green Glen Fernait, for the remote shooting-lodge of Falar, which is beyond Carn an Righ and quite close to the head of Glen Tilt. From this road, with the indispensable help of a bicycle—one would hardly be allowed to make use of it in a car—I have several times approached the Beinn Iutharn group. The walking distance is a good deal less than from the Spital, but since (measured from my base, three miles south of Kirkmichael) some thirty miles of bicycling has to be taken into account, I cannot say that there is any particular advantage in making the attack on this flank. It is, however, the only possible one from the neighbourhood of Pitlochry, and anyone staying somewhere on that side and desirous of new worlds to conquer might do worse than make this expedition.

It would not be worth while to come so far for the purpose, but, if you are staying in the more immediate neighbourhood, another hill which may be done without difficulty from Glen Fernait is Beinn Vuirich, one of those annoying hills which just fails to qualify for the dignity of being a ' Munro '. (I should say for those who do not understand the expression, that it is applied to any Scottish hill over the sacred level of three thousand feet in height, after the late Sir Hector Munro of Lindertes, who held the proud record of having climbed every one of them in the course of his life.)

Unfortunately my acquaintance with Glen Fernait dates

much farther back than my notes, and I have no details of the various days. There was one on Beinn Vuirich, and one spent in crossing to the Spital and back over the fairly high chain between Glen Fernait and Glen Lochsie ; and more than one other day besides these, because I well remember being caught on Glas Tulaichean in quite a heavy snowstorm, though it was but the middle of August, and I am certain that this was not when I did the round of the Glas Tulaichean, the two Beinn Iutharns and Carn an Righ ; for then the weather was a great deal kinder, though almost sunless, as I have not forgotten for the following cause : I had broken my watch and my father had firmly declined to lend me his, so that to find out the time I had to make the best of the compass, a blade of grass, and a poor head for mathematics. In consequence, thinking it was much later in the evening than it was, I raced home as fast as I could down Glen Fernait, only to find, to my joy, that I was in perfect time for dinner. But midday I did establish accurately, for the sun happened to be out, and at that moment I was somewhere on the way up Glas Tulaichean (having left my bicycle at the highest part of the road, at just about 2000 ft., where it crosses the shoulder called Carn an t-Sionnach, right opposite Loch Loch and the highest part of Beinn a' Ghlo). So, allowing an hour and a half for bicycling home downhill, the walking must have taken me about six and a half hours. This corresponds fairly well with Naismith's formula, and would seem to be rather on the fast side.

After the short pull up Carn an t-Sionnach three miles of a gentle grassy ridge bring you to Glas Tulaichean—the name means ' Green Hillocks ' and is a fair description. There is a drop to 2600 ft. just west of Loch nan Eun, before the climb on to the ridge of Beinn Iutharn Bheag,

Mam nan Carr and Beinn Iutharn Mhor, which on the north side forms the corrie containing the headwaters of the Ey. You may now descend Glen Ey to Inverey and Deeside, or else follow a low flattened portion of the main chain beyond Beinn Iutharn Mhor to Carn Bhac and so down the Allt Connie. But I do not much recommend Carn Bhac, which I have done from the north. This and its immediate neighbours are rather stale characterless hills. Beinn Iutharn Mhor is quite a proud gentleman, though not on the face of him so closely related to the Prince of Darkness (and of gentlemen) as to deserve the name ' Great Hell Mountain ', which is what the Gaelic means. The northern corrie holds a little tarn called Lochan Uaine, which seems to establish some sort of cousinship with those *grands seigneurs*, the Cairngorms, across the way; but the family likeness is not otherwise apparent.

Carn an Righ is in several ways the most interesting of the group. It lies detached to the west of Mam nan Carr, between that and the Falar road. Unlike its neighbours it is boulder-strewn, and at the western corner more or less precipitous ; and this makes its shape stand out in more vigorous lines. The king after whom it is called is supposed to be Malcolm Canmore, who was fond of hunting in this forest. But if my inferences are right, it is also connected with at once a more romantic, and a better authenticated, story, in which the most famous poachers of the seventeenth and nineteenth centuries are the chief characters. I have a distaste for the Ossianic heroes, and have consistently omitted any anecdotes about them, where they try to intrude ; these stout realistic fellows are much more to the point. Yet can I hope to do justice in a page or two to a subject which R. L. Stevenson would certainly have thought well worth a book—and a book by Stevenson ?

The poacher of three hundred years ago was a Mac-keracher of Athole, better known throughout Mar, Athole and Gaick by the Homeric nickname of *Lonach-Fhiadh* (Anglicised, ' Lonavey '), meaning ' Hungry after the Deer '. Many were his exploits of skill and prowess in the art of stalking, such as it was at that time of doubtful firelocks, but most remarkable of all was the genius with which for years he evaded all traps, all efforts to effect his capture. Indeed it might have seemed to be genius border-ing on magic, but in this direction Highlanders have never been superstitious (nor are they at all in any bad sense), for on many occasions he disappeared amongst the rocks in a place from which there seemed no possibility of escape unobserved, and yet the most diligent search proved quite in vain.

But at long last taken he was : I suppose, like all heroes, by treachery or else by a conspiracy of the gods—perhaps his devotion to Diana had offended Venus—and in prison Lonavey, who had never known what it was not to breathe the air of the hills, soon pined away. But before he died he spoke words which caught the ear of a fellow prisoner and seemed to him somehow strange enough to remember and report. Yet they were only those, natural enough in the circumstances, in which Lonavey lamented that he could not be ' where his trusty gun awaited him on Carn an Righ's fair height '. The precise significance of these words remained long undiscovered. But the story of some secret hiding-place had been set in motion, and persisted.

Two centuries later there was another poacher, as great a man in his day—and in his way. I think he was a Farquharson, but his name has escaped me. One day while desperately trying to hide from some gamekeepers who were hot upon his track, this man stumbled unawares upon Lonavey's secret refuge. The entrance was beneath a boulder, under which he had to crawl, so that it would be passed a hundred times unobserved. There was a vertical shaft leading into a water-tight cavern of some size, lit by a single crack high up in one of the walls. The poacher's first emotion must have been one of relief at finding himself in such a perfect hiding-place ; but it changed to wonder, when his eye fell on the remains of an ancient gun, placed, as he noticed later, just where the rays of the midday sun would fall on it through the crack ; and he remembered the story of Lonavey, now so remarkably confirmed. He must have been sorry too that his own delicate legal position made it impossible for him to publish such interesting news. The discovery was of course too valuable a trade-secret for him to communicate except to one close associate. For years the cave served him as faithfully as it had Lonavey, but after a while it happened that some emergency compelled them to take the risk of using it in time of snow, and by this means they were eventually tracked to their lair. And so at last the curious story was complete.

Whether the exact whereabouts of Lonavey's Cave is still known to the Athole keepers I am not sure. If so, it is probably a well-guarded secret tradition. Its general position should on the evidence be somewhere beneath the crags on the west side of Carn an Righ ; but you would probably waste your time in trying to find it for yourself.

CHAPTER XIII

GLEN TILT AND BEINN A' GHLO

PITLOCHRY is the next place north of Ballinluig on the Inverness line. Being the tourist centre of the Perthshire Highlands, the modern town is something of an upstart. The old village where Robert Louis Stevenson stayed is Moulin, up the breakneck hill on the way to Kirkmichael. Needless to say, there are hotels and boarding-houses of all grades in both. The immediate neighbourhood though pretty, is not one that will much please the determined walker. The elegant but not very lofty quartzite cone of Ben-y-Vrackie dominates and gives it style. This is a popular expedition ; but on the whole the place is best suited for those with other interests than climbing hills. Beyond Pitlochry comes the celebrated Pass of Killiecrankie, the scene of the battle. Here in a succession of pools like black coffee and cataracts like cream the Garry flows in splendour ; the gorge is thickly wooded to the top of the small rocky hills which lower above the road. It is just at the issue of the Pass that the Tummel, with ' the Road to the Isles ' beside it, enters from the west.

Through the Pass, seven miles from Pitlochry by the aggressively ' first class ' road, we come to Blair Atholl. This is a comparatively small place to-day, but at one time ' the Blair of Athole ' was the effective as it is still the

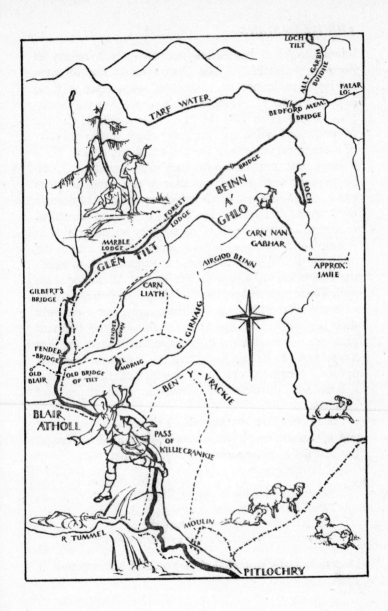

LOCH
TILT

ALLT GARBH
BUIDHE

FALAR
LO:

TARF WATER

BEDFORD MEM.
BRIDGE

L. LOCH

BRIDGE

BEINN
A'
GHLO

FOREST
LODGE

CARN NAN
GABHAR

MARBLE
LODGE

AIRGIOD BEINN

GLEN TILT

0

APPROX:
1 MILE

GILBERT'S
BRIDGE

CARN
LIATH

FENDER BURN

G. GIRNAIG

FENDER
BRIDGE

L. MORAIG

OLD
BLAIR

OLD BRIDGE
OF TILT

BEN - Y - VRACKIE

BLAIR
ATHOLL

PASS
OF
KILLIECRANKIE

R. TUMMEL

MOULIN

PITLOCHRY

moral capital of the Athole country, which means all northern Perthshire. The Duke's castle was of great military importance in a series of wars, since it is so placed as to command all the main routes over the Grampian range : Glen Tilt, the Pass of Drumochter, and the Mounth road called the Minigaig, which was in old days of more importance than the present thoroughfare. It is a large but not strikingly handsome building in an acquiescent setting—for this part of the strath is green and civilised, but not so intensively civilised as to deserve the honours due to art. The castle contains an unrivalled collection of stags' heads—' harts ' they are still called in Athole—and amongst various more or less interesting museum-pieces, one real curiosity, a round bed, in which the twelve sons of a very remote Earl of Athole (or some such Homeric number) used to sleep. It is built round a central pillar which supports the canopy, and apparently they lay with their feet towards this on the bell-tent principle. For economy of space and mattresses the idea has so much to be said for it, that it is a wonder more has not since been made of it by those with large families ; but I conceive difficulties in connection with sheets and blankets.

I like better than anything else at Blair the ruined chapel and graveyard which lies out of sight behind the castle, but just inside the policies. There it is that

> " fiercest of old soldiers lies,
> Dundee, beside the foamy banks of Tilt.
> (With what superfluous mourning in these trees
> The ivy crowns the yew ! There the bee sucks
> His strangest honey, playing sweetheart to the dead)."

He was mortally wounded at the battle of Killiecrankie, at

the moment of victory, and died either at the Castle or
at Urrard House nearby.

Behind this is the main road to Glen Tilt, but a private
one. The public road keeps to the *east* bank of the Tilt,
not crossing the old bridge of Tilt half a mile up, but
bearing to the right very steeply up to Fenderbridge,
where it crosses the Fender ; thence climbing farther
across the corner of the hill, and coming down again to the
Tilt at Gilbert's Bridge two miles farther on. Here it re-
joins the private one. The road continues four miles
more to the Forest Lodge, eight miles from Blair Atholl,
and a mile or two beyond, after which you must walk.
There are gates across it for the benefit of the Duke's
prize herd of Highland cattle, which are really a magnificent and to the stranger possibly rather an alarming
sight. These beasts are much less common in this part of
Scotland than in the west.

It would be a bold thing to put a name to the crowning
glory of Perthshire, but the country about Glen Tilt, and
especially Beinn a' Ghlo, has always struck me as at once
the finest and the most typical example of the sort of
scenery which seems to me characteristic of the county.
The more sensational effects of naked rock are absent.
Instead there are immense fields of soft rich colouring,
broken by contrasting flashes of pale grass or bursts of the
red soil beneath, which are equally dramatic in a different
way. The luxuriance and special variety of tone in these
hills is due less to the reactions of a moist atmosphere, as
in the green hills of the west, than to their own heavier
texture, and their qualities are saved from cloying through
excess of sweetness by the height and sharpness of the
slopes. They thus retain a healthy firmness of outline
and do not relapse into the heather seascape, somewhat

173

monotonous except when the heather is actually in bloom, into which the lower parts of the western Athole forest, towards Drumochter, do incline to degenerate.

If you walk south into Glen Tilt from Aberdeenshire, the contrast between the kind of scenery you have left and that in which you find yourself is as if you had passed from the hall of some great old house, stately but severe and bare, into the elaborate, though still spacious, drawing-room, which the modern lady who has married into the house has made her own : a room such as poor Mary Queen of Scots might have had furnished for herself in Holyrood.   North of the march is a formless region of broken bog and heather, where the headwaters of the Dee should be ; for not only the Feshie, but the Tilt also, appears to have been diverted from a former tributaryship to the Dee. The watershed is quite flat, and its level only a little over 1500 ft.   On the edge of this region lies Loch Tilt, a shallow patch of water surrounded by low feature-less moor.   It is full of trout, and so there is a boathouse, despite its great distance from the nearest lodge—for the loch is on the Athole side of the march, but so close to it that I suspect the water is badly poached from the north ; more than suspect, indeed, for I have seen men there with rods who certainly did not look like close personal friends of the Duke's.

But though Loch Tilt shares the name of the much more celebrated glen—a name whose origins are shrouded in antiquity and are probably pre-Celtic—the burn which comes out of it is a mere trickle.   The main stream of the glen is that roaring ' Bull ' of a river, the Tarf, which drains the main Grampian chain lengthwise for a distance of at least nine miles before bursting into the Tilt through a deep canyon two miles from its head.   One look at the

Tarf is enough to show how apt was the Greek sense of illustration which represented the gods of Achelous and others of their torrential rivers in the forms of bulls. Christened Tilt, it still remains a swift and strong, but less tempestuous, stream of amber water—and I do not mean water the colour of ' warning ' traffic-signal lights, but water the colour of amber, preferably the more expensive lighter variety ; but of course it varies according to the state of flood. And if the Tarf has a personality which falls for deification under the superb symbol of the male, some of the smaller streams which join its course, such as the Fhearnach from Carn nan Gabhar of Beinn a' Ghlo, and the Mhairi and the Diridh from Beinn Dearg on the other side of the glen, suggest perfect counterparts. All these flow down steep winding gullies, fringed with over-hanging alders and rowans, which in the Pagan age of faith must surely have concealed the grottoes of the Caledonian nymphs, or even—forgive my fancy, but in Glen Tilt these things do not seem so far-fetched as perhaps they sound when read about in Wolverhampton—in some final unexplored recess, the dream-place of Baudelaire's exotic, but otherwise un-Baudelairean, poem,

BIEN LOIN D'ICI . . .

C'est ici la chambre sacrée,
Où cette fille très parée,
Tranquille et toujours préparée,

D'une main éventant ses seins,
Et sa coude dans les coussins,
Ecoute pleurer les bassins :

C'est la chambre de Dorothée.
—La brise et l'eau chantent au loin

175

Leur chanson de sanglots heurtée
Pour bercer cet enfant gâtée.

Du haut en bas, avec grand soin,
Sa peau délicate est frottée
D'huile odorante et de benjoin.
—Des fleurs se pâment dans un coin.

If Shiehallion is the Parnassus of Perthshire, Beinn a' Ghlo, ' Ben of the Veil '—the Gaelic is of the same root as our word ' cloth ', and refers to the veil of mist commonly to be seen upon its head—surely deserves the rating of Olympus. Really a group of three well separated and two subsidiary summits, each of which should rank as a mountain in its own right, it makes up the whole eastern side of Glen Tilt. The two northern summits are the highest, and there are the twin peaks of Beinn a' Ghlo which stand up as such a notable landmark in the southward view from the Cairngorms. Their names are Carn nan Gabhar (3671 ft.), ' Goats' Cairn ', and Braigh Coire Chruinn-Bhalgain (3505 ft.), ' the Head of Round Pocket-Corrie '. South of these is Carn Liath (3193 ft.), which is the hill generally pointed out as ' Beinn a' Ghlo ', being the only one of the several points which is visible from the main avenues of civilisation in Glen Garry. The ridge of Carn nan Gabhar runs south for over a mile, and ends in a point called Airgiod Bheinn (3490 ft.), ' Silver Mountain '; and between Airgiod Bheinn and Carn Liath is the lower point of Beinn Bheag (2350 ft.).

Carn Liath is a short and easy climb from Blair, and my wife and I have done it even from Kinloch Rannoch with the assistance of bicycles. We took these up the hill through Fenderbridge as far as Loch Moraig, which would be rather over two miles from Blair. This is the obvious

Grace D'Arcy

IX. GRASS OF PARNASSUS   COTTON GRASS

route ; but it is better to follow the road a mile and a half farther than the loch before taking to the heather, to get the most direct ascent. It is then steep but quite straight-forward, and should not take more than an hour and a half. On either side of the hog's-back ridge fall the steep and equally graduated slopes which are characteristic of Beinn a' Ghlo, heathered to the very top, but planed off with a smooth regularity which seems to leave not a scrap of cover for man or beast. Yet the variety of the several corries in depth and height prevents the slightest sug-gestion of monotony, and the curl of the ridge gives the hill a calm dignity of movement—a movement leading as inevitably to the higher peaks as the path of an eighteenth, century garden to its little summerhouse in the classical style. I know of nothing quite like Beinn a' Ghlo for such serenity of design upon so large a scale.

It was several years since I had been up to Fender-bridge, and on this clear late June day I was astonished that the beauty of the upland fields of oats and sheep-pasture, which here border upon the open moors, could possibly have been so far forgotten. How readily the best things slip from us ! (But it must be admitted that the addition of a very pretty woman in vogue-pattern green velvet shorts would tend to brighten the colours of the picture as a whole.) There is a view both downwards, across the green strath and the low hills beyond, with the spearhead of Shiehallion in the distance, and upwards to the upthrust blue shoulder of Carn Liath. I think such places are the best of all to live in : at the bottom of a valley you have not the same feeling of liberty, and at the top of a hill you have none in fact, for every foot you descend in the freshness of the morning brings a penalty of what seems like ten more to climb back at the end of the

M

day. If you agree with me you will find Fenderbridge a much better place to stay than the extremely neat and rather too trafficky village of Blair itself, where the hotels are. It should generally be possible, except perhaps in August, to find quarters in one of the few cottages near the bridge or in one of the farms higher up the glen.

Always with due regard to the absence of beer, I recommend these considerations to the particular notice of walkers coming from the north through Glen Tilt, but from Blair also the extra climb is worth while. There is a procession of roses, tame and wild, white, pink and saffron, all the way up the hill, and in the meadows a Swiss abundance of gowans, poppies and flowering thorns. Why is it that there are so many more really conspicuous wild flowers in Scotland than elsewhere in Britain? Except inside woods, the earth elsewhere seems to be dead by comparison. Nor, in spite of the climate, or because of it, are there any lovelier cultivated gardens.

For Carn nan Gabhar, which is the ' real thing ' and a full day's walking, there are several possible routes from the south. The most direct is perhaps by Glen Girnaig, which leads right to the foot of Airgoid Bheinn, either starting from Killiecrankie at the entrance of the glen, or from Blair, taking the road past Loch Moraig, which comes into the glen four miles up. From Strathardle, you could approach by Glen Fernait, turning off along the Glen Loch burn at Daldhu, just before the road goes up a very steep little bit of hill. Or it could be reached from the bridge in Glen Tilt a little above the Forest Lodge by way of Braigh Coire Chruinn-Bhalgain.

The day we went up Carn Liath enabled me to reconstruct the route from Fenderbridge which Jock Stewart and I took the first time I ever was on the hill, and this is

178

probably the best. It is one that is not very obvious from the map, and that day is so long ago that I had forgotten it. The route is as follows : Take the road up the *west* side of Glen Fender as far as it goes, and then follow the main burn up to the neck which connects Carn Liath and the Braigh. There is no real path, though there are traces of one. Then either climb the Braigh, or work round it on the east side to the broad col between it and Carn nan Gabhar. This is called Bealach an Fhiodha, the Pass of the Timber. I don't know why, nor do I remember whether there are any traces of a wood having ever been there ; but if the name is evidence for the past existence of trees, it should be a most interesting and exceptional datum for the calculation of the former tree-level in the Highlands. I have never seen any wood-remains at such a height as this (2893 ft.). As the summit is some way to the north of the bealach, it will not save trouble to scale the very steep and stony side of Airgiod Bheinn, confronting you on the opposite side of the little glen in which you will find yourself after crossing the first col : not that there is any harm in it, if the hill tempts you, only you may as well take it with your eyes open. The route described should bring you to the top of Carn nan Gabhar in roughly five or six hours, and if you then returned over the Braigh and Carn Liath, which would take perhaps an hour more, you would have made a pretty thorough exploration of the whole of Beinn a' Ghlo, and have one of the finest days in your history to look back on. You could of course save yourself a great deal with the aid of some kind of vehicle, and an appreciable something by making your base at Fender-bridge.

Beinn a' Ghlo is not generally regarded as one of the hills within the Braemar radius. It belongs strictly to

179

Perthshire, and any part of it except Carn nan Gabhar is practically out of the question from the north, on account of the great distance involved from the nearest point to which one can drive ; this being the White Bridge in Glen Dee, or perhaps the Geldie ford.

I have, however, done this walk on two occasions and first-rate days they both were. The first time, Robin Gerard and I were almost more pleased with ourselves for having conceived the idea of this rather unusual expedition than for carrying it out with success. Yet for the season of early October, when winter is already in the air and the days have shortened, it was perhaps too big a day's undertaking, as we might have found to our cost if anything had gone wrong and held us up. However, even in the dark the Glen Tilt path can hardly be missed.

We bicycled to the Geldie Ford, and left there at 9.5. The track passes through the Bynac, where the larches planted to shelter the solitary shepherd's house (which is unoccupied in winter), make a conspicuous landmark on the open moor. It then makes its way through two miles of broken ground, keeping well above, and to the west of, the meandering burn, as far as the county march. The route is fairly well cairned, and there is a large cairn on the summit (such as it is). The Cairngorms behind become lost to sight as we enter the narrow defile of the upper Tilt, and Perthshire starts up suddenly in all her glory. Here the path is very narrow. It is beaten into the side of a hill so steep that any loose stones will splash right down into the water. The opposite face of Meall na Caillich Buidhe is of the same type.

About two miles of this bring us suddenly to the falls of Tarf, but the sound of the water can be heard some time before the falls are reached. Across the Tarf is the

180

Bedford Memorial Bridge, an iron bridge built in very sensible commemoration of an English tourist who was drowned here a good many years ago, and from this there is a good view of the lower falls. There are, as a matter of fact, some perhaps finer falls above, and some magnificent bathing-pools, entirely hidden from the world at large if accessible at all. I have never been far up the long Tarf valley, but once spent a day which I do not regret, in investigating the best places in the lower ravine. Even this means a short steep climb along the north side, as well as difficult, and—if you choose badly—dangerous, descents and re-ascents.

Two hours is easy time to allow for the distance as far as the Bedford Bridge. We arrived in an hour and three-quarters and had a rest on the seductively green smooth turf below the bridge, leaving again at eleven o'clock. Now comes the main reach of Glen Tilt, which after one slight bend, lies dead straight ahead for six or eight miles, like a vast trench, the tops of the hills on either hand being on the average well over two thousand feet above the glen. No such perspective is to be found anywhere in Scotland. The reason for the peculiarity is that the erosion of the glen—and particularly rapid erosion it must be with such a river as the Tarf as fretsaw—is taking place along the line of a great fault which runs right across the Highlands from south-west to north-east, and indeed is known to geology as ' the Glen Tilt Fault '.

For Beinn a' Ghlo the best route is up the long shoulder of Meall Gharran from the junction of the Allt an Loch with the Tilt, a mile below the Bedford Bridge. But we chose a slightly shorter and steeper way from the foot of the next burn to the south on that side, a mile farther on. In either case the Tilt has of course to be crossed, and this is not an easy business. It is normally both swift and deep—well up the thighs at least—and there do not seem to be any particularly good fords. In a spate it would be hazardous to attempt it, as the late Mr. Bedford would have been fortunate to realise. Upon this subject, I was told a better and less ' tragic ' story (as the newspapers call it) of a party who once upon a time thus crossed the Tilt to climb Beinn a' Ghlo. While they were on the hill there was a severe storm, and when they got down to the glen again they found that the rain had raised the level of the water to such an extent, that in order to re-cross they stripped naked and tied all their belongings as high as possible on their necks, or perhaps carried them on their heads. Whichever it was, they had to let them go in order to avoid being carried away themselves by the force of the water. They got across safely, but were unable to re-cover a single stitch ; clothes, maps, food, flasks, sticks and all were gone ; and in this state they had to face the long miles back to the Bynac shieling. Their arrival there must have been somewhat embarrassing both to host and guests, but if he was a Highlander I am sure he was fully equal to the occasion, and they were no doubt by that time too tired and too relieved to be much troubled.

It was midday before we started the climb along the south side of the gully. The first five hundred feet were very steep, and the rest more than moderately so. By following the bluff between the burn and its next neigh-bour it is impossible not to arrive at the top eventually. But it is quite two miles off, almost due south. At least twice our hopes were raised and dashed by false appear-ances of the top. It is that kind of hill. A point at about 3000 ft. where the bluff joins up with Meall Gharran was particularly deceptive. We arrived at the summit of

Carn nan Gabhar at 1.30. As this was in mist, we did not stay there long, but long enough to admire Coire Caseagallach. This eastern side is the only part of Beinn a' Ghlo which is in any way precipitous—the name means ' the Corrie of the Dreadful Steep '—and this contrast, the enhancing power of mist, and the vision of Loch Loch lying far below, conspired to make a deep impression even on eyes accustomed to the Cairngorms. The curious name of this loch is explained by the fact that there is a now obsolete Gaelic word *loch* meaning ' dark '—and dark it looked under the heavy shadow of the cloud.

We badly needed lunch, after eight hours since break-fast, and found a good stream for the purpose near the top of Meall Gharran, which we then descended. We got our kilts pretty wet in fording the river once more, and by the time we started the tramp homeward it was four o'clock. We reached the Geldie at 5.55 and Braemar at 7.15. It was nearly dark already as we hurried through the dreary pass beyond the march ; for it was the first day of ' winter ' (solar) time. In every direction invisible stags, down from the hills for their evening drink and shelter, were roaring at one another from glen to glen, with that broken winding bellow, which is one of the weirdest and most mournful noises imaginable. Nothing could sound less like the war-cry and love-call which it is. I have never heard it in such full force and so close at hand, and with the hour and the place to help out the effect, it seemed unearthly.

There was a more cheerful tone about the second Beinn a' Ghlo day from Braemar ; for it was a perfect day of that same perfect September in which we went to Sgoran Dubh. This time I was with Bernard Cook and a Gentle-man in ' plus fours ' (which in those days gentlemen were still known to wear). His respectability extended to a tie and a soft felt hat, which he did not once trouble to remove. What caused still more admiration was that, in spite of a disdain for the removal of shoes and stockings where the Tilt was concerned, he arrived home as immaculate, and to all appearances as fresh in wind and limb, when we got back to dinner at nearly eight o'clock, as when we had started from Braemar at seven in the morning. Bernard on the other hand suffered from severe internal disorders as the after-effect either of a record-breaking attack upon Meall Gharran in which he left us both far behind, or of consuming unaccustomed quantities of the bitterly cold water from the springs. Even for walkers, *Surtout pas de zèle* is not at all a bad motto.

After the first steep bit, the climb by Meall Gharran is a long steady pull. We came on herd after herd of deer, one in every pocket of the ridge, and amused ourselves, though we wasted some time in this way, by a little amateur stalking—but with the purpose of trying, not to approach, but to avoid them. Though the summit for some hundreds of yards all round is steep and boulder-strewn, Beinn a' Ghlo is a hill which is heathery almost to the top, and we found white heather three times. It was a mark, even if not an omen, of good luck, for the weather and our form were as good as could be. The sun was roasting, yet once more the ben lived up to its name, and there was mist upon the top, though none to be seen in any other direction. But there was haze coming up from the south. This was a pity, as the view from Beinn a' Ghlo is particularly fine. It stands by itself, and its height, which brings it into the first rank of Highland mountains, is sufficient to overlook all other hills within at least ten miles in every ' airt '. But the panorama of the

184

Cairngorms, which occupy the whole of the northern quarter, was splendid enough to content us.

Rounding the north end of the crags, we started down the steep eastern side. There we found a ledge thickly carpeted with cranberry plants, where we lunched and smoked in deep satisfaction. Then we dropped beside Loch Loch, which is well worth a visit, and went on down the burnside for the two miles back to Glen Tilt. As we started to cross (in a fairly advanced state of undress, for I was warned by experience) our eyes fell upon three clothed in bright raiment—' female of sex it seemed, ornate and gay '—sitting in idleness on the other side not far off, and not looking in the least like a party engaged on the rather serious undertaking of walking through Glen Tilt. It never struck me at the time that they might have been the Baudelairean nymphs of whom I have been talking ; but I suspect, as a matter of fact, that they were part of the domestic staff of Falar Lodge, which is but three miles away. (A shooting-path comes from Falar along the Gleann Mor, which joins Glen Tilt nearly opposite the Falls of Tarf.) If so, how they must have been hating their exile in the wilds ; for the famous lodge of Falar, the scene of some of the most historic sporting exploits (told in length in McConnochie's *Deer and Deer Forests of Scotland* and elsewhere) is one of the most remote lodges in Scotland, and I believe the highest, now that the old lodge of Corrour on Rannoch Moor is abandoned.

I cannot leave Glen Tilt without recalling the one time I took a bicycle through it. It happened that I had to get from Braemar into Argyle, and the thought of the tedious train journey all round Scotland dismayed me. I thought I could get there as quickly and far more pleasantly on my own, for Scotland is the only part of the British Isles where one's legs are still useful upon occasion. My plan was to take the bicycle through Glen Tilt, which is easy enough, ride down to Blair and on to Rannoch Station, leave the bicycle there to be sent on by rail, and end the day by walking across the Moor of Rannoch to the Kingshouse Inn.

I left Braemar at seven, and expected to be at Blair by midday. But although midsummer was not long past, I had eighty or ninety miles before me and time did not weigh heavily on my hands. So, to save time, I started to ride along the smoother sections of the Glen Tilt path ; but they were not smooth enough, for only a mile beyond the Bynac I caught on a stone which buckled the front wheel and in one blow put a finish to my plans for the day. I thought the matter out : the weather outlook was bad and a drizzle was coming on ; but I decided that at this stage, with no bicycle—for the wheel would not go round and so it could not even be pushed—to go back ' were as tedious as go o'er '. Making the best of a bad job, I therefore set out on the remaining eight miles of the path, carrying the offending machine on my shoulders. I need hardly say, this did not add to the pleasure of the walk, but when after all the weather changed and turned out perfect, I could not help enjoying it despite all disappointment. At the foot of the gully of the Tilt proper, I stood for a few minutes to watch a family of stoats playing together, apparently quite unaware of me, on a sunny green bank at the water's edge.

At Forest Lodge I found the keeper's wife working in the hay, and arranged with her to have the bicycle sent down on the next convenient occasion to the Tilt Hotel at Blair, where Miss Christie kindly took charge of the rest of the funeral arrangements. It is not the only good turn she has done for me and many others. As I walked down the road, which is good for two miles north of Forest Lodge, glad as I was to part with the bicycle, it annoyed me a good deal to think how quickly it would have enabled me to cover those ten miles.

As it was, I did not get to Blair until nearly three. From there I rang up friends in Perth and invited myself to stay the night. Apparently, however, I did not make the circumstances of the case fully clear over the telephone; for when I arrived, with only the disreputable clothes I stood in and a little satchel (which held nothing whatever but cheese, raisins, several flasks of whisky ' in case one was bad,' and by a stroke of fortune, that one emblem of salvation, the Old School Tie) my hostess started the conversation by asking whether I would mind very much if the maid did not unpack for me as it was her day out! It was my turn to apologise, and to explain that she would have thought me a very queer, and quite unnecessarily provident visitor.

CHAPTER XIV

THE REST OF ATHOLE, AND GAICK

FOR some twenty miles west of Glen Tilt, as far as the Drumochter pass, and south to that main track of civilisation, Glen Garry, spreads one of the largest unbroken stretches of forest in Scotland. The chief drainage channels to the north are the Feshie, which separates this region from the Cairngorms, and the Tromie, both tributaries of the Spey. Although this huge expanse of county is entirely uninhabited except for the few shooting-lodges and their accessories—and on the Perthshire side most even of these are situated in the main glen—and although it is larger than the whole space occupied by the Cairngorms, it does not offer temptations to the walker in any way commensurate with the difficulties of access. The general level of the main Grampian chain seems to diminish, as it approaches its central watershed, by several hundred feet as compared with the average, for in all this region there is not a single hill of outstanding distinction, whether in height or character.

The highest is Beinn Dearg, close to Blair Atholl, which is 3304 ft.—little more than An Sgarsoch (3300 ft.) and Carn an Fhidleir (3276 ft.) across Glen Tarf to the north. These last have the bad luck to face directly on the Cairngorms, which make them seem very small fry. One of the hills next to Glen Tilt, opposite Beinn a' Ghlo, Carn

188

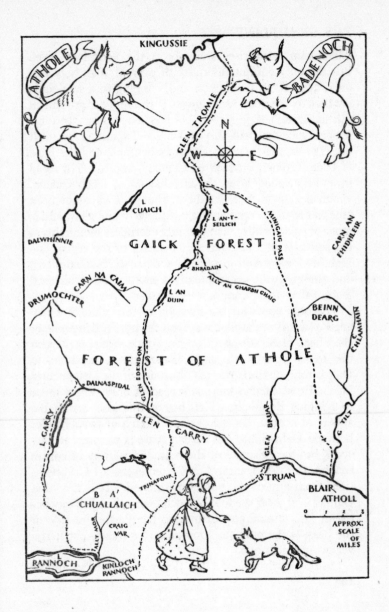

Chlamhain, also rises well above the 3000-foot level. But the only continuous range of over, though only just over, 3000 ft. is at the west end, running in a semicircle parallel to the road and railway; the highest ground of this flat stretch of peat is A' Bhuidheannach Beag (3064 ft.). Probably better than this and higher, standing by itself not far into the forest, between Dalwhinnie and the head of Glen Tromie, is Meall na Cuaich (3120 ft.). This bold little hill, called after the cup-like loch, Loch Cuaich, which lies at its foot, I believe, though I have not been able to prove it, commands a particularly fine view, and is more of a personality than the rather formless mountains to the south of it. The general character of the region is a high level moorland dissected by deep steep-sided glens, and the glens are consequently a more striking physical feature than the summits.

The only bases for the invasion of this country where good quarters are available are, on the north, Kingussie or elsewhere in Strathspey; on the south, Blair, or Struan five miles west of it; and between them, the hotel at Dalwhinnie, on the Inverness-shire side of the Drumochter Pass. From Struan there is a road of only twelve miles to Kinloch Rannoch, which brings this also within the sphere of action. In the desolate stretch of twenty miles between Dalwhinnie and Struan there is nowhere to stay at all, but the existence of the road and railway of course reduces this disadvantage, and extends the area of operations from any of the points mentioned. It is true that Dalnaspidal, near the foot of Loch Garry, just halfway between Dalwhinnie and Struan on the Perthshire side of the pass, is the only stopping-place for trains, but it is a very convenient one.

On the south side of Glen Garry also, over an almost

190

equal area, the country is at once wild in reality and tame in effect. In the triangle formed between that glen, Loch Ericht and the Tummel valley the only high hills are those of the horseshoe just to the east of the Drumochter Pass, which encircles the great corrie or glen called Coire Domhain, and ends in the two wardens of the marches known as the Sow of Athole and the Boar of Badenoch. Apart from these and their outliers, the only hill of substance is Beinn a' Chuallaich, immediately above Kinloch Rannoch. Otherwise the general level of this triangle is insignificant, and east of the Struan-Kinloch Rannoch road it even becomes quite civilised. If then a single chapter is made to stretch all the way from the Cairngorms to the Moor of Rannoch—and that despite the fact that this is the very heart of the Grampians—the reason is that, having much better fare yet to offer, I do not want to waste too much time on that which is worse. It is true also that I have not explored very much of the ground— and few people have except the stalkers—but then again the reason I have not done so is that I never found it sufficiently tempting ; as is betrayed, I fear, by the unusually clean and untorn state of this alone amongst my one-inch maps.

I do not, however, wish to imply that it is not good country ; only that there is better. It is of the type that is likely chiefly to be visited by way of pass-walks, and of these there are some of the very best : in particular the Minigaig Mounth-route, where the older military track crossed from Blair to Kingussie, and the more westerly pass at a lower level, which follows the chain of lochs, Loch an Duin, Loch Bhradain and Loch an t-Seilich. These are both a full day's walking. Of the Minigaig, which goes first to the head of Glen Bruar, and thence has to cross two or three miles of high moorland, not much under 3000 ft., before dropping to the Allt Bhran and so into Glen Tromie, I have no first-hand knowledge. It should be an interesting route, and is one which the through-walker, who has no time or no taste for climbing as such, would probably rate as a first-class experience. But to my mind, if you are going to do so much climbing in any case, it is a pity not to throw in a few real summits. It looks as though in mist the path would be an easy one to lose, and in wet weather there must be some very bad walking. For it takes very few years to obliterate even made roads across the open hill; and I know of one which was a favourite drive with friends of mine thirty years ago, and is already in parts indistinguishable. Of the other pass, by the lochs, I shall have more to say. For a shorter day there is also the well-known track from Dalnaspidal by Loch Garry to Loch Rannoch. And for completeness I should mention the paths from Struan and Milton of Invervack (near Blair), which lead past Loch Bhac over to the Loch Tummel Inn.

The Loch Garry path is one of the best known rights-of-way in the Highlands, and forms part of the old drove-route, still used, which continues past Loch Rannoch and along the edge of Rannoch Moor to Achallater and the West. This pass would be of great service to anyone wishing to reach Rannoch from the north as quickly as possible, even with a bicycle. From Dalnaspidal at the northern end, for five miles there is only a track, to the cottage of Dunish—and it should be noted that just before Dunish there is a ford to be crossed—but from there on (passing Beinn Mholach, which it would be worth while to climb if you had time to spare) there is a good road to the shooting-lodge of Craiganour on Rannochside. The road is nominally a private one, but there can be no objection in

192

reason to your taking advantage of it. The right-of-way, which, though suitable for walkers, and rather shorter, would be out of the question for anything on wheels, turns off to the left about three miles south of Dunish beside a sort of mile- or head-stone, bearing a white sign, " No. I ", of some obscure significance. As you approach Rannoch, Beinn a' Chuallaich looms up before you, and there is also a glimpse of Shiehallion over its shoulder, but nearer at hand there is nothing of special interest.

Beinn a' Chuallaich is enormous in area, though in height it is a tantalising seventy-five feet short of the Munro qualification. It is made up of three ridges rising northwards to a connecting wall, in a formation something the shape of a trident, so that its *penetralia* lie open only to Loch Rannoch on the south. The central prong ends in the rocky eminence of Craig Var, once wooded but now ravaged by fire, which almost overhangs the village of Kinloch Rannoch, and between this and the western one, still a thousand feet or so above the valley, a broad hill-meadow is enclosed. This could not very fairly be described either as a glen or a corrie. It is drained by two main burns, which unite to form the torrent of the Allt Mor, whose thunder in time of flood can be heard for miles and is the music of the village. This enclosure may possibly supply the reason for the name of the hill, which seems to mean, ' the Hill of the Cattle-herding '. It forms a natural corral, very perfectly concealed, which would have been a most suitable place to hide ' lifted ' beasts in the old foraging days, as the Macdonalds of Glencoe used to hide them in the high recess of Bidean nam Bian. But this is pure guesswork. Being so completely sheltered on all sides but the south, it would be a good quiet place to camp in, if you wished to camp for camping's sake and not for any motive of mere convenience—the only motive which, I must admit, would ever lead me to do so. The top of the ben is at the base of the eastern prong. There is a shooting-path to it from Dunalistair, but from Kinloch Rannoch it can more easily be reached by way of the eastern branch of the Allt Mor, though it is somewhat difficult to avoid wet feet in places. Unlike the rest of the hill, the summit is a steep cone of quartz. The view is particularly good owing to the long stretches of low country which surround it in most directions, the Cairngorms appearing to special advantage ; while to make a foreground, on the neck of the north-eastern spur lies a little shallow tarn, where the deer love to wallow.

One almost too cloudless day I lay on the north side of Beinn a' Chuallaich ; the air was overcharged with an excess of ultra-violet rays, streaming down on me from the sky in such concentration, that, though the temperature was not so very high, I was obliged to cower under a rock for shelter ; and thence I spent a long time taking in all the details of the prospect before me with glasses and the naked eye in turns, identifying every ridge and glen, every snowfield on the plateau of Moine Mor and the corries of Cairn Toul and Beinn Muichdhui. But one feature due north in the middle of the landscape seemed to have risen from nowhere : a fair-sized loch at the head of a long winding glen, deep-set against the foot of what was apparently a closed barrier of steep blue hills. For I had not realised, until I looked at the map, that the Cairngorms lie as much east as north from this point, and I had altogether forgotten the existence of Loch an Duin. For this reason it somehow captured my imagination. I determined then and there to visit it at the first opportunity ; and a few days later carried out this intention.

194

Three miles east of Kinloch Rannoch the road for Struan turns north over the shoulder of Beinn a' Chuallaich from the main road to Pitlochry. It rises fairly steeply, but not so steeply that a cyclist is ever positively forced to dismount, though probably he will do so ; and reaches a height of over 1000 ft. before making a sharp descent into the clachan of Trinafour, near the head of Glen Erichdie. The road is one of the prettiest in Scotland, especially where it winds round the top of the glen of the Allt Moine Buidhe, which falls away to the right, with a view down into Strathtummel. (It was in this glen, by the way, that the last wolf of Perthshire is supposed to have been killed—by a woman with a wooden spoon— ending then, I suppose, like Mr. Eliot's world, ' not with a bang, but a whimper'.) But I am describing the road in the wrong order ; the proper way to take it is undoubtedly from the north, for then you meet the broad triangle of Shiehallion face to face as you breast the top of the hill, and all the way down, from there on to Kinloch, can rejoice in the changing phases of that model of shapeliness amongst mountains.

Trinafour is village to the house of Auchleeks, formerly the chief seat of the Struan Robertsons. I mention this in pious memory of the most famous of them, who built the house of Mount Alexander, now called Dunalistair. His character was compounded of poet, rake and Jacobite, in that order ; for the instinct of creation cannot exist upon terms, and if it is present in a man at all, it must be the motive power of his nature in its other aspects. In wastage it may well give rise to disinterested political ardours (as it did with Byron, Shelley and Wordsworth, to count a few) and more often still, to passionate experiments in sensation ; whereas neither of the latter, no more

195

at least than other human activities, are in the least degree capable of generating poetry, perhaps are more apt to act, in time, as brakes upon its momentum. Scotland has produced few poets of merit, and none of the first, or even the second, rank ; and of those in the series, such as it is, Alexander Robertson may reasonably be thought to stand pretty high. I have never seen a complete copy of his works, but some of those which I do know are distinctly worth knowing ; and I cannot do better service to his reputation than by advertising the probability that the best of them (which I have so far missed) were in a vein of what was in better days called gallantry. Struan's *Chloris vagabondes ou imaginaires* preserved him from matrimony ; which, again, would very likely have saved him from becoming ' the beautiful but ineffectual angel ' of the Jacobite cause. But by starting young and ending late he set up a record for warlike attendances in its behalf, turning out first with Dundee, next in the 'Fifteen, and finally, as an old man, in the 'Forty-Five. I say ' ineffectual ' by inference, because he survived them one after the other with no worse penalty than sequestered estates.

At Trinafour the road to Struan turns down the quiet little glen of the Erichdie (either from *eireachdas*, ' handsomeness ', or I fear more probably, for it is a pleasant, but not a striking, valley, from *eireachda*, ' a gathering '.) But we are now on the route of General Wade's junction road from Crieff to Inverness—there are still traces of a road-side barrack to be seen in the Moine Buidhe glen—and this road offers a short cut due north over the hill into Glen Garry. It rises to a height of 1500 ft. on the bare moors, and the gradient on both sides is so severe that it is surprising to find it kept up at all nowadays ; I noticed close beside it one very good example of glacially marked slab,

196

the striations running north and south. The General's original bridge spans the Garry, and brings you out on the main road at the house of Dalnacardoch, now a shooting lodge, but in the old days successively a smithy (as it is named), a military roadhouse, and a coaching inn.

It has over the door an almost obliterated inscription in Latin. The self-conscious use of the language of imperialism *par excellence* is well enough justified, for there was indeed something of the true Roman spirit in the eighteenth century penetration of the Highlands, till then, though but four hundred miles from London and for more than a century nominally subject to the British Crown, almost as unaffected by civilization as America—I mean America then, not America to-day, though in a slightly different sense this comparison might equally well be drawn. With whatever sympathy for the more romantic cause, one can but admire the extraordinary efficiency with which the country, once subjugated, was held by small pickets of English and German soldiers, separated from one another by long miles of desolate country and absurdly handicapped in every movement by the scarlet of their uniforms.

The road up Glen Edendon to Loch an Duin starts through a gate below a plantation, almost opposite Dalnacardoch, and is one of the roughest imaginable ; but of course these shooting-roads vary very much from one season to another, and are apt to be allowed to pass into disrepair if the shooting is unlet for a year or two. It is steep at first, afterwards less so, and passes only one cottage, and that deserted, before you come to the lodge of Sronphadruig, now used only as a keeper's house. This is as ' far back ' as any dwelling in Scotland, yet the stalker there told me that he stays there all the year round. Consequently it is a substantial settlement of its kind, and he has apparently to be something of a farmer into the bargain. At this point the river-bed is broad and flat, and for a wide space the glen is strewn with boulders carried down by spates. Many of these were of an unusual brick-red colour, which is very noticeable, and apparently consist of some very hard type of sandstone. Behind Sronphadruig the Edendon curves round westward into the steep and narrow inner corrie of the Carn na Caim-A' Bhuidheannach range. On its left bank, where the stream has cut into the shallow watershed on the outer curve, is a high wall of peat from which the roots of old pine-trees protrude like bones out of a cemetery after a landslip. In time, if the process continues, the Edendon may cut through this neck of peat altogether and start to flow into Loch an Duin, which lies just beyond it, and so to the Spey.

The loch, which lies right on the march between the counties of Perth and Inverness, is a peculiar one, and typifies the general characteristics of the Gaick country. Open at both ends, it lies in a clean cut right through the backbone of the Grampians, and from the water's edge the sides of An Duin, on the one hand, and Creag an Loch, on the other, rise to about an equal height at the very sharp angle which is characteristic of the glens in the neighbourhood. The Creag an Loch side consists of inaccessible craggy screes. The colour of the water is an unusual greenish blue, discoloured by the mud and gravel continually swept down into it by the burns. At the southern end there is a curious underwater shelf of rock which is visible for some distance, and at the north some small tussocky islands, amongst which men were fishing from a boat. As there was a strong and cold east wind, it looked a thankless task to me, and I was glad enough to keep myself warm by fast walking.

The path is a good one, and from the foot of the loch becomes a regular shooting-track, leading to Gaick Lodge. Loch Bhradain, two miles farther on and only a hundred feet lower than Loch an Duin, is reedy and probably much shallower. Here too there was a boat. The glen between is flat and swampy, and here I saw a pair of wild duck escorting their young in their first essays upon the wing. There was no sun, so that the general effect of these abrupt bare hills was drab and somewhat gloomy, but enlivened by one touch in the foreground, a large mound of the moraine type, which was dressed from head to foot in golden flowers looking as if they had been hand-planted there purely for decoration ; for apart from that one spot there was no sign of colour. The hills seemed deserted even by deer, for I scanned every corner with the glass and saw only a single hind ; but I have no doubt that the level tops held them in large numbers.

I went as far as the corner of the hill past Loch Bhradain, where another path turns up the Allt an Gharbh Ghaig to join the Minigaig route near the head of Glen Bruar. This would have made a good round back to Glen Garry, but I had to fetch my bicycle at Sronphadruig. I had my lunch looking north to the severe form of Gaick Lodge, a mile ahead, and, beyond it, to Loch an t-Seilich, finely enclosed, like a broader and longer Loch an Duin, between the great crag of Creag Liath and bluff Bogha-cloiche.

This glen, Glen Tromie, is supposed to be peculiarly subject to avalanches, but it is hard to understand why this should be so more than in the other glens of the district, which so closely resemble it. It probably owes its reputation (but not, as the sound of the word suggests, its name, which simply means ' gloomy ', ' melancholy ') perhaps to the fame of one particular incident sometime in the last century, when an avalanche came down on a stalking-party who had made a bothy in the glen their quarters for the night, and killed every one of them. This happening was known as ' the loss of Gaick '.

I had plenty of time to enjoy the vista, which is in any case very satisfying to the eye, and seemed the more attractive for the simple reason that I was about to turn back from it as I had come. While I did so it amused me to think that I was within a few hours' easy walk from the centre of Strathspey, a district which one thinks of as far remote from Rannoch, and as hardly in the same world with Loch Tay, by whose waters I had stood only yesterday. It is wonderful what a difference a bicycle can make in covering distances, even when the road part seems to be more walk than ride.

On the way back, beside Loch an Duin, I saw something which may sound too trifling even to mention, but which seemed to me at the time remarkable. This was merely a common, or ' garden ', blackbird, obviously with a nest somewhere in the heather, close to the water. (' For many miles around there's scarce a bush.') I am no naturalist, but to find such a bird in such a place struck me as quite an event, and its presence seemed to give an almost uncanny significance to the general absence of life even in its customary forms.

After four hours' walking, not counting the time taken for lunch, I was back at Sronphadruig by four o'clock, and should have been at Kinloch Rannoch about three hours later, although I went by the main road and round by Struan, had I not taken one of the few chances of the kind which offer themselves in the Highlands, and stopped at Struan for a pint or two of beer. As I crossed the

200

X.   THE CENTRAL GRAMPIANS FROM BEINN LAWERS

Trinafour hill, I passed a family of curlews still in the midst of the same keen educational controversies in which they had been engaged when I had passed them in the morning. I believe curlews take two years to mature and I think by the size of the young that these were in the primary stage. The sun was showing for the first time in the day, and the wind, having blown savagely against me all the way down Glen Garry—as it always does when one is on a bicycle—had fallen at last, so that only the changing notes of the curlews were to be heard ; and Shiehallion before me—but Shiehallion is a new day, and a new chapter.

Before this one ends, I will say something of the other main groups of hills in the western Athole area. Beinn Dearg and Carn Chlamhain go together, though there is a two hours' stretch of rough country, with big dips, between them. If taken singly, the former can best be approached from Glen Bruar, from which there is a pony-track to the top—it lies but little off the Minigaig route—while the latter (curiously unnamed on the one-inch map) is directly over Glen Tilt, opposite Beinn a' Ghlo, from which it shows as a definite point with a fairly rocky face. A shorter descent from Beinn Dearg would be by way of Beinn a' Chait, with an opportunity to explore the interesting ravine of Glen Diridh. But here are pastures new to which I have yet to look forward.

An Sgarsoch and Carn an Fhidleir, to the north of the Tarf, I have explored from the Braemar side. They are unspectacular peaty hills, taking about six hours of mostly bad walking from the Geldie ford. Carn an Fhidleir is the meeting-place of three counties, Perth, Aberdeen and Inverness. Next to it westward above the Feshie is a flat-topped hill called Meall Tionail, the Hill of the Gathering, where it is supposed in old days a periodical market used to be held, at which the men of Deeside and those of the Spey would meet on more or less neutral ground for the exchange of goods and cattle. (The name is also given on some maps to Mullach Clach a' Bhlair, just opposite, across the Feshie. There are several such Meall Tionails in various parts of the Highlands, and I think I am right in saying that they are always to be found at a similar point on the borders of two clan-territories, and were no doubt given the name for the same reasons. The only example which at the moment occurs to me is one close to Beinn Doireann between Glen Lyon and Glen Orchy.) An Sgarsoch and Carn an Fhidleir could also be reached either by way of Glen Feshie ; or, from Glen Tilt, along a path which strikes across into Glen Tarf by a burn a mile below the Bedford Memorial Bridge.

Although the country east of Loch Ericht is less striking than that on the other side, it should be interesting to explore, and it is my regret that I have not done so. As I have mentioned, the chief hills are those round Coire Domhain, which can be done in a comfortable circuit from Dalwhinnie to Dalnaspidal. Naming only the highest points, these are Geal Charn (3005 ft.), A'Mharconaich (3185 ft.), Beinn Udlamain (3306 ft.) and Sgairneach Mhor (3210 ft.). The Scottish Mountaineering Club's Guide contains a valuable warning as to the inaccuracy of the maps with regard to these hills, so it would be wise only to undertake them in fine weather ; for to the south lies the trackless expanse of the Corrievarkie and Talla Bheith forests, in which it would be very easy to be lost. (The Corrievarkie forest must be the only deer-forest in Scotland to which there is no approach by land ; the only means is by boat along Loch Ericht ; it must for this

202

reason be a paradise of game-preservation and require a very small police-expenditure.) One point of error, and a very obvious one—that is, if you notice it—to which the Guide calls attention, is that the maps show the Allt na Glaise *crossing* the bealach between Beinn Udlamain and Sgairneach Mhor, and thus apparently flowing *uphill* for 150 ft. of the northern slope ! I don't, however, understand what the Guide means by saying that this area is ' not a deer forest '. So far as I know it forms the main part of the country stalked from Dalnaspidal Lodge.

With a bicycle, this circle of hills could also be reached from Rannoch by the Craiganour road. In this case the best course would appear to be north-west from the head of Loch Garry up the ridge leading to Meallan Buidhe (2850 ft.) and thence on, in much the same direction but with slightly more west in it, to Sgairneach Mhor, rather than from the north side of the Dunish ford by way of Meall Doire. I should imagine that the tour would be well worth while for the sake of the view down Loch Ericht and of the Beinn Alder group, from several angles. But with those stirring places closer acquaintance is yet to come.

CHAPTER XV

RANNOCH

OUTSIDE the window by which I sit down to write, the hydrangeas trail on towards November, still in the full portent of their fleshly bloom. They have lasted since July. The chrysanthemums, which in Japan are most admired when withering, also remain in evidence. But for the rest of the world decay moves at a more healthy pace. I am reminded that according to Lady Murasaki the ancient Japanese, amongst other civilised habits astonishing to us, used to hold a solemn annual festival for the purpose of ' viewing the autumn-leaves '. The Japanese and I are at one in this matter, for autumn is the pride of the year ; I would give ten springs for it.

But for that very reason it is the time when my desires set towards Scotland in the most restless impatience of my surroundings. Southern woods have perhaps a wider selection of deciduous trees, with a better range of blends and contrasts in emblazonment : the oak and the ash, beech, elm and sycamore, maple and creeper, the sanguine berries and hedges flushed as though wine ran in their veins. I like especially those long leaves of the Spanish chestnut, which are shaped like Mycenæan swords and coloured in a cold individual bronze. But the spirits of the season run cleaner in the northern air. A fine day there at this time of year sets a standard of its own.

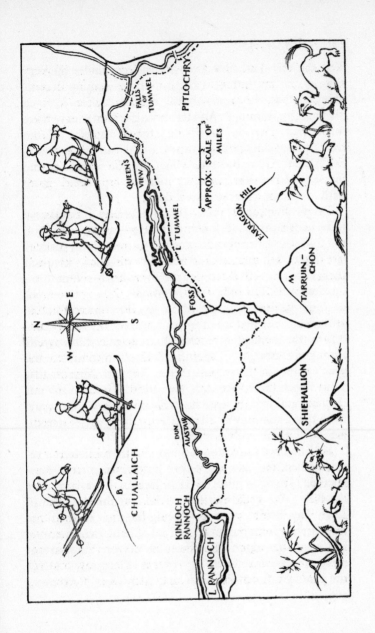

You can feel that it has been stolen from under the very nose of the impending winter, of whose coming descent upon the fold *vi et armis* already reconnaissances-in-force give nightly warning. Any day now the farmer may wake to see that snow lies on his ungathered ' stooks ' (if the harvest has been late) and then the oats will be good only for fodder. It is the time when the rifle speaks in the forest, and the deer know it ; but they are crazed more with love than with the fear of death.

On the phantom of such a day, as it is here, it is not easy to be content with a few mental images—an egg-shell sky, the folds of the hardly still glowing heather (for a spark of late ling or bell in its second flowering still shows here and there) and, in such a setting, the silver birch-columns exquisitely veiled in gold, and the rowans, like dancers even to their painted lips, posed in gay but uncomfortable attitudes. The picture inflames desire for the reality, and it is for the moment as much as I can do to restrain myself from going straight off again to Rannoch to complete the year's trinity of the seasons there. For it so happens that I have been there twice this year already, once to spy out the land and once to taste the milk and honey. But apart from that I knew it well all my life, up to the age of sixteen, and such places are persistent.

So I had the combined feelings of a first visit and a return, when, one day just before Easter, we entered Rannoch once more in quite the right fashion, by walking over the hills. We could not leave Killin, at the west end of Loch Tay, before 11.30, that being the time at which the train arrives from the south, or from Crianlarich where we had spent the night. For the time of year this was not early enough, since Loch Tay diverges a long way south of the parallel to Loch Rannoch, and Glen Lyon intervenes ;
206

there are thus two crossings to be made and the distance is considerable. But it could not be helped, and as we should be on roads or good tracks except for the first part of the day there was no chance of being lost in the dark.

Loch Tay and Glen Lyon are separated by the high range of Beinn Lawers and Meall nan Tarmachan, now under deep snow and practically impassable. But there is one low pass, and through this a road, which leaves Loch Tay four miles up from Killin. This was clear enough of snow for motors ; but as we were walking we preferred to look for a short cut to the summit of the pass across the lower slopes of Meall nan Tarmachan. There is a path of sorts this way from Tirarthur, which I think is an old right-of-way. Unfortunately we fell for a deceiving gate a little too soon and found ourselves in for some rough going through the lower scrubby woods, where we put up one or two pheasants, and then along the wall which divides the woods from the open moor. We joined the track at the crossing of the Allt Tir Artair. But we were only the worse off from that point on, for it is almost impossible to follow, and indeed seems to have disappeared altogether. Perhaps the impression was partly due to the snow, for now at over 1000 ft. up, we were in the region of deep drifts, and had hard work for over an hour in successively fording these and the very soft places between them. We only reached the top of the pass above Lochan na Lairige (about 1800 ft.) at three o'clock, and by this time were quite ready for lunch.

As we ate we had the chance to watch a pair of stoats courting in the channels of the snow near to the road. The scene in all directions was Alpine, and the illusion was completed by the fact that people were attempting to ski on the smooth slopes of Beinn Lawers above us. On the other side of the lochan the abrupt precipice of Creag an Lochain looked the more formidable underneath its crusted architrave. The lochan itself is a pretty one, with a frieze of alders or some such trees. But the classical beauty of the view is the peak of Beinn Vorlich framed between the two sides of the pass, looking the taller, like one of Metternich's Austrian grenadiers, in its white uniform ; and when the sun once caught it, for a few moments this seemed to lift it higher still. Nearer at hand the savage tooth of Meall nan Tarmachan and the ridge behind it thrust boldly, with a gleam of blue ice to maintain the Swiss illusion. This is visible most of the way down to Glen Lyon, and, if we turned to look at it once, we did so a dozen times.

The Brig o' Balgie, where the road crosses the Lyon, is the centre of the remarkable glen, known in Gaelic as ' the long, crooked glen of the stones ', which continues above the Brig for another fifteen or sixteen miles. The upper part is open sheep-country ; the lower, a narrow wooded gorge—a show-place which motorists can take in easily in a round from Aberfeldy. Fortingal, at the entrance of the glen, is also a historic spot, and gives its name to the old parish which includes most of Rannoch. It possesses a yew tree ' which is probably the oldest specimen of vegetation in Europe ', and the remains of a Roman camp. There is even a story that this was the birthplace of Pontius Pilate, which has actually found recent supporters ready to overlook the fact that the Romans did not penetrate so far, nor even conquer England, until a much later date. The part of the glen around Brig o' Balgie is narrow and the hills on either side are high, but it has an air of dignity and ease, to which the vast sweeping pool below the bridge, the great beeches and the fine avenue of limes

208

leading to Meggernie Castle make their contributions. In its setting these make the village (if it amounts to a village) one of the most agreeable little places in the Highlands. It is a pity there is not an inn there, for it is also a good centre for a variety of hills. Quarters can, however, be obtained at Innerwick farm, where we had some tea, and elsewhere ; the Post Office would be helpful in this respect. But you would have to go a very long way for a drink.

And now for the second part of the day's journey. To anyone coming from the green hills of Glen Dochart, a richer and more interesting type of country seems to open up on the north side of Glen Lyon, which comes within the aura of Loch Rannoch's own effulgent beauty. The change depends also on a geological difference, and the well-known hill-path from Innerwick to Carie on Loch Rannoch runs along a belt of limestone, into which the burns have cut deep and picturesque ravines.

This pass is known as the Lairig Chalbhath. The path, which rises to a height of about 1600 ft., is good and clear all the way. It starts in two branches just by the war-memorial, where the main road crosses the Allt Chalbhath. For half a mile these run parallel, one inside the wood along the river, where there are attractive pools, and the other just outside. Where the wood ends, both turn up hill northwards and unite. This is the only point where it is possible to go wrong, for there is a wooden bridge over the burn which you may be tempted to cross. It is true that it also leads to Loch Rannoch, at Camghouran farther to the west, by another recognised pass, the Lairig a' Mhuic, which you could take if you wish to reach the west end of the loch. But for the direct route to Kinloch (which in spite of its name is at the foot of the loch, not the head—that is, at the east end) remember to keep the main burn on your left hand.

By the time we left Innerwick the upper sky had cleared, and we saw the banks of cumulus, rolled back on the eastern horizon, show first a deep scarlet against a china-blue, then a greenish-grey on a background of paler rose, with an afterthought of aquamarine before transparency and the final stages of fade, dim, black-out. It was already dark when we reached the top of the pass at half past six, rather more than an hour from Innerwick, and we had still rather a longer walk before us than we then realised. (I had been over from Rannoch and back at least once before, but that was long ago.) As we came along the edge of the Black Wood, where there were a number of startled hinds, Beinn a' Chuallaich rose in front of us before the light failed. It seemed to get very little nearer to us, however far we walked. The road from Carie to Kinloch also seemed a very long three miles. It was quite dark by now, but one dazzling illumination across the water, like a liner at anchor, broke the peace of the night. What it could be, we guessed in vain, and not until we reached the village did we discover that it was the new hydro-electric dam at the outlet of the Tummel. I do not know why it should be necessary to force people's attention so aggressively to this structure, but for some reason or other it is kept lighted at night by four exceedingly powerful lamps. We were very glad eventually to reach the Bunrannoch Hotel ; and at nine o'clock sat down to an excellent dinner and an excellent fire, all most hospitably provided for us at short notice, in spite of the fact that we were the only guests at such a time of year. At the Bunrannoch you ask for whisky and they bring you Talisker in a lordly glass ; just as I suppose they would serve you with nectar to drink, as a matter of course, if you somehow happened to stumble into the celestial regions.

Moments like this finally damn the puritanism, or cant —that ' unconfessed injustice ' which, as Saintsbury says, is only worthy of a teetotaller—which, notwithstanding professions of devotion to the cause of prosperity, yet impedes it wantonly by maintaining the duty on whisky at a now unremunerative level ; and this merely to gratify certain low passions of impertinent spite, and to deprive the peoples of Scotland and Ireland of their national drink, in their climates a rational, a natural and a noble drink, and one which, if rejected by some epicures, is everywhere welcomed by the greatest.

In the morning I went in fear and prospective indignation to assess the damage to the scenery done by the Grampian Electricity Company. The dam is the worst feature visible at Kinloch Rannoch ; for the row of pylons, which conducts 320,000 volts from the power-house nine miles up the loch, somehow fails to offend me particularly. But no more the swirling pools of the Tummel, into which it used to be a delight to gaze after salmon from the old bridge or from the turfy banks— they lie buried in a fast but thoroughly well-disciplined canal, with wide borders of the dredged-out gravel. The fishing seems also to have suffered, especially since the flow of water is dependent on the dam, and therefore displays what must from the point of view of the fish be startling eccentricities. The level of the loch was expected to rise, but the ironical angel who lies in wait for technical experts has instead caused it to fall several feet. This does little harm and the fishing in it is as good as ever. There are worse results closer to the two power-houses at Killichonan and Tummelbridge, far enough away from

Kinloch Rannoch to be taken more philosophically. But I cannot see how the people of the district of whom not one, except the lairds, is a penny the better off for the injury that has been done to their country, can ever really forgive it ; and the old can hardly bring themselves to refer to the subject at all, or only with traces of an inexpressible bitterness.

It is a wonder that these things should be ; for since the price of the electricity produced is as high as eightpence a unit and is in any case supplied mainly to people who could do very comfortably without it, no great social benefit seems to result ; but it is still more of a wonder that, with the worst will in the world, attempts to deface the Highlands really have so little effect as a whole. The beauty of Rannoch has so much vitality that after all it is almost possible to ignore the existence of the scheme.

One's disturbance of mind is due rather to a moral feeling of resentment, than to purely aesthetic causes. But nowhere will the mind prove to be an entirely satisfactory companion if it is permitted to air moral prejudices at the expense of natural satisfactions. So I contented myself with the pious hope that the wicked shall be turned into hell (including the stupid also in the commination, if that is not too much to expect) and there and then decided to come back and make Kinloch Rannoch my summer-base.

True, it is not a very good point of access for any particular group of hills, except Shiehallion and its neighbours. Crianlarich or Tyndrum is better for those about the head of Glen Lyon, Killin or Kenmore for the Beinn Lawers group, Dalwhinnie for the Beinn Alder neighbourhood, the hills east of Loch Ericht and the western parts of Athole, and Blair or Struan for central Athole. But Kinloch Rannoch is just within range, though long range, of all these fairly well separated groups, besides being in itself far more attractive than any of those places, and offering more choice of accommodation. For these reasons the remaining chapters of this book will be constructed round this general headquarters.

Rannoch is part of what seems to be a natural open thoroughfare from one side of Scotland to the other. The Tummel, though it only bears that name from Kinloch Rannoch to its junction with the Tay, has its real source in Coire Ba, deep in the Black Mount forest on the far side of the great Moor—less than ten miles from the nearest arm of the Atlantic. Yet neither road nor rail have made use of this apparently tempting route ; the western part of it, across the Moor, would, I suppose, mean very high engineering costs, and so, thank God, remains impassable except on foot. And in the other direction, north and south, across the Moor, there is the railway only, no road. Rannoch therefore retains the peaceful charm of a backwater from the tourist point of view. For the normal visitor from the eastern parts of Scotland it is a kind of land's end, from which he looks out across the obliterated levels of the Moor to the solemn, monumental hills about Glencoe and Glen Etive, on the west coast, with much the same sense of distance and enchantment as if he were gazing from that coast across the open seas to Morven and Mull. Rannoch can of course be reached at the western end by the railway, and this is the best way for scenery *en route*, though not necessarily the quickest, even from Glasgow. But many more people arrive for the first time from Pitlochry or Struan, and this is undoubtedly the right dramatic approach. After the first sight of the distant Watchers, Sisters, or Shepherds of Glencoe, as they are variously called, with a ten-mile stretch of loch, and

213

such a loch, as foreground, you will not need to envy the experience of mystics.

From Pitlochry, twenty-two miles from Kinloch, the main road along the north side of Strathtummel is a very pretty one, ' starring ' a view down Loch Tummel to the knobbly hills of Farragon and Tarruin-chon, with Shiehallion beyond, which is known as the Queen's View —which queen, it is unnecessary to specify. But for walkers and cyclists a by-road along the other side is much to be preferred for the usual reasons and others ; except that it misses Killiecrankie. It goes close past the Falls of Tummel, where Swinburne bathed when he was staying at Tummelbridge Inn on an undergraduate reading-party with Dr. Jowett. They are supposed to be the highest falls in any river which a salmon can leap. There is now a ' ladder ', but some of the fish still try the feat out of enthusiasm or ignorance. I can't say I have ever seen one succeed, perhaps because the bigger ones have learnt by past experience to take the path of least resistance. The track keeps close to the edge of Loch Tummel, through pastures rich with a mixed perfume of birches, sheep, thyme, and heather-honey, to the unspoiled old Highland village of Foss, the early home of Mrs. Kennedy Fraser. It joins the Aberfeldy high road, which in turn connects with the main Pitlochry road at Tummelbridge, eight miles from Kinloch Rannoch.

The fine bridge is one of General Wade's, on his road from Crieff to Dalnacardoch. The Latin inscription composed by the Headmaster of Westminster for the famous Adam bridge at Aberfeldy—art and science were both art still in those days—speaks of ' the indignant Tay '. Indignant of a mere bridge—and a bridge by Adam ! What words then would the learned divine have found to express the indignation of the Tummel in this year of grace? For here you pass the lower power-house of the hydro-electric scheme, and the neighbourhood is quite spoilt with works of construction and workers' houses in connection with it. Jowett's hotel is closed, and the licence transferred to an inn very prettily situated on the Pitlochry main road, perhaps three hundred feet above the loch. The power-house is fed by a canal running along the side of the hill above the river on the south side, from the huge dam that has been built to form a reservoir just below Dunalistair House. This dam can also be seen from the main road, and I must admit that I find it rather impressive. The pity is in the destruction of the once fine stretch of river between it and Tummelbridge.

Dunalistair is on a rocky barrage, the glacial wall of the original Loch Rannoch. The scheme has made a somewhat unsuccessful attempt to turn the level fields above it once more into a lake. It was thought that this might have made a new and useful fishing-ground, but I am told that something in the feeding was apparently sour, and that the fish killed there had an unpleasant flavour. But I suppose no man knows definitely how the country will eventually settle down from the fishing point of view, and I have been told by a high official (not in inverted commas) of the Scottish Fishery Board that in his opinion it will be much improved. The great Jimmy Scott in Kinloch will tell you all about it year by year, and much else besides.

So far we have been on the wrong side of Shiehallion; for no mountain, not even Shiehallion, is sculpturally perfect; but by the time we reach a point about two miles short of Kinloch Rannoch it reveals what I hold to be its most finished lines. From farther up Loch Rannoch it is a narrow spear-like point, clinching the view at large and holding it in focus. But from here it must be taken by itself and as a whole, and the broader three-quarter angle is more satisfying to the eye. The cone is all but symmetrical, but the emotional curve of the upper shoulder intercepts Euclid just in time.

No one can remain long beside Shiehallion without fascination, but the strongest feelings very often find a man ' feebly inexpressive ', as Aldous Huxley says, and I suspect that I should have been wise to make no attempt to describe its effect ; if only I could have denied myself the indulgence. My fumbling attentions will probably fall in the same category as those of an old minister of Rannoch who has given to the world (or to such small part of it as is comprised in what was his own parish, for I am sure no copies are to be found elsewhere) an imposing volume under the title *Shiehallion*, consisting mainly of compilations of his own, which may, perhaps too generously, be described as sonnets. It seems unkind, besides being a direct invitation to Nemesis, to say that they are quite worth looking at for amusement ; but, after all, what one says of the dead does them no harm.

The conquest of Shiehallion is naturally the first ambition of all visitors to Kinloch Rannoch who are fond of mountains, and of many who are not. The most direct way is by the Tempar burn, two miles from the village along the road on the south side of the Tummel, taking about five hours from Kinloch and back. It can, however, be climbed almost equally well from any direction, and in any case there is a steep steady pull to be faced. The longer north and south sides are the steepest. There is plenty of loose rock and scree, but no real crag.

I have been up it a good many times, generally from Tempar, with variations in descent. I think the first time

XI.   SHIEHALLION

was from Blair Atholl with the help of a bicycle. It was a still, cloudless day even on the summit, and the Argyle peaks swam in haze. We found a flourishing wasps' nest amongst the piled rocks which form the last hundred feet, one would have thought an inhospitable place for heat-loving insects,

and fled indignant to the shades beneath.

One of the latest times was with Mary in the snow at Easter, the second day after we arrived from Killin. There were deep drifts on the exposed shoulder, filling the cross-channels, which on the way up we did our best to avoid, not knowing their depth. But we gradually dis-covered that they were frozen hard enough to bear our weight, and so came down again very much more quickly. As we were in ordinary dress, that is to say, skirt and kilt, and shoes, not in proper climbing clothes, the scramble over the snow-clad rocks to the summit was quite tricky and rather uncomfortable. It was not so cold on the top as we had expected, but we left it at once because a fresh snow-storm was bearing down upon us from the north, hiding the Cairngorms in a flurry of white. In all other directions spread line upon line of the silver hills, with less monotony than that of the Alps because the glens and most of Rannoch Moor were clear of snow and contrasted in their dead winter brown; while in the Tempar glen and at a dozen points at all distances rose the smoke of heather-burning. There were a few ptarmigan, all in white of course, and many white hares. (I saw one of them still in his winter dress, through some freak of nature, much later in the year, and very self-conscious and awkward he seemed to feel.) The snow that started to drive once more over the edge of the hill reminded me of the hares'

217

habit in such weather. They crouch on the leeward side and allow themselves to be buried, but edge forward little by little in such a way as always to keep a breathing-hole in front of their noses ; and by this simple, yet ingenious expedient succeed in keeping themselves warm and comfortable without the risk of suffocation.

Shiehallion owes its pointed, regular shape to the fact that it is entirely composed of quartz, that hard splintering rock which amongst commoner rocks is so peculiar that, when I was small, I used to think of it as a precious stone. It is generally found in smaller outcrops, not in a solid mass such as this. Errigal in Donegal is another example of the same rather rare formation, and indeed a better one ; for, whereas the top of Shiehallion is several yards long east and west, that of Errigal is a platform so small that if you lay down on it your head would hang over one side and your feet the other. Beinn-y-Vrackie is also of the same type. But Shiehallion is of an individual rose-coloured quartz, which gives it a faint warmth and radiance even in grey lighting, and takes on before sunset a peculiar depth of colour which might be painted but cannot be described. It is this characteristic combined with its form which makes it perhaps the most beautiful of all mountains.

The view is good, because it stands fairly well apart from other hills, though less so than people are apt to imagine ; in fact the view from either of its neighbours, Carn Mairg and Beinn a' Chuallaich, though they are lower, is rather better, because they cut off a good deal of what you should see from Shiehallion, whereas Shiehallion, owing to its narrow tapering form, is very little of an obstruction, besides being itself an improvement to any view. I am inclined to think that Shiehallion's reputation in this respect is partly inferred from the fact that its distinctive shape is so easily picked out as a conspicuous feature of the landscape from so many quarters.

The name, like all names that matter, has no known meaning, but all reasonable men are agreed that it has something to do with the *sithean*, that is the fairies. There is one part of the female anatomy of which etymologists, like the rest of us, are particularly fond ; and I suppose it was inevitable that some of them have suggested the too specious explanation *sidh chaillean*, ' a virgin's breast ', in this case also. Women's charms are dangerous enough ; they would be fatal, if this explanation were physically possible. A decent obscurity of meaning is therefore to be preferred. As to spelling, I have chosen the simplest of several variants, the word being in any case fully Anglicised. ' Shichallion ' is perhaps nearer to the probable Gaelic ; but there is no justification for the merely pretentious ' Schiehallion ', in which the presence of the *c* after the initial *s* is neither English nor Gaelic (which requires *s* alone) so far as the pronunciation, which is universal, is concerned.

But our homage has been paid ; we cannot stand gaping for ever ; and I proceed.

CHAPTER XVI

CARN MAIRG

THE casual visitor to Kinloch Rannoch will hardly realise that Shiehallion, which seems to stand in such conscious and conspicuous isolation, has in fact some quite important neighbours. They are farther to the north, right on the edge of Glen Lyon, and are completely hidden from any-where close to the village by the lower hills near at hand, which front on the loch between the Innerhadden and Carie burns. The most striking fragment of this on the whole conventional mass is the irregular rocky bluff of Creag an Fhithich, over Innerhadden House, which is more generally known as ' the Giant of Rannoch ', from its supposed likeness to a huge recumbent figure seen in profile. The hills behind form a continuous ridge with several points over 3000 ft. of which the highest is Carn Mairg (3419 ft.). In saying that they are completely hidden I was not quite accurate, for there are one or two points near Kinloch from which you may catch a glimpse of this summit, especially in the early part of the year when a long belt of snow runs across the hill-face below. The corrie which holds it is for that reason called Coire Cruach Sneachda—a name reminiscent of more than one corrie in the Cairngorms.

This range can be reached at either end, that is, either by the Carie burn, or by Allt Coire Cruach Sneachda, the

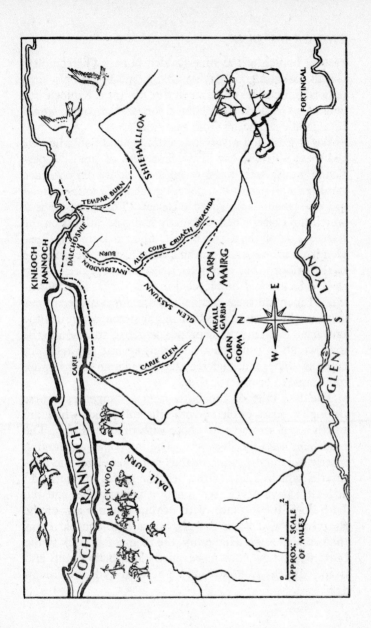

eastern branch of the Innerhadden burn. The complete circuit makes a good day's walking, and is the only such tour which can be undertaken directly from Kinloch. It could also be done from Glen Lyon, and of course would be a good deal shorter from that side.

We at least had a very interesting expedition when we did these hills one day in the first week of June. A particularly early start was not called for, so we did not leave until ten minutes to ten, covering the three miles of road to Carie by about a quarter to eleven. This is the point at which the Lairig Chalbhath path diverges, but it is on the farther side of the Carie burn. The track up the Carie glen itself is a separate one and starts just on the *near* side of the bridge. For two miles it also is a very presentable road, which could be bicycled in comfort, at least downhill. I mention these details because the existence of *two* good tracks so close together might perhaps confuse the unwary. It is true that a proper degree of attention to the map would as usual be a safeguard against any such deception—but, then, such remedies for human weakness are too simple to be often applied.

The last mile of the burn runs a dangerous course through a series of clefts, with falls and rapids which are worth a wet scramble for those with time to spare. The road here keeps its distance. The intervening ground is mostly bog, and prolific in that delicious plant, the bog-myrtle, which is one of the peculiar graces of Scotland : at least I have never seen much of it elsewhere, and the Irish bogs, for instance, with neither this nor any of the thirty-nine wild water-flowers, are as drab and barren as they are extensive. Higher up, the road comes back to the burn, which now flows more quietly in a shallow gully and is an excellent trout-stream. The road ends at a rough

222

shelter. A path of sorts is traceable for a short distance farther, but soon peters out in the midst of a fairly broad broken stretch of peat and tussocky grass, headed by a semi-circle of hills. The central point of these is the rising cone of Carn Gorm (3370 ft.) which has been visible all the way from Carie, and adds a touch of distinction to the little glen.

This was our first objective. We chose a route less direct, but firmer, than the beeline across the flat upper glen, by turning off towards the well-defined buttress which projects north from the western ridge, between Carn Gorm and the part marked on the ordnance map as Meall Droilichean, Oyster-catcher's Hill—a good name if the right one, for there are several families of these pretty birds in the glen, and we sometimes watched them conducting fishery-classes for the young ones in one or other of the little sandy bays near its outlet into the loch. I notice, however, that the version given by the half-inch Bartholomew map is ' Meall Dronn a' Chinn '. I have reason to believe that in these matters this map is very often right, and so it may be here; but in that case ' Meall ' is redundant, since Dronn a' Chinn by itself means ' the Bluff at the Glen-head '.

We reached the foot of this slope about an hour after leaving Carie, and climbed it by a little burn which rises on the level platform at the top of the buttress. This flows underground for the greater part of its course, gushing out at intervals in cool green beds of moss. The day was clear and fine and quite still in the valley, but as we reached the heights we came in for a light but rather chilly wind from the east. Where the inner slope is steepest, at about the 2800 ft. contour, I almost stepped on a nesting ptarmigan. She ran off, cowering with half-spread wings,

223

and we took a quick glance at her nest with its eight eggs neatly arranged in a circle, the points inwards. At a few yards range, it was practically indistinguishable from the grey stones, and traces of snow in the interstices perfected the illusion. It would have been easy to pass close to the nest a dozen times without either noticing it or rousing the parent-bird to move.

Thence we followed the ridge on to Carn Gorm. At the foot of the culminating three-hundred-foot rise we passed a wretched old hind. Her senses had, it seemed, so badly failed that she did not realise our presence until we were very close to her; and then she had hardly the strength in her legs to carry her to a safe distance. We reached the top of Carn Gorm by twenty past one. It is a well-shaped hill, with a good drop on all sides of the summit. On the south, steep grassy slopes, made interesting by several winding ghylls, fall directly into Glen Lyon; the great mass of Beinn Lawers is in opposition. To the east the view is obstructed, but it is open north across Loch Rannoch to the Beinn Alder and Beinn Nevis groups and the Athole forest, and west to the high hills of the Beinn Doireann group round Glen Lyon's distant head. Beyond these last rise the twin peaks of Cruachan.

After lunch in a rather damp, but sheltered, place on the Glen Lyon side of the top, at two o'clock we went on north-east to the col below Meall Garbh, a descent of about six hundred feet. We stopped to listen to the piping of a couple of golden plovers who apparently had a nest thereabouts, and had just picked out the elegant male bird with the field-glasses, when we suddenly became aware that we were not the whole audience; two men on the hillside opposite were training their telescopes in our direction. When we came up to them we found that one was a naturalist, fully equipped with photographic apparatus in a green watching-tent, and his companion one of the Dall keepers. There are unthought-of moral perils in the close season ; but we were reassured to be told that we had not, as it happened, done any harm to the cause of research. We were even able to assist it by telling them about the ptarmigan's nest, and indicated its position by sighting it with the keeper's gun as precisely as the inevitable conjugal disagreement allowed.

Meall Garbh is very rough and stony, as its name shows. It has no very definite summit. In fact it is really no more than the western finish of the broad three-mile ridge of Carn Mairg. There is a wooden shanty under the rocks just on the south side of it, which might be worth bearing in mind in bad weather ; and a little farther on towards the east we met first a collie and later three Glen Lyon shepherds making in that direction, apparently for their midday meal, for they carried kettles. We made various voyages of discovery and slow progress—finding nothing but a great number of hares and some pretty lichens—and once succeeded in losing each other for several minutes. Consequently it was half past four when we arrived on the actual summit of Carn Mairg (3419 ft.). Although this is ill defined, a hundred yards or so to the north of it, there is a sharp projection of disintegrated crag which, though it is not on a big enough scale to show up remarkably from a distance, at shorter range succeeds in giving the hill a character which it would otherwise have missed. This makes the approach more tempting. Nor is the temptation delusive, for the top of Carn Mairg is a place where it is well worth while to spend half an hour. We did so, and I also explored the craggy point, which has a better command of Glen Lyon. But most of the time we passed in a careful scrutiny of the surrounding country in all its details.

All reasons for climbing mountains that can be stated, like all the reasons that can be given for liking a poem, are necessarily inadequate, and to try to justify one's predilection at all is to deliver oneself bound into the hands of the enemy. The view in particular, however good it may be as such, is generally one of the least plausible of possible excuses. But in the case of Carn Mairg the plea becomes defensible, for the view is quite unusually satisfying. There is much of it and what there is is all good ; except that Shiehallion shows its least affecting side, and becomes for once almost a dull hill. (But it is perhaps true that the capacity for occasional dullness is a final mark of genius !) Shiehallion hides nothing, so that except southward, where Beinn Lawers of course holds the field, the eye can travel in every direction to the full extent of its powers, encompassing the Highlands from Beinn Nevis to the Cairngorms and the Lowland country round Perth up to the Sidlaws, the Firth of Tay and the Fife Lomonds. Past Beinn Lawers there is also a glimpse of the upper end of Loch Tay. There was still a great deal of snow on the high tops, and I was rather surprised to see more remaining on Lochnagar and the Glen Shee hills than on the Cairngorms ; but there was a solid bank of it along the southern edge of the Moine Mor. The prospect to the east was unfortunately a little dimmed and flattened by the wind which was coming up from that quarter with a burden of North Sea haze.

At five o'clock we started on the return descent. Immediately north of Carn Mairg there is a corrie which seems the natural way down, but the burn which rises in it flows north of Shiehallion towards Fortingal ; and although it would be possible to follow this to the foot of Shiehallion and then cut across the col to the north and so down to Tempar, the most reasonable route is by Coire Cruach Sneachda, the next corrie to the west. At the top the two corries are not very distinct. They are connected by a few hundred yards of broken hummocky ground where the snow lay in patches, soft and springy underfoot and pleasant to cross. True to its name, Coire Cruach Sneachda held a long wreath of snow,

> unde loquaces
> lymphae prosiliunt tuae

—' from which your burn leaps in full song '—and now you have only to follow this down to Innerhadden and Kinloch Rannoch. But it is a good distance, and took us another two hours or more to cover.

Not far down the glen, just between the burn and the steepest part of that rocky little eminence, Meallanan Odhar, I chanced on the entrance of a fox's earth. It was half-covered with sphagnum moss and long strands of heather. As I probed into it with my long stick, suddenly *an sionnach* himself appeared from the backdoor a little farther down, and bounded away over the deep heather, casting the right crafty look back at us several times before he disappeared. His pale red hair showed up vigorously against the dead browns and greens. Holding ourselves in duty bound to repay the hospitality of the soil by lodging an information against such an unwelcome neighbour for the young grouse, we looked about for some means of marking the place, and by a curious chance found a beam of rotten wood big enough to stand at the mouth of the earth, like an oar set upright on the grave of a Homeric sailor. But it is a thousand to one that the earth was deserted that very night. If so, I am sorry, for it seemed a good one, and even rogues might as well be comfortable.

This was the last of our encounters, human or divine, and we reached home in nice time for dinner at half-past seven. Before the burn joins the one which comes down the flat open glen on the left, it swings rather in that direction and its channel deepens. Instead of following it we held eastward across the hill; and this proved to be the right course, although it entailed a small climb, because we soon hit on a shooting-track which took us comfortably for the next two miles to Dalchosnie; a name known to history as the site of a minor encounter in the wars of independence, but now appropriated to a modern lodge of the ' Scottish baronial ' persuasion. The circumstances of the engagement were as follows : The English party came down upon the Tummel valley from the south on a surprise attack, but were not quick enough to forestall resistance ; and the women who were working in the flat meadows round the mouth of the burn, and where the new loch is now, joined in with their sickles and turned the scale of battle. The English escaped up the west-hand glen (which runs nearly to the head of the Carie glen) and so, presumably, over the high chain of hills down to Glen Lyon ; and the glen by which they went is named after them, Glen Sassunn, to this day.

I am glad to say that Englishmen are now received more cordially in Rannoch. Indeed they own the best part of it. While I am on the subject I should like to mention that one of them, Captain Wentworth of Dall, upon whose land we have been trespassing during most of this chapter, has as fine and well-kept an estate as any I have seen in Scotland. The cottages, paths and fences are all of the best, and do no dishonour to one of the most attractive of the

228

typical Scottish castles. This is halfway along the loch on the south side. It has been greatly improved by the use of small cypress-trees as an inner setting to the great outward frame of the Black Wood, the primitive forest of Rannoch, and looks out to the loch across a judicious foreground of park-land. The gardens are a show-piece. There are also plantations which, I have been told, reproduce the arrangement of the troops engaged in one of the battles of the Crimean War—a pleasant curiosity well worthy of the great but absurd traditions which still keep a few English heads looking over high collars.

CHAPTER XVII

THE LOCH TAY HILLS

BEINN LAWERS and Meall nan Tarmachan can be done from Rannoch by crossing the Lairig Chalbhath, but of course this adds very considerably to the day and puts it virtually out of the question to tackle more than one of them at a time. A bicycle can, however, be taken as far as the top of the pass for riding back ; rough riding, it is true, and rather dangerous in places where the track runs, with many twists and bends and ups and downs, along the edge of the deep gully in which the burn flows ; but quite feasible and a good deal quicker than walking. To take a bicycle so far should shorten the time for the day from Kinloch Rannoch and back by almost an hour and a half. As you come down the south side of the pass into Glen Lyon the twin symmetrical buttresses of Meall Ghaordie, Creag an Tulabhain, and Creag Laoghain, show to striking advantage rather farther up the glen. The green winding channel of the Dathaig in the side of Beinn Lawers opposite looks like the route of the Loch Tay road, but this is really more to the west, concealed by the rise of the ground on that side.

These hills can, however, be better approached from some point on the side of Loch Tay, which they dominate. Or, if one is staying actually in lower Glen Lyon, this is nearly as good.

230

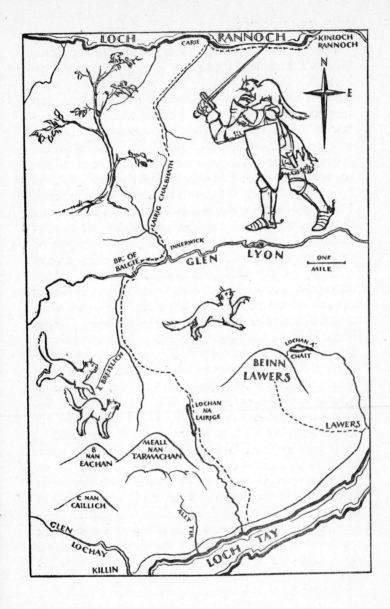

Beinn Lawers is not only the highest hill in Perthshire, but, after the Beinn Nevis group and the Cairngorms, the highest in the British Isles. It is only sixteen feet below the four-thousand-foot line, and it is claimed that the enormous cairn built on its summit makes up the deficiency. The view is certainly remarkable ; yet otherwise it is rather a disappointing hill, with grassy featureless slopes which do not impress the eye in proportion to their size and height, and, except for isolated fragments here and there on the north side, are practically free from crag. The manner in which its various summits (you may count them as half a dozen in all) are arranged along the basis of an almost S-shaped ridge suggests a passing comparison with Beinn Cruachan. But from a thorough exploration of Cruachan on both sides I can vouch that that splendid hill is much its superior in all but the literal sense. I confess, however, that I have not the same familiarity—a familiarity which has only bred admiration—with Beinn Lawers, which indeed I have climbed but once, and that only by the most obvious route : that is, from the Temperance Hotel at Lawers, whence a well-worn path leads directly to the summit. There is apparently a second path half a mile or so to the north-east. This is a steady and distinctly monotonous ascent, but on a clear day the top has its rewards ; and behind the top there is a respectable, though not a noble corrie, where lies the loch which is the source of the Lawers burn.

This is called Lochan a' Chait, a name which is common in this part of the country—there are almost as many of them as there are Lochan Uaines in the Cairngorms. It is one of many examples of a fashion for certain prevalent names which may be noticed in various districts and has often struck me as curious : sometimes I have suspected that these vain repetitions are as much the fault of the surveyors as anything else. There are other ' Cats' Lochs,' for instance, under Stuchd an Lochain between Glen Lyon and Glen Daimh, and on the north side of Beinn Heasgarnich.

No doubt this is evidence of a kind that wild cats were numerous about these parts in former times, as indeed they were all over Scotland when there was more forest in the old sense, and less in the new—more shelter and fewer keepers' guns ; although they are naturally less disliked in deer-forests than on grouse-moors. It is rather surprising to learn that cats are still indeed to be found on the bare and empty hills between Rannoch and Tay— though I could believe anything of Beinn Heasgarnich. But these fierce little beasts (one of which has according to legend been known to kill a knight in full armour) after verging on extinction, seem to have been on the increase again in late years, and perhaps to have extended their territory. In Rothiemurchus, where they were thought to have died out altogether, one at least appeared in 1925, while in Western Rannoch and Badenoch they seem to be almost common ; and in 1934 there were several of them amongst the executed criminals on the keeper's gallows at Dunan, between Rannoch Station and Bridge of Gaoire.

I am reminded too of an account of surely the strangest of those strange battles, futile and desperate almost as the wars of men, which sometimes (but rarely) take place between members of different predatory species of animals— the best I have ever been lucky enough to *see* in this line was an encounter between a pair of hawks and a pair of crows, high over a little lough on a remote island off the Irish coast. Interesting enough ; but the Scottish episode, which took place, so far as I remember, close to Loch

233

Ericht, must have been ten times more so, for in it the combatants were nothing less than an eagle and a wild cat. The eagle, it seems, swooped down upon this unlikely quarry, presumably by mistake, and must have been unpleasantly surprised when the cat reared up and struck out ferociously with its claws. One would have thought that even so the eagle still had most of the advantages of the position ; but they are not morally enterprising birds, and the cat, which was after all fighting for its life—and a cat —had the best of things in the end.

But even with these recent reappearances the decrease of the wild cat during the last century has been very marked, especially as compared with others of the rarer animals ; and it is far from unlikely that he will follow the martens and his merely nominal relations, the polecats, into oblivion, except in so far as these place-names shall preserve his far from pious, but romantic, memory. This may be my excuse for introducing this digression in his favour, and for concluding it by quoting in evidence the following picturesque catalogue of the vermin trapped in Glengarry (not the Perthshire, but the Inverness-shire, Glengarry) during the three years from 1837. It is derived from the *Gazetteer of Scotland*, but my direct source is Malcolm and Maxwell's book on *Grouse and Grouse Moors* :

11 Foxes.	3 Honey buzzards.
198 Wild cats.	462 Kestrels.
246 Marten cats.	78 Merlin hawks.
106 Polecats.	63 Hen harriers.
301 Stoats and weasels.	6 Jer falcons.
67 Badgers.	9 Ash-coloured hawks or
48 Otters.	long-tailed blue hawks.
78 House cats (going wild).	1431 Hooded crows.

27 White-tailed sea-eagles.	475 Ravens.
15 Golden eagles.	71 Fern owls.
18 Ospreys.	11 Hobby hawks.
98 Blue hawks.	275 Kites or salmon-tailed
7 Orange-legged falcons.	glebes.
63 Goshawks.	5 Marsh harriers.
285 Common buzzards.	35 Horned owls.
371 Rough-legged buzzards.	3 Golden owls.
	8 Magpies.

From this list it appears that, while there has been an all round decline, on the whole the creatures that are rare now were rare then, and that the cats, with the martens and polecats, have come off much the worst proportionately.

But to return to the more immediate aspects of Beinn Lawers :—Rather than simply to climb from Lawers to the summit, it would be better worth while to make a whole day of it, and to cover the full length of the hill across the various tops, starting from somewhere on the east side of the Lawers burn, and working round to Lochan na Lairige, or down to Brig o' Balgie. The map makes the way quite clear, and a public motor which plies along this side of Loch Tay could be pressed into the service if your base were not convenient. If the former course is chosen, a moderate day could be turned into a long one by continuing the walk across the pass to the Meall nan Tarmachan chain. But this is no task for tired legs, as we shall see, so that if the whole circuit is to be attempted I should advise that it be taken in the reverse direction, Meall nan Tarmachan first : then if you must leave out something, you will have missed least in leaving out part of Beinn Lawers.

For Meall nan Tarmachan is a very different type of hill. It is a sharp-backed ridge with an almost continuous

235

line of precipices on the south side, and the peculiar difficulty in handling it is due to the fact that these intrude themselves at intervals across the ridge northwards, and break it up into awkward sections—a queer rugged formation, which I may say, without attributing any inaccuracies or lack of skill to the Ordnance Survey, makes the map very difficult to read, and an inadequate guide to the true character of the ground. Seen from the north the whole length of the ridge is corrugated to a fanciful degree, which to the knowledgeable eye infallibly reveals the presence of the crags beyond ; but this indication is not enough to tell you what the top of the ridge itself is like. In short, though not in any way dangerous for the ordinary walker with some sense—he need not, I mean, possess any technical climbing qualifications—it is definitely a mountain to be avoided in mist or bad weather or in snow. In good conditions, taken by itself, it is quite a short expedition from Killin, though a considerable one from Rannoch.

The ridge therefore demands a more detailed description than is always called for. It runs roughly in a northeast to south-west direction from the north end of Lochan na Lairige—the cairn half a mile above the loch marks the watershed—towards the junction of Glen Lochay with the Tay valley, a distance of some six miles. It continues the general formation and direction of Beinn Lawers (the lowest point between the two groups being as much as 1800 ft. up) but is to Beinn Lawers as a sharpened pencil is to a blunt-ended one or, if you like to put it that way, as different as chalk from cheese ; which means, very like indeed—up to a point. The northernmost part is Creag an Lochain (2742 ft.), a broken lumpy strip of coarse grass with a western flank of terraced sheep-pasture, and on the east the fine cliff above the lochan, down which a waterfall descends with some ceremony. From this point I have looked half through, half across, the mists, which had started to swirl up the Lairig from Loch Tay, towards the shadowy mass of Lawers, looming enormous like the hooded spectre in Goya's picture, ' Death and the Soldiers '; while across the peak of Meall nan Tarmachan itself a storm-cloud was breaking, and the first drops of rain plumped into Lochan an Tairbh-uisge, heavy after weeks of hot summer as long pent up tears. It was as good a moment as I remember.

Between this lower part of the ridge and the steeper rise of seven hundred feet or so to Meall nan Tarmachan is something more than a col, several hundred square yards of peaty ground much broken up by hillocks and outcrops of rock. From this point to Meall nan Tarmachan the way is by no means direct, but involves two or three rises and dips ; some rocks have also to be negotiated, but the less the farther you keep to the north side of the hill. An easier route is to climb directly from Coire Riadhailt on the north without touching Creag an Lochain. Though this is steep enough, there are no severe obstacles to encounter ; but you will miss the abrupt view down on Lochan na Lairige.

The actual top of Meall nan Tarmachan (3421 ft.), above the loftiest cover of Cam Chreag precipices (' the Twisting Crags '), is a dizzy place, but is not quite so uneasily close to the edge as several other tops farther along the ridge. The starkest of all is Meall Garbh, less than half a mile to the south, which is all but a sheer rock-pinnacle, and a very conspicuous point on the crest of the hill. The slope towards Coire Riadhailt at this point is not only steep but excessively rough and stony. You must descend it a little way in order to work round Meall Garbh to the sort of col before the next rise to Beinn nan Eachan. Here there is a break through the crags of Coire Fionn Lairige to the south ; you may say the only one in three miles. To the north, beyond the gully of a burn, you are confronted by the western wall of Coire Riadhailt, a distinct ridge called Meall Ton-each projecting from the main mass, also faced on this side with impregnable rocks. Between these and the edge of Coire Fionn Lairige the way must now be picked, within a very narrow frontage, amongst a series of overlapping rock-terraces. This section is, however, a good deal easier to go up than down. The point of Beinn nan Eachan, grassy on the side away from the cliffs, is just beyond the roots of Meall Ton-each ; and past it again, the ridge works round comparatively without incident for nearly another mile to Creag na Caillich, where it comes to an end.

I have taken the ridge in the reverse direction in the course of a walk from Killin to Kinloch Rannoch. It was not the best of days ; the rain had been pouring down all night, so that the Dochart, making the best of the only really lively part of its long course, foamed and thundered under Killin bridge ; and morning saw the hills still wrapped in ponderous clouds down to almost the 2500 foot level. But a light wind coming down the glen from the west just saved the situation, and when I started, the tops, except Beinn More, were clear ; although the deep blue linings of the clouds and the close appearance of the horizon were more than suggestive of bad weather still to come. Meanwhile beside the pastoral banks of Loch Tay (which is over 300 feet lower than Loch Rannoch) the air was warm, and I was sweating uncomfortably before I pushed my way through the woods and deep bracken of the lower slopes east of the burn which comes down near

238

Bridge of Lochay hotel, into the first layer of the aether. I am not sure that this is the easiest route to Creag na Caillich, for it entails a slight detour to the left across a stretch of grouse-moor, rather irregular ground, and then there are one or two depressions which cannot be avoided and therefore add to the amount of climbing to be done. There should be a better way from Glen Lochay a short distance up, but it may be that part of the hillside is private.

Being in rather a hurry, I did not actually go to the summit of Creag na Caillich, but traversed the shallow grassy corrie behind it, and so reached the edge of the cliffs just short of Beinn nan Eachan. As there were signs of the mist falling again, and I had no intention of undertaking a lonely venture across Beinn nan Eachan in such conditions, I occupied myself meanwhile with taking in the lie of the land northward. There I could see the long dreary pass of the Lairig Breislich, which connects Glen Lyon and Glen Lochay, to be reached in case of need by way of Meall Ton-each or of the Allt Fionn Ghleann to the west of it. I do not know whether the name Lairig Breislich is intended to mean ' the Pass of Dreams '—a name in the true spirit of the Celtic twilight—or with more realism, ' the Pass of Madness '—the pass which no one but a raving lunatic would take, when he could go so much more comfortably (though it is a little longer) by the other *lairig* where the road is now. In any case I have not sampled it myself. I thought it looked very wet and nasty, and altogether too much like another ten miles or so to the west, which you shall yet hear well abused.

Beinn nan Eachan rises as a cone on the edge of the ridge. At two o'clock, two and a half hours after leaving Killin, I reached its peaked summit, which all but

239

overhangs the abyss on the south side ; a refined variant
(in the scale of a thousand feet lower) of Sgor an Lochain
Uaine above the great corrie of Braeriach and Cairn Toul.
It is the last hill one would expect to be called ' the Ben of
the Horses ' ; for the ground between it and Creag na
Caillich, though nothing to the east side, is much obstructed
by the cross-grained stratification of the hill, to which I
have already referred : indeed one might fancy that who-
ever invented the names in this region was displaying a
conscious sense of humour.   I suggest, however, a possible
solution in terms of Meall Ton-each, which quite definitely relates to a physical resemblance (to wit, a horse's
rump) on the hypothesis that from some point to the north
Meall Ton-each and Beinn nan Eachan establish the
visual relation of crupper to arching mane.   In that case
the name in its present form is probably corrupt.   One
might conjecture that the original version was something
like ' Beinn Ceann-each '.

In coming delicately through the spurs of rock on the
other side of Beinn nan Eachan (to accept the name without
further speculation) I found myself forced some way down
the narrow spout under the crags of Meall Ton-each.
This could probably have been avoided by keeping well to
the right, as at this point the main cliffs are broken and
that side is safer than usual.   As it was, however, I began
to think that in order to reach Meall nan Tarmachan it
would be easier to go right down into the corrie and up
again, than to undertake the long transverse scramble across
those stony and much scarified slopes.   I considered the
question during the few minutes I took for lunch in a wet
and draughty hole amongst the rocks ; but it was settled
for me by a malevolent gust of wind, mist and rain which
now swept over me from above, and soon hid the summit

Robert M. Adam

XII. THE WESTERN GRAMPIANS FROM BEINN LAWERS

of Meall nan Tarmachan altogether. This decided me that the long march still between me and home was quite enough for the rest of a day of bad weather, and I was only too pleased to have set the now most forbidding ridge behind me before the storm came.

Coire Riadhailt is a gloomy corrie which does not win the heart. It is inhabited entirely by sheep for which there is good grazing and shelter. But I noticed with interest a number of giant boulders broken from the wall of mountain and rolled for quite extraordinary distances out into the green levels. One, the largest single block of quartz I ever remember seeing, lay in isolation so far from the foot of the hill that it seemed almost inconceivable that it could ever have reached its position by natural means. But I suppose its great weight and the hard ice which must in winter encrust this sunless northern corrie would account for this without violence to mechanical principles.

By half-past three, then, I was on the road ; at Brig o' Balgie an hour later ; and, after a slow journey across the hill, reached Carie again at half-past seven. The rain had ceased, and the wind fallen, so that the loch was smooth and reflective, and in its sweetest and most welcoming mood. Most often it has been like this when I have known that in the rôle of fisherman I should have wished it otherwise, but have been quite helpless to regret the passionate beauty which Loch Rannoch at its silkiest cannot conceal. To-night I had no reason to withhold my admiration. It was too early for the deer to be coming down out of the Black Wood to water, as I have often seen them do near the mouth of the burn ; but the oyster-catchers were there again ; the tiny trout in one of the ditches under the road rushed madly out of sight as I passed ; and all round the loch, ten yards out, the larger ones were rising provocatively. In June the birches are so full of sap that their scent yields even to the sunshine of the day ; but after rain on a warm evening such as this it drifts in an almost visible cloud of intoxicating strength. And after those jagged green hills the sensual charm of Rannoch once more claimed me with renewed and irresistible power.

CHAPTER XVIII

RANNOCH TO CRIANLARICH

THE special attraction of the south shore of Loch Rannoch is the famous Black Wood of Rannoch, one of the largest remaining sections of the primitive forests. There is no other example upon a big scale in the southern Highlands; although there are smaller fragments scattered here and there, which add a touch of magic to the scenery wherever they are found. Such are the wood of Cranach, on the bare slopes facing Rannoch Moor across the Water of Tulla, through which the West Highland railway passes; a copse which gives distinction to the entrance of the Coire Ardrain glen near Crianlarich; and a few trees posted here and there on the south shore of Loch Earn. The Black Wood extends from the haugh of Carie as far as the village of Camghouran, a distance of some five miles.

This side of the loch is known locally as ' Slios Garbh ', ' Rough Side ', in distinction from the more open slopes upon the northern shore, which runs up not into high hills but to the lower moorlands towards Glen Garry, and is thus called ' Easy Side ', ' Slios Min '. Although there are glimpses of the Beinn Alder group to be had from the south bank, Slios Min has much the best of it as regards distant views, and is for that reason in a way the pleasanter. But there are roads (and reason) on both sides, and the

243

motor which runs four times each way daily from Kinloch to Rannoch Station pursues a sensible, if complicated, system of alternations. This makes it easy even for those who have no means of transport of their own to make the best of both worlds. But if you wish to make sure of the motor to or from any point short of Bridge of Gaiore, you should be careful to make sure of its intentions. They are always honourable, and punctiliously (if not punctually) fulfilled ; but vary according to the day of the week.

It took me by the northern route, early one morning in June, to the start of a great journey across the hills ; one which I was reluctant to undertake alone, for, especially when so far from the beaten track, solitary walking is in principle a most unsound proceeding, besides being less agreeable. I am sorry to say that in this way the rest of this book will be one long shocking example. Only let me warn anyone who follows it at least not to do so without being to some extent prepared for emergencies. It is necessary to make up your mind to take far too many clothes, and more food than you suppose you are at all likely to want ; and then not to use it all up out of an instinct of frugality, laudable enough in itself, but in other circumstances. Extra slabs of chocolate, raisins, and the like, are the easiest things to manage ; and a copious flask is really a necessity, although it is very rarely wise to use it in the course of a long day, except perhaps in the last three or four miles. I also like to have some vaseline and some sticking-plaster, and have often been glad of them. These precautions mean of course that you have to burden your self with a rucksack which you might have done without ; but it cannot be helped, for as a member of society you have no right to neglect them however tiresome they may seem. It is also well to take someone of reasonable

244

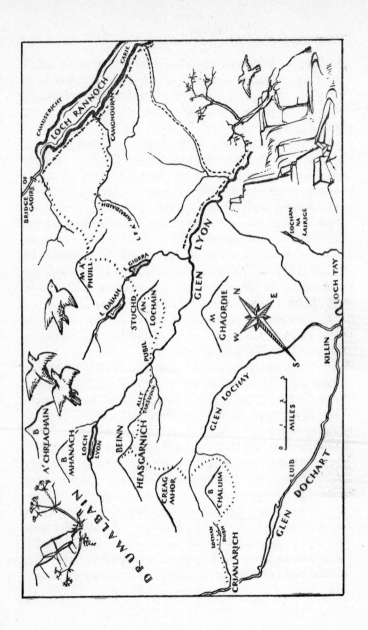

intelligence into your confidence as to the route which you mean to follow—not that it will always be possible to carry out your exact intentions. In case you are aiming at a distant destination, you should also arrange to send back a message to say you have arrived.

Loch Tay and Loch Rannoch are on divergent lines, so that their distance apart, measured from the western extremities, is about half as much again as from the eastern, but within these limits there is only the one intervening glen, Glen Lyon. As the crow flies, the distance from Kinloch Rannoch over Carn Mairg to Fearnan on Loch Tay is about ten miles, while from Bridge of Gaoire to Killin would be about fifteen. The actual routes to be followed would of course be much longer, but in the latter case either of the following alternatives would still be within the compass of a fairly long day's walking :

1. To Camghouran, over the Lairig a' Mhuic to Innerwick, and so by Lochan na Lairige, the Lairig Breislich or the Meall nan Tarmachan range.

2. By the path up the Allt Eas Stalchair and over the Lairig Meachdainn ridge, between Meall a' Phuill and the Cam Creag, to the Bridge between Gallin and Moar in Glen Lyon, and thence over Meall Ghaordie into Glen Lochay at a point three or four miles from Killin.

But west of this line, not only does the distance progressively increase (so that to Crianlarich, which was my objective, it is over twenty-two miles direct) but two more glens have found room to insinuate themselves. These are Glen Lochay and a northern branch of Glen Lyon called Glen Daimh. I had therefore an unusually long day before me, and, as I did not know any of the country except Glen Lyon itself, quite an adventurous one. The programme included not the passes, but the highest peaks, of the various lines of hills ; and one of these was Beinn Heasgarnich, the second highest of the Glen Lyon group and a ben which I had long wished for the chance to climb. As sometimes happens, my imagination had fixed on it without any apparent reason ; I daresay the strangeness of the name may have had something to do with it. I have not been able to discover its meaning. The best I can do in the way of conjecture is *beinn na-h-eas garbh an each*, ' the ben of the rough waterfall of the horse ', which seems to me to make reasonable sense. Apart from this question, Beinn Heasgarnich is an inaccessible, and, for its size, a little known hill, and these circumstances are also of a kind to provoke inquiry ; an inquiry which, as it turned out, had exceedingly interesting results.

It was a tolerable morning, though cloudy, as the bus rattled along from Kinloch Rannoch to Bridge of Gaoire ; not the best type of day, nor the best method of travelling to enjoy the scenery. But even so at this early hour it is always disturbingly beautiful. All the way there are the birch trees ; behind, across the rim of the Innerhadden foothills, the more and more acute pinnacle of Shiehallion, and in the far distance down Strathtummel the supporting cone of Ben-y-Vrackie ; while intermittently the Glencoe giants disclose themselves ahead. (Far away as they are I have seen them reflected in Loch Rannoch as clearly as if they rose from its edge—not indeed in the morning, but *à contre-jour* in the low light of sunset.) Some way above the road run the pylons, but man's improvements do not weigh heavily with nature until you come to Killiechonan seven miles on, where a row of modern suburban cottages prepares you with an unpleasant kind of tact for the tall ungainly structure of the main power-house which lies in wait a corner or two farther on ;

247

behind it the double columns of eight-foot black piping descend the hillside with all the water of the once proud River Ericht prisoned in their iron guts. The little strand of Camusericht (Ericht Bay) quivers sensitively in the presence of the intruder. Yet, one more bend of the road, and even this injury may be forgotten : especially since the spirited skyline of Beinn a' Chreachain, with its sharp summit and long angular wing, here comes into sight to the south-west as a new and dominating feature of the view. Opposite, at the back of the Camghouran glen, the Cross Craigs rise like the Bastille, above the woods where this morning a cuckoo was still advertising himself, as they do in these latitudes even into July—a few days later, when we landed there to shelter from a storm, I had the rare chance to catch sight of him flitting from one tall birch-tree to another—and before you reach Bridge of Gaoire, near Camusericht Lodge, there is a pine-wood where long after they had faded in the lowland woods, the bluebells still shone like rifts in an unearthly sky.

I started walking at 8.20, crossing the Bridge of Gaoire, and taking a short cut across the moor for a few hundred yards from opposite the post office, to join the private road along Allt a' Mheanbh Chruidh. Just beyond are the grassy pasturages of the Braes of Rannoch, where there are a considerable number of cottages and one or two sub-stantial farms. Indeed, I should say that this end of Loch Rannoch, which is low and sheltered, with the Camghouran glen two miles to the east, is the most populated part of the Rannoch district ; for Kinloch would hardly exist but for the tourist trade. The road was good easy walking, and in under an hour I reached the bridge over the Luban Feith a' Mhadaidh, by which another road comes up from Camghouran—a name which, by the way, has nothing to do with ' Cameron ', although it is pronounced almost like that, and by a coincidence happens to be full of members of this clan, as is its little walled burying ground near the lochside ; not that Rannoch was ever, properly speaking, Cameron country.

Not far past the bridge I crossed the burn, struck off to the left on a short, but at first rough, climb up the side of the Garbh Meall, skirted its stony summit, and reached the top of Meall Buidhe (3054 ft.) a little before 10.30. This ridge of smooth turf runs south like a level road for nearly a mile, before turning east to the point called Meall a' Phuill ; a name given presumably with reference to the ' pools ' in Glen Daimh below which it probably commands better than any other point (the lower of the two lochs, Loch Giorra, not being visible from Meall Buidhe) —for there do not seem to be any tarns closer at hand. But it should here be stated that the Bartholomew half-inch map, omitting ' Meall Buidhe ' altogether, gives the name ' Garbh Meall ' to the summit, and extends the name ' Meall a' Phuill ' to the whole of the southern part of the ridge. From the character of the hills, as I have described it, I should judge that here Bartholomew is in both respects less accurate than the Ordnance Survey.

As this ridge lies almost on the edge of the mountainous mass before the great waste of Rannoch Moor begins, for the height the view is surprisingly good in that direction, and the summit is just in the right line for seeing actually into Glencoe. It must be the only position from which such a thing is possible. To-day, unfortunately, the visibility was far from perfect. I had only my little telescope, which is quite strong but has only a small field of vision, and had not burdened myself with field-glasses. But in any case there was little enough time to spare ; so without much delay I went on down the slope of rank grass and peat, where, although we are coming into what is primarily sheep-country, there were a few parcels of deer.

I soon came within sight of the one homestead in the secluded glen below. This is not even named on the map, and I forgot to ask its name in the few minutes' conversation I had with a man at the side-gate. I had expected it to be an insignificant cottage. But it is a regular ' toun ' capable of accommodating a small army of people, as it probably does at least at such times as those of shearing and dipping. It stands between the two lochs at the end of the road which branches off the Glen Lyon road three miles down, well sheltered by one of the small plantations which alone break the uniformity of this little upland dale, so tightly enclosed between the steep sides of its smooth green hills. Though rather like some of the Lakeland valleys, Glen Daimh is at a much higher level—the lochs are both over 1300 ft. up : and it is quieter than the quietest and more, infinitely more, remote. It must, in fact, be almost free from intrusion, for it leads nowhere ; and has thus more of the character of an obscure Alpine *tal*, only visited in high summer, than of anything at all common in these islands. I noticed that there is a boat-house on Loch Giorra, and guessed that the fishing belongs to Meggernie Castle, the most famous of the great old houses in Glen Lyon, which would be about five miles from here, a mile and a half short of Brig o' Balgie.

Shortly after 11.15 I crossed the river between the lochs, and started on my second climb of the day, a steep 1800 ft. to the summit of Stuchd an Lochain (3144 ft.) . This is at the western corner of the corrie which in its upper terrace, a flat peaty place, contains another Lochan nan Cat.

Just halfway up I came within sight of the loch, which lies back nicely framed against an incisive ridge ; and glad I was to do so, for I found this part of the walk hot and tiresome—for encouragement I had kept my eye on a lively little double waterfall, which plashed down on me coolingly from a height of ten or twelve feet as I crossed the burn. But above the corrie, although the slope was steep, the ground was firmer underfoot, and this part of the climb was quickly over. Towards the top the hill narrows to what in Cumberland they call an ' edge ', with very rocky, but hardly precipitous, sides. There I met a covey of young ptarmigan, just on the wing ; they sailed above my head in quite good style on the upthrust of the light south-west wind from beyond the Stuchd.

I reached the top at 12.30, and found that here again the view is remarkably fine. Near at hand your gaze falls in two sharp dives, to Lochan nan Cat and thence to Lochs Daimh and Giorra, while, on the other side, Loch Lyon shows at greater distance. But the great asset of Stuchd an Lochain is its command of the vast amphitheatre from Beinn a' Chreachain to Beinn Doireann, across the gap beyond Glen Lyon, and then round to Beinn Heasgarnich ; the last almost opposite across the glen, but a little farther to the west. These hills form the romantic region known as Drumalbain, ' the backbone of Albainn ', which divides Breadalbane from Argyle and the east of Scotland from the west ; a no-man's-land whose green hollows have been the immemorial scene of forays and conflicts without number, to turn out at last in the twentieth century, but for the storms of nature, the quietest places under the sun, where not even the stags and hinds have much to fear.

South-west towards Glen Lyon the incline is a very gradual one at first, and there is a two mile stretch of boggy ground to be covered ; nor do I think there can be any dry way to Stuchd an Lochain from the south. Even after several weeks of fine weather this bit was disagreeable to cross. The only thing which interested me was the discovery of some old tree-roots, so fragmentary that, it must be admitted, I could not swear that they were not the remains of large heather-roots, though there is little or no heather here now. By the aneroid I placed the level of the highest at 2300 ft. This conforms with various other observations which seem to go to show that the tree-line in Scotland in old days was at about this height, and it seems probable that forest at one time covered almost the whole area of the Highlands up to that limit. Other comparable data of which my memory is certain are the remains in Glen Guisachan (Cairngorms) at 2000 ft., those in the Carie and Innerhadden glens at between 2000 and 2200 ft., and those on the ridge of Meall Breac, south of Loch Rannoch, at 2200 ft. There is also a Lochan Soir *a' Ghuibhais* (or Lochan Coire an Lochain), just east of Loch Treig under Stob Coire Sgriodain, at 2444 ft. As I have already mentioned in writing of Beinn a' Ghlo, if the name of the Bealach an Fhiodha, at a level of 2813 ft., is relevant at all in this connection, it should be taken as evidence of a singular exception to the general indications.

The lower course of the Allt Camaslaidh, which I had been following, is quite excitingly pretty and varied after the morasses above. It is one of three burns which here converge and execute the last part of the descent in parallel ; they make a really delightful place of the little sheep-farm of Pubil at the foot. Gathering was in progress, and the long narrow glen echoed and overflowed with the drowsy pastoral sound made by score upon score of sheep as they were herded in. I stood on a knoll for some minutes to watch the collies at work, and applauded the initiative and athletic skill of a single individualist lamb, who seemed to be giving more trouble to society than all the rest of the flock put together. I concluded that even sheep have an evolutionary future.

I had not been in the upper part of Glen Lyon for many years ; not since Jock Stewart and I did the whole length of it with bicycles, camped in the rain beside Loch Lyon, and struggled on next day, with much encumbrance, through the hills to Bridge of Orchy. It is the most interesting section of the whole glen : open country like Glen Daimh, but with so many hillocks along the foot of the hills on either side, covered either with short heather or the light turf of the downs and terraced intricately with sheep-tracks, that it is hard to say which are the numerous ancient forts, ' duns ' or ' raths ', and which are merely *sithean* or ' fairy knolls '.

The glen is well known as a site of early civilisation, and was one of the first parts of eastern Scotland to be touched by Christianity, its local missionary-saint being Adamnan or Eonan, the biographer of Columba. His name is commemorated in many a legend and place-name in these parts. But I like to think of its inhabitants in their yet more primitive state of nature-worship, which seems so reasonable and appropriate in such places as this, where there is no need of even the best manufactured theology to uplift the soul. It is possible that traces of this golden age are to be found in some of the local names, such as Pubil, meaning ' tent ', or perhaps ' encampment '—in which the initial *p* is, I imagine, a trace of the pre-Gaelic Celtic dialect of the Welsh type perhaps used by the Picts— and An Grianan, the hill just to the east of Pubil, which

253

means ' the Place of the Sun '. Now while this can be interpreted simply in the sense of a sunny place (what we speak of as a ' sun-trap '), this kind of description, even if reasonably apt, would, I fancy, be of a very rare type ; and it is quite ' on the cards ' that this flat-topped rocky eminence may have been a place of sun-worship, for which it would certainly have been both suitable and convenient. However that may be, this last still reach of the longest glen in Scotland, so far out of the main-stream of modern interests, exhales a sensible bouquet of mingled fairy tales and prehistory which is altogether charming. And moreover, there is little in the externals of life as it is lived there now to distinguish the present from those distant periods of time to which such Homeric simplicity essentially belongs.

The light road runs all the way close by the Lyon's vigorous, though moderately winding, course. My intention had been to follow this for the three miles up to Loch Lyon and thence to make the direct assault on Beinn Heasgarnich by the rather steep shoulder, Stob Garbh Leachtir. But a careful inspection of the hill made during the descent from Stuchd an Lochain had decided me that a better route offered on the east side, by the Allt Tarsuinn, which joins the Lyon almost opposite Pubil. There is a wide shallow pool at a bend of the river just above the confluence. A boat lay in the foreground, on the farther bank ; but beyond this was a wide curve of stepping-stones which I used to cross. Between the bleak hills behind and before, this spot made a friendly picture which I long carried in the mind's eye.

By the burn a rough track climbs the pastures into a narrow glen. Here there is an easy pass over to Glen Lochay, rising only seven hundred feet or so from Glen

Lyon. This strikes across to the left-hand slope, opposite Beinn Heasgarnich, after crossing the burn. But at that point (where there is a sheep-fold) I of course turned up to the right with the burn, which rises just below the top of my mountain.

It must now have been about three o'clock, for I had spent about three-quarters of an hour at lunch in a cleft beside the water. I was beginning to be disappointed in the moderate promise of the day. The sun, which had gleamed once or twice, now seemed to have retired for good, and the sky was haggard.

I was faced by a curious range of contorted hillocks about a thousand feet above me and a mile or so distant. These filled the whole sky-line ; except that far beyond, like a peak on a separate supporting range, showed a distinctive hackle of rock which I thought must be the top of Heasgarnich. (As a matter of fact the actual summit turned out to be higher and more to the right.) The going was very heavy, and many minor ups and downs were not to be avoided ; for the only route seemed to be to hang as close on the flanks of the burn as its often steep banks allowed.

For the last half-mile before coming up to the long broken rampart above, I was intrigued by the behaviour of a family of little smoky-blue birds, some kind of dippers or else water ousels, which kept fluttering on just in front of me from pool to pool. The parents could, of course, easily have outpaced me and gone far ahead, but they kept stopping and coming back to titter agitated encouragement to a particularly feeble young one, which could only just fly and struggled up each of the little cataracts, one at a time, with a pathetic intensity ; I think I could easily have caught it in my hands. Their proceedings were

255

touching but betrayed some lack of intelligence. Finally I passed the lot of them by short-circuiting a bend in the stream and left them behind me, no doubt much relieved.

The burn led through a narrow pass in miniature into a labyrinth of peaty mounds, extending perhaps half a mile forward and a mile from side to side between the wings of a higher encircling ridge. Here for a time I ignored the course of the burn, which dissolves into a series of meandering tarns. The place was laborious enough to cross, and meanwhile I could not yet make out what the route ahead was like, certain only that it was still no direct ascent. But I was overjoyed to have discovered so strange a fragment of the world, and was only sorry that I had it all to myself. I was in luck besides, for only a few hundred yards ahead an eagle suddenly made his appearance. He dropped from some distant corner of the sky, and came to rest just beyond the next big hillock. I ran ahead, and crept carefully over the rise. I was not quick enough to catch him on the ground, but was only a few yards off when he rose awkwardly out of the heather ; and I could see from the white bars on his tail-feathers that he was not a full-grown bird. Indeed this was clear enough from the difficulty which he seemed to find in gaining height. Once a few hundred feet up he floated off rather unsteadily towards the east, and I saw him no more. I do not know whether eagles still nest in this part of the country, but in any case, I believe, the young are apt to stray far afield experimenting for new territory after leaving the parental nest. The one I saw may have been setting out upon this difficult stage of life, and he certainly had a lonely, uncomfortable sort of look with which I sympathised.

I picked up the line of the burn again—it is well called ' Tarsuinn ', ' the Oblique '—and went by various farther

XIII.

HEAD OF THE LONGEST GLEN IN SCOTLAND
GLEN LYON, PERTHSHIRE

stages up the north side of its northern branch, through a series of two or three more shallow corries descending in steps, with some scrambling to be done on the steeper slopes between them. The main burn here runs in a considerable chasm. I noticed one or two small cairns which seemed to mark a route on the other side, but could not see that it had much to recommend it over my own. At last I came to a little lochan which is the source of the burn and beyond this rose the summit-ridge to a height of another two hundred feet.

This last corrie is a clean-swept little hollow, quite different in character from any lower part of the hill. Above the lochan lay two long snow-wreaths, and where the snow had lately melted at their lower edge were fresh mosses of an Alpine type which reminded me of some to be found, generally at a much higher level, on the Cairngorms. One was in delicate green bloom. Other flowers, such as the cushion-pink and the heavy cups of the greater celandine, lay like nosegays about the greyish sward. One huge clump of bright cushion-pink, lying on top of a rock as if swelling over the brim of a huge basket, quite startled me at a distance with its resemblance, at first sight, to some curious beast couchant.

I reached the top of Heasgarnich (3530 ft.) with elation ; for the climb had been both arduous and unusually full of interest, and so combined the only two good grounds for retrospective satisfaction, something enjoyed and something done. It was just five o'clock. I now considered the possibility of making the easier, though rather longer, journey down Glen Lochay to Killin instead of proceeding to Crianlarich, but was soon determined in favour of my original goal by the sure and certain hope of a warm welcome, however late I might arrive, in the Crianlarich

R

Hotel, where I knew that both food and drink would be good, the rooms comfortable, the water hot at all hours, and the service quick and intelligent—an almost unknown concentration of the desirable qualities.

The sky was growing black and there were a few drops of rain, so I only stayed long enough on the summit to walk the few yards north to a point from which I could look down the steep Coire Heasgarnich to the head of Loch Lyon. As I returned, the most conspicuous object in the landscape was the mass of Beinn More thrusting high into the clouds only ten miles away ; I need hardly say, Cruachan was also well to the fore ; and from one point on the ridge south of the cairn I caught a glimpse of the head of Loch Awe down the course of the Argyle Lochy, where run the road and railway-line to Oban.

I dropped quickly down the Eag Uillt to the Allt Bad a' Mhaim, crossed it, and traversed the bracken-covered slopes beneath Sron nan Eun to a point in the upper part of Glen Lochay half a mile or so above the red-roofed cottage of Badvaim, which is the last human outpost in the glen. Here, if I had only had more time, I should have liked to call for a few minutes' local ' crack '—and should then perhaps have found out something more to tell of Beinn Heasgarnich ; but it was after six o'clock on a somewhat gloomy evening and I had still to get myself over from Glen Lochay into Glen Dochart.

On the way down I tumbled almost on top of one herd of about a dozen deer, stags and hinds ; they raced off up-wind towards Creag Mhor (3387 ft.). This is part of the range extending south from Heasgarnich, which also comprises Cam Creag (2887 ft.) and Beinn Chaluim (3354 ft.), and forms a second line of defence inside the main fortification of Perthshire facing on the West Highland line. Of these Beinn Chaluim is the most imposing, and towards Beinn Heasgarnich especially presents a very savage appearance. It is a green shiny peak much scarred on all sides, but with a convenient long shoulder of approach from Crianlarich, which is at an easy distance. This compact region of high hills about the head of Glen Lochay is, I think, the only part of the whole great tract between Rannoch and Tay which is still shot from as a regular deer-forest. On the map it is shown as the Forest of Mamlorn, but is generally known as the Forest of Borland. It forms part of the still very extensive Breadalbane property, once of such remarkable size as to become the subject of a fairly well-known song, whose words are no longer quite as true as they were. The song begins :

> From Kenmore to Ben More
> The land is a' the Markiss's.

But that presumably gives only the greatest single dimension and certainly does not do justice to the full range of the Marquis' territory, which included the Black Mount forest—that is, half the Moor of Rannoch as far west as the hills on the Argyle coast—and ran southward as far as Loch Earn.

South of Badvaim is a mile of dead flat marshland dissected by trenches. These might be difficult to cross but luckily there are planks laid over them, which is better than one would expect of this apparently trackless area from a distance ; but it is still nasty. At the crossing of the Allt Chaluim, a large burn draining both sides of Cam Creag, the ground begins to rise again. Here I halted for a few minutes' rest before the last step. After the grand manner of the day's work up to the present, I was inclined to regard the crossing of a mere pass—all that now lay

259

between me and supper—with some contempt. It was twenty-five to seven when I started ; I did not trouble to make a proper calculation to avoid the necessity for getting out a new sheet of the map (I was just on the last inch of No. 55) but from memory, or mere optimism, I judged I should be at Crianlarich by eight at the latest. As a matter of fact I was not there till ten minutes to nine, and upon mature consideration I now think that this was very good going ; indeed I confess there were moments before I crossed the watershed when my heart (and my feet) sank so low that I wondered whether I should ever get there at all.

For perhaps a mile the remains of an old cart-track or road of some kind are just traceable along the left bank of the Lochay, though this is of more use as a moral re-assurance than as a practicable path. Why there should ever have been such a good road up there rather puzzled me at first, but its purpose became clear—and at the same time, fulfilled, for the road now vanished—when I reached the melancholy ruins of what had once been a considerable clachan ; I should say probably something more than a mere summer sheiling. Though perhaps on a smaller scale, such sights are common. But in this bare and dreary glen the silent heaps which may, though I think not, have been so since the 'Forty-five, had all the indecent mournfulness of unburied bones ; such as priests in their morbid preoccupation with the materials of love and death—for them equally unknown quantities—even now like to expose. Some such inscription therefore seemed appropriate to the ruins in this derelict glen as Samuel Butler quotes from one Italian charnel-house of the kind :

> Quales vos estis nos fuimus
> Et quales nos sumus vos eritis

(which, like the best of art, is a well-stated lie with some truth in it) and with these words coming and going in some confusion on the threshold of my mind, I passed on in truly a sombre mood.

But Latin and righteous indignation are robust company, and beyond the fountain of these ghostly thoughts I pushed vigorously ahead. Such vestiges of a track as there may be seem to be on the right bank of the stream ; but this is a doubtful piece of inference, and the question is in any case merely academic, for above the clachan the glen becomes almost contourless on the map and so rough and heavy underfoot that no path has a chance. Once I nearly trod on an old cock grouse. He looked round with an expression of surprise and consternation more definite than I should have thought possible on a bird's face. Once I thought I heard ahead of me—could it be possible ?—the noise of the train running down from Tyndrum to Crianlarich. But it was actually an aeroplane, an odd but comfortless apparition, which in a few minutes had passed over me and beyond Beinn Chaluim. It returned again, flying in the direction of Glasgow, before I had yet crossed the Dochart, no doubt in the meanwhile having been at least as far as Fortwilliam or the isle of Skye. When I reached Loch Chailein I thought at last I was near the watershed. (By now I dared not open the map in case the glen on the other side should have the same appearance and rob me of my remaining spirits !) But I was wrong—there was an even worse stretch of sodden land, about a mile of it, between this loch and the two small Lochan Dubh, which might equally well flow in either direction, and, as it happens, are the source of the Inverhaggernie burn to the south. This Despond I crossed diagonally to the edge of the slope on the Beinn Chaluim side, which looked the firmest route, and so passed to the west of the Lochan Dubh. It was lucky that I did so, for all in a moment I found myself on a reasonably steep, dry, heathery hillside, and, what is more, an excellent path. I need hardly say I went off down this like the wind, and made excellent time to the bridge across the Dochart at Inverhaggernie, and so along a horribly hard bit of the main road into Crianlarich.

A great blaze of broom along the roadside gave me a fine welcome, and I enjoyed the feel of the soft gloaming— since it no longer mattered to me whether it rained or not. It was not long before a small mountain of the sweet mountain-sheep and how many pints of beer I did not count had put me into the best possible vein of self-appreciation ; which so far as it related to my own efforts, was justified—and so far as to the more excellent gifts of Providence, was excusable. For in twelve and a half hours I had covered some thirty miles, for the most part of worse than average going, with a total climb of over seven thousand feet—and, what is more important, I had enjoyed every yard of it but the last few thousand.

Crianlarich stands almost on the Glen Falloch water-shed—an artificial watershed formed of deposited moraine-material, which to all appearance has diverted the Falloch south from an original course into the Dochart. Tyndrum, at the head of Glen Dochart, just short of the county march, shares with Crianlarich the distinction of possessing two stations, and for the five miles between them there is a railway-line on either side of the glen : one, the West Highland, coming up by Loch Lomond from Glasgow and running on to Bridge of Orchy and across Rannoch Moor, and the other, the Oban line, from Balquhidder, by that remarkably steep glen, Glen Ogle, and through Killin

Junction. Apart from this disfigurement Glen Dochart, green, desolate, and flat and marshy at the bottom, is not to my mind in itself an endearing valley. The Dochart is of course really the upper part of the Tay, and its name, *tamh*, ' the Water of Sloth ', is here particularly well justified. But any of these places—you will find another hotel at Luib, half-way between Crianlarich and Killin, as well as cheaper miscellaneous accommodation here and there—is an admirable centre for many high hills ; while from Tyndrum there is also the new highroad to Glencoe, of which enormity, as a walker, and even as a man, I cannot trust myself to speak with moderation.

CHAPTER XIX

DRUMALBAIN

' IT is difficult to feel the same intimate affection for mountains whose names we cannot pronounce as we can feel for Scafell or Snowden ', says Mr. Arthur Gardner in his *Peaks, Lochs and Coasts of the Western Highlands*—a book which yet contains many lovely and understanding photographs. ' The Gaelic language ', he continues, ' never seems to have been meant to be written down. It abounds in sounds that no tongue not brought up to it can pronounce : its genders are chaotic and its inflexions affect the beginning or the middle of the word rather than the end, making the ordinary type of dictionary almost useless.'

I suppose all Mr. Gardner says is true. I cannot find a single statement with which I don't agree. For as to the initial remark, I have exactly the same feeling myself about Welsh, which is meaningless to me and looks ugly ; although in some languages quite unintelligible words can be warmly suggestive. As to the second, it is certainly true that few natural Gaelic-speakers can read and write, and that the academic rules of orthography are abominably artificial ; although there may be some excuse for them, having to make some attempt to represent sounds which seem to be directly taken from the variety of nature and will not readily submit to the dictation of mere vowel and consonant. Of the negative usefulness of acquired Gaelic there is clear evidence. I have known several people who

264

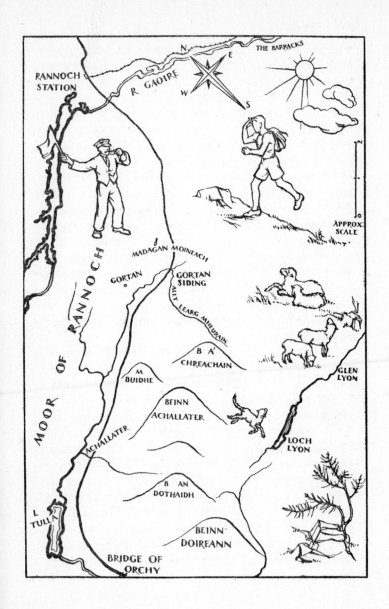

THE BARRACKS

RANNOCH
STATION

R GAOIRE

N
W E
S

APPROX.
SCALE

MOOR OF RANNOCH

MADAGAN MOINEACH

GORTAN

GORTAN
SIDING

ALLT LEARG MHEURAIN

B A'
CHREACHAIN

M
BUIDHE

BEINN
ACHALLATER

GLEN
LYON

ACHALLATER

LOCH
LYON

L
TULLA

B AN
DOTHAIDH

BEINN
DOIREANN

BRIDGE OF
ORCHY

were under the impression they spoke it fluently, and could read it aloud, but could not make any Gaelic-speaking person understand a word. This does not mean that the fault is entirely on their side, for in the first place it is essentially a dialectic language and varies appreciably from glen to glen, and in the second it is spoken only by the uneducated who are always unadaptable to slight departures from their particular conception of ' the only right way '— in language as in religious and moral habits. The same thing might happen to an English ambassador talking French to a peasant of, say, the Limousine. Even so, the difficulties of imitating the vocables to the satisfaction of a native are unusually great. I once spent many minutes in quite unsuccessful attempts to pronounce the single word *laogh* (a calf). The sound as I heard it was simply a prolonged *l*, sounded far back on the palate, without any particular vowel attached, just like the low of a young calf, and my own ear (but mine only) entirely approved the efforts of my tongue.

Yet there strikes me that something is badly wrong with the general tone of Mr. Gardner's remarks : at any rate I find myself out of sympathy with them. This is probably because, without pretending to know Gaelic either conversationally or to read, I have taken the comparatively small amount of trouble necessary to understand its phonetics in theory, and can therefore, with the help of experience in particular cases, make at least an imperfect attempt at most of the pronunciations. And far from finding that the names detract from my fondness for the places to which they belong, I must say that I derive a greater satisfaction from the mere sound of certain Gaelic words and names than is to be gained from such an elementary knowledge of most languages. In this degree

266

Gaelic words relating to simple things have often struck me as peculiarly expressive. The initial *ch*s and *t*s (pronounced like ' tch ' before a slender vowel) as in the well-known lament, ' Cha till MacCruimein ' ; the deep *o*s, the long *i*s, the strange effects of the various diphthongs, ro concatenations of diphthongs separated by aspirated (and therefore generally elided) consonants, and above all the rising and falling accentuation, have a direct emotive effect like that of music. Let me quote one verse of a Gaelic song, a specially fine and dignified combination of sounds which succeeds without any help from suggestion or symbolism in making poetry out of what, judged by the standard of prose, is a statement of little significance :

> ' O chi chi mi na mor bheanna,
> O chi chi mi na cor bheanna,
> O chi chi mi na coireachan,
> Chi mi na sgoran fo cheo.'

All it means is :

> ' I shall see, see the great hills,
> Shall see, see the proud hills,
> Shall see the corries,
> See the rocks under the snow.'

It will look absurd in an attempt at English phonetic spelling, but I suppose I should try to show how it would sound to the English ear :

> ' Ó hee hee me na móre venna,
> Ó hee hee me na core venna,
> Ó hee hee me na core-ahan,
> Hee me na sgore-an fo hyo.'

The devices used are almost childishly simple, yet the repeated *ee* and *ore* sounds in each line are certainly telling,

267

and they lead up constructively to the final smash of *cheo* —a sound which in itself I dearly love.

The present chapter will be concerned with the chief range of Drumalbain, the watershed of Scotland, which roughly forms the Perthshire-Argyle march. This contains some hills with very peculiar-looking names, which will make a good object-lesson in the infinite possibilities of concealment offered by Gaelic spelling to any sound which has a fancy ' to make itself scarce '. We have Beinn Achadh-Fhaladair ; which by the disappearance of the aspirated *d* and *f* resolves itself simply into ' Achallater '— and to save paper and ink this is how I shall spell it—; Beinn an Dothaidh, which on similar principles becomes just ' an Doey '; and Beinn a' Chreachain, pronounced ' a' hrayhan ' as nearly as I can render it.

On the morning of the day on which I went to these hills I spent some time talking to the head keeper at Rannoch Barracks (a true Highlander from the western island of Luing) and in the course of conversation referred to this hill as ' Cre-achan '. He was far too polite to show more than the mildest surprise, but told me that, if that were so, it would be a long step, and presumed that I could hardly expect to be back that night. This opinion coming from an expert puzzled me very much ; until I found out that he thought I meant Beinn Cruachan—a feat which the heroes of Ossian would not have despised.

But before we come to Beinn a' Chreachain and his peers I am reminded that earlier in this book I made some remark as to the number of words for ' hill ' with which Gaelic is equipped. Meanwhile curiosity has led me to re-examine the point, and as I am already on the subject I think this may be an appropriate place to summarise the result of my researches. I will do so as briefly as possible in tabular form,

268

and if your interest is in no way roused, there is nothing in the world to prevent you turning over the page. Here is my list—I do not pretend that it is exhaustive, especially in the latter sections which are capable of almost indefinite extension, or that the classification is anything but arbitrary.

1. *Specific terms* (mostly implying some individual characterisation) :

aonach
ard (height).
bac (bank)
barr (high ground)
beinn (the most general word)
bidean (peak)
braigh (upper part)
bruach (bank)
carn (cairn)
carr (a shelf)
cnap ⎫
cnoc ⎭ (hillock)
creag (rock)
creachan (windy summit)
cruach, cruachan (stack)
dronn (bluff)
eiridh (rising ground)
fireach (high moor)
garbhlach (rough hill)
leirge (hillside)

leacainn ⎫
leacach ⎪
leathad ⎬ (stony slope)
leitir ⎭
lurg (rising ridge)
maol, muil, maoile, maolinn, mill (bare hill)
meall (generally, ridge)
moine (moor)
monadh (flat hill)
mullach (summit)
ord, uird (round steep hill)
sgor, sgur (sharp rock)
sliabh, sleibh (rare, but common in Ireland)
slios (slope)
stac, stuc, stuichd ⎫ (jutting
stob ⎭ hill)
torr (abrupt hill)
tuim, tom ⎫ (hillock)
tulach ⎭

2. *Metaphors* accepted as almost synonyms :

aghaidh (face, brow)
aodann
drum (back, spine)
socach (snout)
sron (nose)

cliabh ⎫
uchd ⎪
mam ⎬ (breast)
sidh ⎭

3. Other occasional *metaphors* :

aran (loaf—as we say ' sugar-loaf ')	dun (fort)
	fad (turf)
bachd (crook)	fiacaill (tooth)
bod (cod)	gob (beak)
buchaille (herdsman)	guala (shoulder)
caisteal (castle)	sgiath (wing)
cladh (sepulchral mound)	sidhean (fairy knowe)
ceann (head)	suidhe (seat)
cir (crest)	tal (adze)
cleit (quill)	taobh (side)
cul (back)	tiompan (drum)
diollaid (saddled)	ton (buttock)

4. *Allied terms*, implying height :

aoineadh (steep cape)	feannag (strip of high ground)
cadha (steep path)	uachdar (upper part)

I see that, taking all in, these nearly double the rough estimate made in Chapter II—enough to go on with, and we shall.

I left my bicycle in the care of my friend at the Barracks—which I should perhaps explain is a shooting-lodge occupying the site, but retaining no more than the name, of the Barracks set up here after the 'Forty-five—and after prolonged meditation on the swirling black pool through which the peat-laden waters of the Gaoire arrive in Loch Rannoch, caught the second bus of the day on to Rannoch station. The plan was to take the train, which runs along the edge of the Moor close to the Drumalbain range, to Bridge of Orchy, almost sixteen miles down the line (opposite the head of Glen Lyon), and thence to walk back along the range and (if need be) across the corner of the Moor to Bridge of Gaoire ; or preferably to catch the north-bound evening train at Gortan siding, which is about half-way between Rannoch and Bridge of Orchy stations.

Although one might not at first realise it, an arm of the Moor of Rannoch runs out as far as Bridge of Gaoire. Topography is confused by the vast debris of what must have been a monarch amongst the glaciers of the world even in a glacial age. The road picks its way through a wilderness of *tumuli*, clustered so thickly with grotesque boulders that in places it would be difficult to find a way between them. The predominant type of rock is a curiously heavy granite of a sombre red colour, which seems to contain considerable metallic deposits ; and this may well be so, if I am correctly informed that no rock like it is found nearer to Rannoch Moor than the Ural Mountains. There is but one house, the lodge of Dunan, in the five and a half miles, but several woods make for variety. In any case the sense of the primeval, which cannot but be felt, and the views ahead as the station is approached, are more than enough to prevent monotony. Besides, for the last few miles of its course, after the long sluggishness of the Moor, the Gaoire rushes grandly alongside like a giant refreshed. It used to be a fine salmon-river, but the pike from Loch Rannoch have now made their way far up and to a great extent spoiled the fishing.

A rather sordid little settlement, such as the picture-goer would expect to find in ' the Middle-West ', has germinated on Rannoch station. It has no other *raison d'être* whatsoever, for there is nothing but the extreme of desolation for many miles around. It can, however, boast the possession of a useful shop and a bar, with a small hotel attached, where people stay chiefly for the excellent fishing in Loch Laidon and the other lochs scattered everywhere about the Moor. In all directions across the wide flat spaces encircling masses of high hills stand out on the horizon, especially on a fine spring or autumn day when the snow on the tops brings them closer and makes them easier to pick out and identify. The station is the starting-place of a track across the Moor to the Kingshouse Inn, the better of the only two practicable routes across the Moor from east to west.

The walker will find Gortan halt, lying as it does at the butt-end of the high chain along the march of Perth-shire and Argyle, a most useful point of contact between civilisation and the heart of the wilds—if they have such a thing : for this region, I must say, shows little enough sign of sympathy with any human ideal. But discretion is required, for the trains do not regularly stop there, nor will they do so merely on request made locally : you are supposed to write to the head-office of the company in Glasgow and arrange in advance. But there is a reason for everything ; and the reason for this is that when the rail-way was made the company were bound under contract to the Marquis of Breadalbane to observe these inconvenient formalities, his object being to preserve his forests from the inroads of poachers ; and therefore before you can get the train to stop, you are also supposed to convince the company that you are a person of respectability. I don't know whether walkers come into this category or not, so it is safer to describe yourself, as I did, ' friend of the signal-man ', which, if not true *in puncto temporis*, had at least the great merit of becoming so before that day's sun had set on my iniquity. I should add that the time-table is sus-ceptible to one semi-official influence for good, which is that the Gortan children (believe it or not) go to school every day at no less distant a seat of learning than Fort-william. On this account the morning train north and the

XIV.

THE SPINE OF SCOTLAND, FROM RANNOCH MOOR

LOCHAN NAH-ACHLAISE

evening train south can generally be trusted to stop at Gortan. There is also a shepherd to be brought to Rannoch on Saturday nights. But I will not trouble you further with these refinements.

My problem then was, first, to arrange for the evening train from Glasgow to stop at Gortan, and secondly, to be there in time to catch it. For the train from Rannoch does not arrive at Bridge of Orchy until 11.40, and this left me less than seven hours for a walk of thirteen miles covering four, fortunately well-united ' Munros '—the total climb amounting to about 5400 feet. This works out at rather over seven hours, by Naismith's formula, so there was just time to do it but none for loitering on the way ; which was a pity, for the day was one continuous blaze of sunshine, morally a temptation to indolence and physically a handicap, from the point of view of speed : emphatically a day for shorts. But if I had missed the train in the evening, I should have had to face nine or ten miles more across the Moor from Gortan to Bridge of Gaoire, and this addition I was inclined to spare myself if possible, as it would have meant a very late return to Rannoch.

At any other time this section would have tempted me. The track is part of the drove-route leading from Bridge of Orchy, the last outpost of Argyle, past the sheep-farm of Achallater and the Fletchers' ruined castle from which— to mention the most sensational incident in its by no means peaceful history—Campbell of Glenlyon set out on the last stage of his journey to carry out the Massacre of Glencoe ; and so by Loch Rannoch and Loch Garry to the north. It is still used when the sheep of the Grampians are sent to winter in the milder climate of the west coast. I believe the original track and right-of-way runs directly from Gortan, crossing the railway at Madagan Moineach ;

s

but according to my information the better route is by the path joining the line at the point marked on the map as ' Soldiers' Trenches ', three miles north of Gortan. (The question as to what military purpose these trenches can possibly have had, may well give rise to a good deal of perplexity ; so it may perhaps be as well to explain that they had none. But they are none the less probably quite authentic and were so-called in no spirit of mere frivolity. The Commissioners of the Forfeited Estates, with the usual ill-informed benevolence of English Government departments in dealing with Scotland and Ireland, for some time employed the troops at Rannoch in a hopeless attempt to drain part of the Moor and reclaim it for cultivation.)

The train was a few precious minutes late at Bridge of Orchy, so I was not able to start until 11.48. But in spite of this I was at the top of Beinn Doireann (3524 ft.) and had most of my climbing behind me, by 1.20. This was twenty minutes to the good as compared with the detailed time-schedule which I had made out in advance in order to keep myself posted of my chances of reaching Gortan before the train. I made up ten minutes more between there and Beinn an Dothaidh (3267 ft.) and another five before reaching the south top of Beinn Achallater. The lead allowed me to slacken the pace a little, but none the less I reached Gortan at 6.5, twenty-five minutes earlier than my reckoning, making a total time of six hours, seventeen minutes. This record-breaking spirit is objectionable in itself, but was the only possible one in the circumstances ; and as the time available for this walk must generally be dependent on trains, it is useful to have ascertained the indispensable minimum—which for the very energetic, without packs and in good conditions, might be estimated, in round figures, at six hours. On a day like this I should have been glad of several hours more, for though there was some haze I could yet see as far as the Cairngorms, and the views, especially of the hills closer at hand, are of an order which does not deserve to be treated with such scant attention.

Beinn Doireann, the Mountain of Storms (which should perhaps be spelt ' Douairain ') is probably the best known of these hills. It is just not the highest, but it is much the most accessible. The normal ascent is by the blunt end of the ridge, the very steep regular bluff which rises due north of Auch on the main road. From this direction it is a bold commanding peak, and it is easy to understand that it should have made a particular appeal to the imagination of Duncan Ban Macintyre, one of the most celebrated of the eighteenth-century Gaelic poets (to whom there is a monument on the side of Loch Awe, not far from Dalmally). It is indeed the nominal subject of what is supposed to be his best poem, although he was nearly eighty when it was written.

Certainly, Beinn Doireann is a fine hill, but the less frequented tops farther on are more fascinating to my mind. From the west the chain is clearly seen to be continuous both structurally and in detail. The railway follows its line with precision, except where the big corrie runs back between Beinn an Dothaidh and Beinn Achallater. A coping of rock is carried out with hardly a break throughout the length of the ridge just below the top, but the crags are so weathered and decomposed that, except in a few places, this obstacle is more formidable in appearance than in fact. On the east, towards Glen Lyon, no such well-defined formation is perceptible and the contours are less sudden and spectacular. Judging by my own observation, for what it is worth, I should say that the geological explanation of these effects is that the strata are tilted upward towards the west and broken off crosswise, the fractured ends becoming the escarpment visible along that side of the ridge. This feature is apparent from the lie of the ground as you walk along the tops, especially between Beinn Doireann and Beinn an Dothaidh.

From the station, I went only a few hundred yards along the road before striking off by one of the dozens of burns which vein the hillside, coming down at a right angle from the ridge of Beinn Doireann. The first part of the climb, to about 2000 ft., is at a very easy gradient, but over rather broken ground. The rest is steep, and the way must be picked carefully amongst the crags and across screes of clinking schist. I came quite suddenly on to the neck of the ridge just north of the top ; I was a good deal impressed. The hill is only a few yards broad at this point, so that all at once I found myself on the edge of that fine corrie of dusky-black rock, Coire Chruitein, which is really rather an innocent place as these things go, but the very devil in looks. It consists largely of loose or hanging rocks, and, with these to play on, so far as noise was concerned the mere zephyrs of the day succeeded in giving quite a creditable impersonation of a real wind.

But I liked better the open hollows on the north side of the hill, through which I had to descend in order to reach the col (at 2500 ft.) below Beinn an Dothaidh. Here there are small tarns, and there were also considerable drifts of snow, caught mostly in the narrow clefts of rock which some of the burns have seized on to make their escape into the lower glen. Here, too, I met a hind, the only creature except sheep which I saw all day ; for this is all sheep-country, and for some reason the grassy hills which suit sheep best seem to attract very little of any other form of life. Yet there must at one time, about two hundred years ago, have been as much game in this neigh-bourhood as elsewhere, for Duncan Ban in his poem speaks of the earlier presence of deer, red grouse, and even blackcock, and laments that they have been supplanted by sheep during his own lifetime. There may well have been more heather in those days, for the predominant vegetation of a locality changes often quite rapidly ; and, as to the blackcock, creatures of the woods, apart from the fact that they were undoubtedly commoner throughout the Highlands generally than they are now, it is likely that the forest, of which the grove of Cranach is a mere remnant, was then still extensive.

The seven hundred feet to Beinn an Dothaidh gave little trouble. There is a very pretty tumbling burn with bright beds of moss along its sides and icy water, which I splashed over myself but with a great effort forbore to drink. I thought of it with regret for the rest of the day, for I never came across another so good or nearly so good. From Beinn Doireann my eye had been chiefly drawn to the spiky Gothic pinnacles of Cruachan. From Beinn an Dothaidh the turreted mass of Stob Gabhar asserts itself just across Loch Tulla, and the spaces of the Moor begin to unfold, showing to better and better advantage as you go farther north. But at this point comes a mile towards the west, along the rocky slopes of the big corrie, during which you have Loch Lyon and Glen Lyon directly in front. In a mist it would be as well to bear in mind that there are three bits of rising ground to be crossed before (bending here a little towards the south and back) you find yourself on the last slope leading to the col (2500 ft.). Here the ridge turns once more due north and enters on its narrowest and finest section. The side of

Beinn Achallater stretches out for a mile beyond the bealach in an even wall, never quite precipitous but none the less unscalable. There is an easy slope along its edge to the south top (3288 ft.) and another mile of level walking brings you to the north top (3404 ft.).

The small cairn marking the north top is on the very edge of the only great precipice of the Drumalbain range. It was here in the spring of 1925 that the young student Henderson was killed. It was three weeks before his body was found, although there was a large search-party out every day scouring the hills. There is a curious story connected with the case, for the body was eventually discovered by the directions of a woman with second sight who lived, if I remember correctly, somewhere near Inverness ; and even in the bright sunlight there was a peculiar grimness about these stark sheer rocks, especially from Meall Buidhe (3100 ft.) (the first point on the ascent of the long shoulder of Beinn a' Chreachain) whence the best view of Beinn Achallater is obtained.

The descent from Beinn Achallater to the col (2700 ft.) requires caution. A perfectly safe route could be found by keeping farther to the south-east away from the edge of the cliff, but this would mean more loss in height. Once over Meall Buidhe, the way on to the summit of Beinn a' Chreachain is easy and straightforward ; and a final climb of three hundred feet from the edge of Coire an Lochain brings you on to its culminating peak.

Beinn a' Chreachain is a masterpiece of natural architecture, steep on all sides except along the ridge by which we have approached it, though the steepness is broken along the line of the zig-zag shoulder which extends towards Gortan and brings the whole range to a triumphant conclusion. Its dispositions are as good. The views in all

278

directions are uninterrupted, since it is not only the highest point of all Drumalbain and the Glen Lyon hills, but stands well apart from the rest on the most open quarter. In particular, it happens to be in the exact line of Loch Ericht, and the vista up that long narrow stretch of water to the sea of mountains beyond is unique.

Content to be within range of Gortan in such good time, but very hot and thirsty, I plunged into a patch of snow only a few feet below the cairn on the north-east side before resuming clothes and comparative respectability—for I had been walking for the last two hours practically naked, with my things in the rucksack. Even in that short time I was annoyed to find afterwards that the skin had nearly been burnt off, leaving the straps of the rucksack neatly stencilled on my back. But such marks as these are honourable stigmata to carry under one's contemptible jacket back into the world of streets.

On the shoulder, which I now started to descend, there is yet one more sight in store ; the view back at the pointed summit of Coire an Lochain in which lies a happy-looking tarn. It is the only corrie of its type in all this country.

From now on my thoughts were set on water, but not one clear spring could I find. The lower slope is gentle and lightly wooded with birches, and the last mile to Gortan is the first of the many miles of Rannoch Moor itself ; so there were only brackish ditches and pools unfit for drinking. At Gortan it was no better. One would hardly have thought it possible that there should be a single dwelling in the Highlands without a good water-supply, whatever else might be lacking in the way of home-comforts. But this is so at Gortan, and all they have to drink there is taken in from the engines of passing trains.

Not that this is the only respect in which the circumstances of living at Gortan are singular, and most people would think intolerable. The little siding is an island in the surrounding expanse of eerie and intractable moorland, connected with the run of humanity by the far-gleaming parallels of steel, which strike the imagination rather as a mathematical symbol leading to an abstract world of infinity than as a physical link with the real one. The intrusion of the railway does about as much to assert man's dominion over nature as a piece of silver paper in the Grand Cañon. If anything, it reinforces the desert solitudes in their mute attack upon the faculties. But although, or perhaps because, they have been in this one spot for I have forgotten how many years, the signalman's family are to all appearance as contented, and even gay, as you could find. It is a rare pleasure to encounter such a surviving fragment of normal family life as it must have been a generation or two ago, when cars and cinemas were not, books were fewer and better, and the minds of country people had no choice but to live like bees on their own honey.

CHAPTER XX

THE BEINN ALDER GROUP

THOSE of my readers who do not know and love their Sidonius Apollinaris will hardly appreciate the compliment which his biographer paid me in undertaking, not indeed to read, but to buy my book, upon one condition : that not a single mention of ' Bonnie Prince Charlie ' should appear. I appreciate his motives, and I think I have done well to carry my respect for them (with my hopes for at least one purchaser) so far as this last chapter ; but it brings me into country where the mention of the fatal name becomes inevitable.

Yet let not romance spring up with too rank a growth. It is time the discomforts and misfortunes which that young man brought on himself deservedly, and on his followers undeservedly, began to be treated in a colder vein of history. The Highlanders certainly fought and died with undoubted gallantry in their enthusiasm for the charm and good looks (not allied with any of the more solid marks of genius) of a Prince who would probably have done even less than Whig imperialism to improve the condition of the Highlands. But the chiefs knew well enough ' which side their bread was buttered '—yet that's an unfortunate phrase, for the fact is generally known, though not often emphasised, that almost without exception they took care to have at least one member of the

281

family on *each* side, in order to assure the succession whose-soever might be the success. Peoples fight always out of sentiment ; rulers never.

No more secret hiding-place could have been chosen for prince, chief or clansman than the fastness on Beinn Alder known to all readers of *Kidnapped* as ' Cluny's Cage ', nor one more strategically posted. It apparently faced Loch Ericht, which in that case defended it on the east, while both the ways of approach along the lochside, from north and south, lie across long miles of exposed waste land ; they would thus be very easy to guard, and at the first sign of danger an escape could have been made into the wilderness of high tops behind. Cluny was in hiding there for some years, but for the Prince it was necessarily but a temporary resting-place, however perfect as such, since the main object of his adherents was of course to convey him, as opportunity offered, to the coast.

It should be observed that the spot on the south side of the ben marked on the map as ' Prince Charles' *Cave* ' cannot be even the site of the Cage, which was an artificial structure of some kind and set, it would appear, on a much steeper face ; very likely round the bend of the hillside north-east of the Cave and a mile or so distant—that is, if Stevenson's imaginative description is to be trusted ; and I think it may be accepted for what it is worth. There happens not to be a more reliable record, and in this case his version, besides being agreeable to read, is also con-sistent with geographical possibilities ; although the trees of which he speaks are gone if they ever were there. He often pays less regard to this kind of correctness : the impression of Rannoch Moor in the previous chapter is, for instance, misleading, especially in the particular that he makes a party of dragoons scour the Moor on horse-

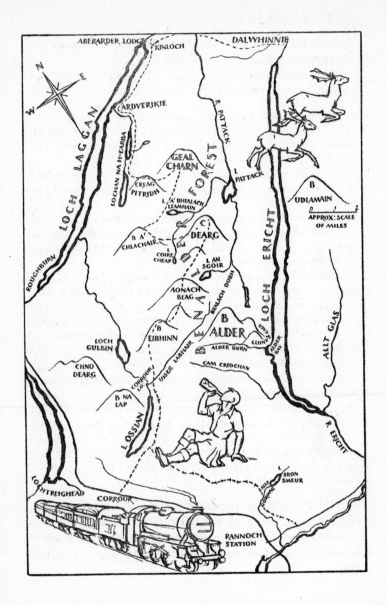

back—a feat which would put the boldest achievements of Dartmoor huntsmen in the shade.

The passage, though familiar, is therefore worth re-calling. It is as follows :

I began to be carried forward with great swiftness (or so it appeared to me, although I dare say it was slowly enough in truth), through a labyrinth of dreary glens and hollows and into the heart of that dismal mountain of Ben Alder.

We came at last to the foot of an exceeding steep wood, which scrambled up a craggy hillside, and was crowned by a naked precipice.

' It's here ', said one of the guides, and we struck up the hill.

The trees clung upon the slope, like sailors on the shrouds of a ship ; and their trunks were like the rounds of a ladder, by which we mounted.

Quite at the top, and just before the rocky face of the cliff sprang above the foliage, we found that strange house which was known in the country as ' Cluny's Cage '. The trunks of several trees had been wattled across, the intervals strengthened with stakes, and the ground behind this barricade levelled up with earth to make the floor. A tree, which grew out from the hillside, was the living centre-beam of the roof. The walls were of wattle and covered with moss. The whole house had something of an egg shape ; and it half hung, half stood in that steep, hillside thicket, like a wasp's nest in a green hawthorn.

Within, it was large enough to shelter five or six persons with some comfort. A projection of the cliff had been cunningly employed to be the fireplace ; and the smoke rising against the face of the rock, and being not dissimilar in colour, readily escaped notice from below.

' Alder ' seems to represent *alld dobhar*, and to mean ' the Mountain of Rock and Water ', a description which, although it applies to all mountains, does for some reason or other seem to suit Beinn Alder particularly well. (I have

seen it authoritatively stated that the name is locally pronounced Ben Yallar ; but as I have only negative evidence
on the point, I can only say that this pronunciation is by
no means universal.) ' Huge, broad-shouldered, the
heavens bowed to meet him '—so begins Principal Shairp's
admirably descriptive verse. And the ben is, I should
think, the most extensive compact mountain in Scotland—
I mean by this expression to exclude long broad ridges
like Beinn a' Bourd and Creag Meaghaidh. In this respect
it considerably exceeds even Beinn Muichdhui—the area
of the summit-plateau, according to the Scottish Mountaineering Club Guide, being as much as four hundred acres—
and in height, at 3757 ft., it ranks with Lochnagar. Yet
owing to the difficulties of access it is not often climbed at
all, and yet more rarely explored as it deserves.

Beinn Alder is at least held in no mean repute. But
divided from it on the north by a pass at the 2300 ft. level
there is an almost equally remarkable plateau which has
not even a name on the ordinary maps, although its
highest point, known as Geal Charn (not to be confused
with Geal Charn, or Mullach Coire an Iubhair, four or
five miles farther again to the north), is only sixty-nine
feet lower.

This union of high plateaux is the nucleus of a system of
mighty hills which form one of the wildest regions in the
Grampians, and part of the main watershed of Scotland.
The track of civilisation hardly touches its fringe : for
from north-west to south-east it is contained between the
eleven miles of Loch Laggan (as it will be once the extension to the new dam is complete) and the seventeen of
Loch Ericht ; Loch Treig divides it from the giants of the
Beinn Nevis group, which are its immediate neighbours to
west ; while on all the intervening sectors tracts of bog

form practically as strong a frontier. The only possible points of approach to any of these hills are Dalwhinnie, Kinlochlaggan, Corrour station (the next on the West Highland line north of Rannoch) and from between Rannoch station and Camusericht. But not one of these could by any stretch of imagination be called convenient. The highest summits are mostly within the Benalder and Ardverikie forests, which are in the same ownership and were originally treated as a single forest. At over 50,000 acres this was one of the very largest in Scotland, after the forest of Mar, which is outstanding in size ; and at a later date the owner decided that the huge area could be better managed in the present two divisions. The Corrour forest on the west also contains some big hills ; one side of Beinn Eibhinn (3611 ft.), Chno Dearg (3433 ft.) and Stob Coire Sgriodain (3211 ft.). The approach from the south is through the forest of Rannoch.

From what has already been said of Beinn Alder it is easy enough to infer that it is a hill which offers a great variety of ascents. In all cases the distances are great : from Kinlochlaggan or Dalwhinnie, approximately seventeen and fifteen miles respectively by either the Bealach Dubh or the Bealach Beithe paths ; from the Rannoch side, considerably less, but much of the ground which has to be crossed on this side is the worst possible going, and this cancels out the preliminary advantage. There is not a great deal to choose between the routes from the south ; but it is safe to say that the best is from Corrour station, the next best from Camusericht, and the worst from Rannoch station or Dunan. If, however, permission can be obtained to use the private road from either Dalwhinnie or Loch Laggan to Loch Pattack, the expedition falls within more normal compass, the distance being reduced to eight or nine miles each way. In this case time would permit of a more thorough survey of the ins and outs of the mountain ; and for that reason alone this method of attack is to be recommended as the ideal.

The Scottish Mountaineering Club Guide devotes several pages to an outline of the majority of the various possible routes. Partly for this reason, and partly because the map itself contains all the information necessary for the intelligent and determined walker—and to be ready to tackle Beinn Alder at all is a sufficient testimony to both these qualities—I shall not further enlarge upon the subject. Some comment is, however, called for with regard to one slightly misleading direction in the Guide's description of the Lochan Sron Smeur route from Rannoch station. What it tells you is : ' Cross the Cam Criochan and go straight down to the lochside [Loch Ericht is meant] and keep to it till you reach Beinn Alder cottage.' Now, as a matter of fact, there is a path for part of the way, not along the lochside but some way above it, and this should be followed as far as it goes. I have called the direction quoted misleading rather then mistaken, because the Guide discloses that it is by no means in ignorance of the existence of the path by referring to it a little farther on in describing the Camusericht route.

It was with sorrow and some anger that I revisited Beinn Alder one day last June after many years ; for between Loch Rannoch and Loch Ericht the worst havoc of the Grampian Electricity Scheme is to be seen. But if people were always above making use of what they hate, life would be impossible ; and on this principle we took advantage of the new road which has been made alongside the black conduit-lines that feed the power-house. True, it was a deadly ride, and it is doubtful if the road is really of

287

much service to walkers, unless they are provided with four-wheeled transport (for which a pass must be obtained either from the resident engineer or from the Rannoch Estate office in Aberfeldy). The river Ericht, which used to be such a fine furious torrent, is no more. As a last insult its channel has even become a grave for the water-pipes.

Loch Ericht has been raised and lengthened about a mile and a half by a great dam placed to the south of the former junction of the Ericht and the Allt Glas. (This has, of course, made the existing maps inaccurate.) Along the new west shore of the loch as far as the next big burn, the Cam Criochan, there are two miles of really appalling bog, made worse still to cross by a series of narrow creeks running inland from the loch. This part of the journey took us an hour and this was tolerably good time, although the weather had been dry for some weeks. The level of the water was correspondingly low ; when this is normal the changes and chances of the ground would naturally be altered, and possibly improved.

At the bridge over the Cam Criochan, the old Camus-ericht path is joined, but is serviceable for little more than a mile. It stops short nowhere, in the middle of a most depressing stretch of country ; for the smiling green strip of plantation, which here shows on the map, in reality suggests nothing so much as a cemetery. With very few exceptions all the young trees have withered where they stand, in bleached and mutilated rows. Numbers of trenches which, off the path, make the bad walking still more difficult, have availed nothing against the almost level morass which they were planned to drain. This no man's land is the edge of the Rannoch Forest and of Perthshire. There is another mile and a half of it

288

XV.   LOCH ERICHT AND BEINN ALDER

beyond the end of the path before you come to the Alder Burn and cross the march into the clean footing of Inverness.

Here there is a very different story to tell. You are now right under the walls of Beinn Alder, which, with one fine rock-chimney conspicuous and heavily shadowed, have loomed ahead all the way for the last two tiring hours. On the left ascends a short narrow glen crowned precisely by the cone of Aonach Beag. On the right is the spiritual haven of Alder Bay, a miracle of a place for solitude, lying as it does on the far border of two forests, protected by so many and such miles of ground. The cottage is a sign of civilisation at first disquieting, but on second thoughts felt to give just the necessary degree of relief to the tension of extreme loneliness. It is not now a ruin, as stated in *Hill Paths in Scotland* (1926 edition), but it is not at present inhabited. I happened, however, to notice some newspapers of recent date inside the windows ; so it is certainly being kept in order for possible occupation in the future. After the climb we spent some time here. We plunged, but not for very long, in the chilly waters of the loch, and raced round the little field of pasture to dry ; and then lay for a long time in the sun imagining what it would be like to live in such a place, and generally building cottages in the air.

At the Alder Burn the worst is behind you ; you must still count something like two hours for the actual climb. The most natural way up is along the left-hand branch of the western of the twin burns descending from the Bealach Breabag directly opposite you, and through the border of rocks on to the easier slope of the summit-plateau. It is then hardly more than a mile, round the edge of the north-eastern Garbh Coire, to the top. This route passes close to ' Prince Charles' Cave ', which I have not, however, identified.

The burn is pretty and interesting. Its course, which is often contained in rather eccentric fissures, is marked by numbers of very unusual composite stones. These are no doubt the result of the junction at this point of the granite, which forms the Cairngorm-like tableland of Beinn Alder and Geal Charn, with the metamorphic rocks. I noticed particularly striking shards of mica, and picked up one in which the silver was continuous from edge to edge, like the reverse side of an eight-inch looking-glass. I found also a lump of almost pure chalk. There are bits of granite, faded yellow or grey in colour, which can easily be crumbled to the lightest of gravel between the fingers, and others as hard and resisting as the polished walls of Aberdeen.

It is worth while to go a little out of the way by proceeding to the summit of the bealach and deflecting on to the slope of Sron Coire na h-Iolaire (3128 ft.) and Beinn Bheoil (3333 ft.), or even to climb one or both of these points, for the sake of the direct view of the eastern cliffs of Beinn Alder. Loch Bheoil below is a large loch for such a high level, and its presence greatly improves the effect of the crags, though it does not lie very close to the foot.

There is no term of general praise in the dictionary which it would be absurd to apply to the distant views, across the rolling foreground of high pasture, from Beinn Alder. The special quality is a superlative wilderness, for in the whole landscape the eye falls hardly on one point of civilisation. But I class without any parallel amongst experiences of the kind the occasion on which this panorama, seen for the first time, combined with a perfect sunset to create a spectacle transcending ordinary conditions.

One of the few of Wilde's paradoxes in which he hit on a lasting truth was his contention that nature copies art rather than art nature—that we do not become aware of the various possibilities of natural beauty until a succession of artists, as it were, turn over the pages for us one by one. But he pushes the argument too far (as, of course, he meant to do) by inferring that because Turner, who taught us sunsets, is *démodé*, therefore sunsets cease to be beautiful. Seen from a study-window, perhaps ; but under such limitations natural beauty has in any case a negligible value for any reasonable man as compared with the more accommodating diversity of art. Mere ' scenery ', as digested from the inside of a car or even from the observation-carriage of a mountain-railway, quickly palls (such at least is my experience), if even for a moment it can be said to uplift the spirits ; indeed it has for me rather the depressing effect of a stuffed bird on a boarding-house mantelpiece. It is, I conclude, a mistake to treat our enjoyment of natural beauty purely as aesthetic. There is an aesthetic element, but more important is a sense of living personal contact, the feel of the sharp air and the hard stone underfoot ; and the whole experience is less analogous to the contemplation of a statue than to the embraces of a woman.

Despite Wilde, therefore, that portentous display, seen across the whole width of the Moor of Rannoch behind its ring of peaks, remains with me as an exciting memory. It has had fourteen years to fade ; for this odd expedition, I need hardly say, was one of the follies of extreme youth— if anything which has earned such a reward can be called folly. There we were, almost in darkness, at the top of this remote ben ! It was light enough to find our way down easily enough, but I remember that we wasted a long time vainly searching for the terminus of the truncated path along Loch Ericht, where we had left our bicycles—having come by the Camusericht route (past the sawmill); which is, or was then, a good shooting-track, though not really suitable for bicycling if you are much over fifteen years old. (I have since made a note that the end of the path is to be found in a clump of the few surviving larches, 237 paces south of the little burn half-way between the Alder Burn and the Cam Criochan.) We fell off at almost every bend, but made remarkably good progress all the same, and reached Kinloch Rannoch at about eleven o'clock; having made a non-stop journey all the way from the summit of Beinn Alder.

From Rannoch the railway has still nine miles of the Moor to cross before entering the defile of Loch Treig, from which it emerges in Glen Spean. It reaches its highest point (1357 ft.—377 ft. above Rannoch station) just beyond the stopping-place of Corrour. The walking-route is considerably longer. It runs about two miles to the east of the railway along the rising slopes on the edge of the Moor to the head of Loch Ossian (a mile or so from Corrour) and thence close to the line to Lochtreighead, from which there are routes on to Roy Bridge, through Glen Nevis to Fortwilliam, and south-west down to Loch Leven. The old thoroughfare to the north seems, however, to have been down Strath Ossian and past Loch Gulbin round to Fersit at the foot of Loch Treig, encircling Beinn na Lap (now the sanctuary of the Corrour Forest), Chno Dearg and Stob Coire Sgriodain. These are hills of which I have no first-hand knowledge, but which obviously could be taken in one's stride from Corrour to Glen Spean.

The route to Loch Ossian from Rannoch strikes off the

road a mile and a half east of the station. There is a gate marked ' private ', but this warning applies only to cars. The road is good for two miles. So far the ground is level. On the left are clumps of birches, behind which the Allt Eigheach makes its way through a hidden dell strewn with rounded lumps of Rannoch Moor granite, the litter of centuries. Where the Allt Gormag is crossed the road, as a road, comes to an end, and just beyond, near a particularly huge square block of stone, is the ford of the Allt Eigheach. The line of the track can be seen running along the fence on the opposite side and starting to climb round the west slope of the ridge which runs continuously, through a series of fairly high and not uninteresting points, Carn Dearg (3080 ft.), Sgor Gaibhre (3124 ft.), Sgor Choinnich (3040 ft.), and Beinn Chumhainn (2958 ft.), almost to join the Beinn Alder mass, and forms the county march and the boundary between Rannoch and Corrour Forests. Once you are on the track, due west and just within sight of the forlorn waters of Lochan Sron Smeur, there is no further difficulty. The way along what was once the road to the old Corrour Lodge is thenceforward unmistakable.

But the journey along this path was as lonely and as dreary as could well be imagined on the day when I explored this region. There was a light drizzle. The mist hid all the hills down to my own level, but allowed me to see below it far and wide across the watery spaces of Rannoch Moor. I looked first down the length of Loch Laidon, and farther on, down the Blackwater Reservoir to where the Devil's Staircase crosses from Glencoe to Loch Leven. But, without horizons, all that appeared might have been the bare substance of a world awaiting genesis. All was so still, that every sound was startling. Many herds of deer crossed the path ahead of me. The grouse whirred over in large packs, one of as many as fifteen, which struck me as peculiar in the early part of the season, even before the nesting was at an end. For a long way a golden plover kept me company with his keening whistle. But what wound through the air most strangely was the loud panting shuffle of a train coming down the line ; and soon its smoking funnel and the long writhing form behind came into view. So near and yet so far !—the passengers and I were in two worlds too disparate for our common humanity to bridge, and for the moment I felt nearer in blood to deer and plover than to them. The vacancy of the clouded hills has a curious power to overawe without depressing, and I have never felt lonely within myself in any unpleasant way even in the farthest parts of the Highlands ; as I must say I have sometimes felt in the mountains of ever-populous Ireland. Perhaps Ireland is peopled with hostile Fir-bolgian ghosts as well as men ; certainly it has few of the living wild creatures who in their own places rouse to the surface a sense of fellowship existing at some deep preconscious level.

The ruins of the old lodge, which, at a height of 1723 ft. almost crown the road, cause more dismal sensations. In its day this was probably the highest human habitation in the three kingdoms. Inside, it is now a mass of nettles. The only other remains of alien vegetation are some gross overseeded weeds which might once have been rhubarb.

At the summit, not far beyond the old lodge, the path twice divides, as the map will show ; the main branch, which I took, drops away rapidly to Loch Ossian. When I came well within sight of its gloomy depths, I had lunch ; and it must have been here that, as I found later, I somehow lost my old battered compass. (If anyone find it he may return it to me, if he will ; or keep it for the little it is now worth and with my blessing, in the name of Pan and Hermes, provided he will but respect its past.) I noticed two buttresses on the north-east of Meall na Lice which are not indicated on the map ; and in general the survey does not seem to have been very careful of crag in this particular region. This point is within half an hour of either end of Loch Ossian, and in about that time I was at the door of the Youth Hostel, which is really what I went out for to see.

This is a reconstructed boat-house, standing by itself in a perfect situation at the end of the loch, but in the shelter of a few trees. I approached with the respect proper in one who had no right to be there, and, finding the door ajar, walked in and looked round. But it seemed to be quite uninhabited, and the stationmaster at Corrour, who is in charge of it, later confirmed that this was so. He was interested to hear about the door being open, and told me that the same thing had happened before, and had at first given rise to the usual kind of speculation. But the responsibility had been traced merely to the wind, which sometimes, it seemed, managed to slip down the inner bolt on one wing of the double door, so that the lock on the other wing would lose its purchase.

I know very little of Youth Hostels generally ; this would certainly be a fine place to spend a few days. There can hardly be another in so remote a place, and here, without it, there would be no accommodation of any kind. But I must say I should require some company. What surprised me most was that the laird should permit such a danger-spot, as it would almost universally be regarded from the sporting point of view, in the very heart of his forest. I learnt, however, that this particular laird,

Sir John Stirling-Maxwell, one of a family distinguished for its broad interests and sympathies, not only encouraged, but to a large extent paid for its construction. Naturally, however, he does not allow it to remain open later than July.

Unlike Gortan, Corrour is a stopping-place for all trains, and the stationmaster, who is single-handed, is kept pretty busy, apart altogether from his subsidiary office as warden of the hostel. When he has time he himself likes to walk the hills, which he knows as natives should, but too rarely do nowadays. The station serves only the lodge—the new lodge built forty years ago, five miles away at the far end of the loch ; which is, rather contrary to appearances, the foot of the loch, not the head. It is thus really a private station, and for a long time did not even appear in the time-tables, to the great inconvenience of strangers invited to Corrour for the stalking ; for except by the railway or across the hills on foot, there is no possible means of getting there.

It was from Corrour a few days later that I started on a memorable day's walking. My destination was Kinloch-laggan, twenty miles distant in the direct line, and the way lay across country almost unknown except to the stalker, and the highest summits of the Corrour and Ardverikie forests. Though the glass was falling and I made my early start from Kinloch Rannoch with some trepidation, the morning turned out fine and clear, with a drifting south-easterly wind, and I was in good heart as at nine o'clock I set out alongside the row of dwarf telegraph-posts which line the road to Corrour Lodge.

On such a fine day Loch Ossian becomes almost cheerful, in the grand manner. It is lightly sprinkled with tiny wooded islands. The western end remains none the less austere ; but half-way along the shore the road enters Sir John's carefully designed plantations of various trees, in which birches predominate. This wood is the product of such understanding art that it has the comeliness of a natural forest, not the uniform forest of northern climates but the ever-changing wild forests of the Mediterranean, which here and there survive from the pages of Virgil. There are occasional splashes of colour, as, nearer to the lodge, broom and honeysuckle become more frequent, with many other flowering shrubs. The house stands at the end of the loch ; it is backed by a supporting settlement of cottages and farm-buildings ; while between it and the water's edge are gardens, which, I am told, are a treasury of Alpine species. And, in a word, this whole establishment of Corrour—the last sign of humanity I was to see till evening—blossoms in the wilderness as ' shines a good deed in a naughty world '.

I passed the back of the house at 10.15, and started along the path which leads beside the Uisge Labhair to the Bealach Dubh, between Beinn Alder and Geal Charn. A black cat brought me the last good omen by crossing my path, and even rubbing against my legs ; the feel of the good familiar granite underfoot quickened my steps ; and I really felt that I was in for a good day.

My first object was Beinn Eibhinn. The most obvious way is to strike north immediately from the bridge over the Uisge Labhair, along the ridge on the east of Strath Ossian. But I thought the walking looked better along the next ridge, Creagan Craoibhe, ' the Rocky Place of the Trees ' (but there are none) ; this also connects more directly with the summit. I therefore followed the path for two miles, and then started an easy and uneventful climb which brought me over the top of Uinneag a' Ghlas

297

Coire (3041 ft.) into the little furrow of a col beyond, which looks as though it ought to contain a pool of water, and perhaps sometimes does. From close range in the bottom of this delightful hollow I watched a large herd of deer, a hundred of them or more and a great many of them stags, pass in single file across the neck of the hill in front of me down into the Glas Coire. I saw them again later on, just below me in Coire a' Charra Bhig.

From the col there is a still gentle, but now rather stony climb of six hundred feet, first north and then east, to the top of Beinn Eibhinn (3611 ft.), which I reached at 12.15. Close to the top there is a little tarn, not marked on the one-inch map. The sun was now shining full from an open sky, though there were clouds about. The distances were perfectly clear, a sign of coming rain ; but as I did not expect it before nightfall, I was more than contented with the beauty of the moment.

I borrow with gratitude the Scottish Mountaineering Club Guide's terse and accurate description :

' The southern spurs of Beinn Eibhinn are comparatively featureless, but the mountain presents a bold front to the north and falls almost from the summit cairn in 1000 feet of crag and talus slopes to the floor of Coire a' Charra Mhoir, a cirque of remarkable beauty and symmetry of form. . . . The view is extremely fine, and there are few points from which the great elevated tableland, that extends in an almost unbroken line from Creag Meaghaidh to the northern limits of the Monadh Liath, can be better observed. The outlook northwards to Loch Laggan and Strathspey is however blocked by the long ridge of Beinn a' Chlachair.'

The view southward, to the Glen Lyon and Drumalbain hills and across Rannoch Moor, was equally good, and the pointing index of Shiehallion showed prominently.

Closer at hand towered the battlements of the Beinn Nevis mass, with large snowfields still covering the greater part of the very high ground. But I was still more interested by the view north-west to the serried line of tops on either side of Glen Shiel, where in the still profounder distances rose a great forked peak, I think, that of Mam Soul and Carn Eige. In that foreground, right from the foot of Beinn Eibhinn to Glen Spean, four or five miles away, spreads the Sliabh Loraich, a green meadow of impenetrable marsh, dejected and subservient to the remoter splendours.

Across Coire a' Charra Mhoir stands Aonach Beag (3647 ft.), the next summit of the range. The route follows the lip of the corrie. The rough descent of about 400 feet, between steep sides bedded in scree and loose rock, requires some care ; and from the tenuous col to the summit there is a corresponding rise.

A shallow depression, and no more, divides Aonach Beag from the elevated prairie of Geal Charn. There is no cairn or noticeable summit to the plateau, but the highest point, which I reached at about 1.15, is at about 3688 ft. This was therefore in one sense the climax of the day. The yet larger plateau of Beinn Alder is now close at hand to the right, and it would have made a fine tour to go on to it across the Bealach Dubh, and so return to Rannoch. It is one which I recommend with confidence. But my own plans now led me away to the north-east over Geal Charn and along the continuation of the ridge, which ends in Carn Dearg, above Loch Pattack.

The north-east face of Geal Charn, like that of Beinn Alder, is precipitous throughout its length ; for in fact the two mountains are a physiographic unity. The abrupt overflow of the main ridge towards Carn Dearg and

' Lancet Edge ', at the extreme east corner of the plateau, offer the only two practicable outlets. Both demand great caution.

Making my way round the obstacles in my path scar by scar, and dropping a little farther than necessary out of the direct line to Carn Dearg, I found myself, still above the main precipices falling to Loch an Sgoir and perhaps a hundred feet below the edge of the plateau, on a small terrace, itself a corrie in miniature, floored with broad slabs, grass, moss and lichen—none smoother—a place possessed of charm beyond the reasonable expectations of this ageing earth. The skyline above my head was crowned by a heavy snow-cornice, a more-than-white resplendent against a more-than-blue. A second snow-bridge half-way down spanned the waterfall which had just room to draw breath in my little corrie, before the cold resolution of its final plunge over the shadowed precipices. Here I took my lunch and bathed, and it was long before I made up my mind to go ; for naked in my serene, yet pendulous, retreat lay Blake's eternal symbolic man, eternally poised between the upper and the lower worlds.

But at 2.15 the sun went for the day, and the matter in hand once more took control. The descent to ' the Saddle ', Diollaid a' Chairn, is closely bordered on either side, at first by actual crags, and lower down by very steep slopes. It commands a remarkable double view of Loch an Sgoir on the left hand and Loch Coire Cheap on the right, both lochs lying at the foot of high and rugged corries and both being visible at one time and at an equal distance.

Carn Dearg is a stony eminence, with two well-marked tops a few minutes apart. The first is a great natural cairn. I reached the second, the higher, at 3.10. It is the perfect standpoint from which to survey the truculent frontage of the Beinn Alder-Geal Charn massif—corrie and spur linked in a long series of alternations. In the opposite direction the country, part of which is well chosen as the sanctuary of the Benalder forest, is low and melancholy enough; but the eye finds relief in the long line of Loch Ericht and the heights of Beinn Udlamain on the opposite coast. Culra Lodge is plainly visible just below, and there, past Loch Pattack, lies the way by which Prince Charles came down to Beinn Alder.

Only to the north are there new worlds to conquer. Right across the straight low cutting of An Lairig, which is the northern boundary of the whole Beinn Eibhinn range, is the unassailable south-east face of Beinn a' Chlachair, Stonecutters' Hill; well so named, for it is strewn from end to end with blocks of masonry that rival Cairn Toul. I meant to turn the crags on one flank or the other, and from Carn Dearg the eastern line of march seemed rather the shorter. I therefore aimed straight across the Lairig for that end of the Beinn a' Chlachair ridge. As a matter of fact there is nothing to choose between the two, since the event proved that I should really have made for the watershed—or rather, the best pretence of a watershed which this sodden pass can show—and this, at about 1800 ft., is exactly below the centre of the crags, nearly a mile to the west of my actual bearing.

In the descent I walked through the middle of a large herd of deer, grazing on the easy slopes. I have never seen deer show so little sign of concern at human presence; perhaps in this forgotten corner of the hills and so early in the year as June they could hardly believe their eyes. Two hinds, who probably had fawns hidden somewhere

301

in the heather, actually nosed after me at only thirty or forty yards' distance, with every sign of inquisitive anxiety. Later I heard them calling that the coast was clear.

It was the only sound that broke the sad stillness of this far glen, where even the water of the burns is silent. The main stream is a broad peaty ditch of considerable depth, with a few sandy places better for fording. Although there is a made footpath along the south bank, there seems to be no bridge or good crossing-place. I wasted some time looking for one ; eventually I waded, sinking deep into soft mud and startling the tiny trout which hovered in shoals over the patches of white sand. It is obvious that except after a prolonged spell of dry weather the crossing would be scarcely possible.

I soon struck the footpath, marked on the map, which rises across the east shoulder of Beinn a' Chlachair towards Loch a' Bhealach Leamhain. But before I reached the first burn, which I should have followed to reach the top of the ben, the lateness of the hour had decided me to omit this climb, which would have taken me farther out of my line for Kinlochlaggan than I could now afford. The burn was a particularly clear gushing stream of such water as belongs only to mountains, and even then only to mountains of the naked virgin rock like this ; and there was all the pleasure of yielding to temptation in the long draughts of it with which I spoiled the remainder of my wind. There was another lying in wait for me in a luxurious quilt of moss, just after my path joined the made track above the loch. Men are lucky with the daughters of stern parents ; and the Naiads of Beinn a' Chlachair should be especially kind to strangers.

The path from Loch Pattack through the Bealach Leamhain to Ardverikie is almost a road. There are
302

eighty miles of such constructed paths and roads within the afforested area of Benalder and Ardverikie. It goes without saying that they are most useful, and indeed without them most of this country would be intractable in the extreme. Here, where the route leads through the lower part of a rocky corrie, five hundred feet above the loch, quite a considerable piece of engineering has had to be done. As I emerged from this Thermopylae, I came close up to a hind with one young fawn, the only fawn which I had seen all day out of very large numbers of deer. He promptly disappeared after her amongst the dangerous boulders with a remarkable display of activity and confidence for his age.

The path now divides, but all roads lead to Ardverikie; one by the head of the upper of the two Lochan na h-Earba—this would have taken you alternatively to the foot of Loch Laggan and Moy Lodge, but will do so no longer with the completion of the big engineering scheme—and the other over the col between the rocky little cone of Creag Pitridh (3031 ft.) and the mightier Geal Charn, or Mullach Coire an Iubhair (3443 ft.) to the point between the two lochs. This latter branch was the one to suit me, since I wished to take in Geal Charn on my way.

The ascent of Geal Charn was direct and not difficult, though the flattened summit is rather stony; the very place for ptarmigan, none of which I had seen all day till now. There is a fine sudden view to north and east, the enormous level mass of Creag Meaghaidh filling quarter of the horizon; and for the first time I had a good look at the head of Loch Laggan and my goal. I could well have proceeded by a path which descends directly northward from east of the cairn, but I had left my rucksack behind me— and without it, after the rather laboured climb from An

303

Lairig, I was feeling as light-footed as a stag. I had therefore no choice but to return as I had come to the col below Creag Pitridh.

The time was now 6.40, and I had still nine miles before me. I should not, however, have been deterred from acquiring the scalp of Creag Pitridh on the way, at the expense of a mere 500 feet, had it not occurred to me that with four more ' Munros ' now to my credit—counting Beinn Eibhinn, Aonach Beag, Carn Dearg, and the second Geal Charn—the number of notches on my stick, by which I rather childishly represent them, had risen to eighty-one, nine times ' the number of the sacred Nine '. This seemed a most propitious figure at which to lay up my laurels for another year, and I yielded gracefully to the omen. Even so it was 8.50 by the time I reached the doors of what seems unfortunately to be the only public lodging in the thirty odd miles between Newtonmore or Dalwhinnie and Roybridge; and that with a lift in a keeper's car down the last mile and a half of the Ardverikie drive.

The upper Loch na h-Earba lies in a bare glen, open at the head, and in the fringe of wood just touching its foot and enclosing the head of the lower loch, there was a radiant stillness and fragrance. Several tall stags bounded away under the trees; the evening rise alone rippled the surface of the water.

But I began almost to suffocate in the dark evergreen thickets, plantations of more recent date, which in every direction envelop the Gothic citadel of Ardverikie.

For the shadow of industrialism lies heavier on Lagganside than on Rannoch. The whole valley is fallen into the grip of the Fortwilliam factories. The waters of Loch Laggan are shrunken and clouded like the leavings of a

304

Gargantuan wash-tub, and Loch Treig is in a yet worse
case. The fishings are all spoiled with mud. Like the
Ericht, the once-roaring Spean has his mouth stopped
with an iron gag. The gods are wounded and the nymphs
are fled. It is satisfactory to know that all this has cost
£5,000,000, and has provided employment for 2000 men
for five years and half that number for an extended period;
that there is a tunnel through Beinn Nevis 15 miles long
and 15 feet in diameter, a displacement of 100,000 tons of
rock per mile; that the dam at Roughburn is 178 feet high;
that the power-house will develop 120,000 h.p.; ' while ',
to quote an official account, ' among the more important
ancillary works may be mentioned the attractive village
which has been built for the employees of the company
on the banks of the River Lochy, and the building of a
pier 1000 feet long at the head of Loch Linnhe.'

As I passed the too, too solid walls of Ardverikie,
spiritual ancestor of these striking results, only a slight
change in gender (hard enough, I admit) would have made
the lines which here must follow a perfect index of the
reaction on my susceptibilities :

> The darksome pines that o'er yon rocks reclin'd
> Wave high, and murmur to the hollow wind,
> The wand'ring streams that shine between the hills,
> The grots that echo to the tinkling rills,
> The dying gales that pant upon the trees,
> The lakes that quiver to the curling breeze ;
> No more these scenes my meditation aid,
> Or lull to rest the visionary maid.
> But o'er the twilight groves and dusky caves,
> Long-sounding aisles, and intermingled graves,
> Black Melancholy sits, and round her throws
> A death-like silence, and a dead repose :

> Her gloomy presence saddens all the scene,
> Shades ev'ry flow'r, and darkens ev'ry green,
> Deepens the murmur of the falling floods,
> And breathes a browner horror on the woods.

But, gentle reader (if I may make the effort at gallantry —an effort which I can only describe as municipal—so much in favour with the generation which planted such woods and built Ardverikie and hung the unrivalled collection of Landseer reproductions in the parlour of Loch Laggan hotel), you feel, gentle reader, that the length of my quotations is good value for an apology ? Then I will compromise in parting.

There are two kinds of quotations ; they are either a setting for the display of one's own learning and intelligence—and of this use I have been sparing, since I disclaim the first and have just enough of the second to be a nuisance to myself, without being of much use to others— or else they are jewels offered for their own worth and beauty, and set as best one can afford. Mine are of this second class ; for doubtful of my own power to please, I am yet honest enough to wish to do you some service if I can. I may not have chosen the right method ; but the discrimination even of those who profess respect for what I might call ' immediate ' values now generally rises so little above the clouds of mere concept and ideal, a long prudery has so far atrophied the sense of honest form which is at once the seed and flowering of all pleasurable experience, that I have hoped to help my design by turning the spot-light on some of the most finished examples of formal beauty in language which I have had the fortune to discover.

Nor can it well have passed unobserved—and it is no accident—that these excerpts have been taken almost wholly from the ' best known ', and therefore neglected, works of one great man ; who is the last of poets to be associated with a subject like mine, but who keenly resented coarse predilections ; who, had his own frailty of body permitted the experience, and the fashion of his time suggested it, would probably have been so deeply moved by the hills of Scotland as—to be unable to speak of them at all ; whose extreme sensibility responded even to the trivialities of thought and behaviour by which he was surrounded, in harmonies of such delicate weave as, it seems, to have become, like his own sylphs,

> too fine for mortal sight,
> Their fluid bodies half dissolved in light,

imperceptible to ears of brass dulled by the successive bombinations of more thrusting versifiers ; and to whose memory, and to whose restoration in his proper rank, I drink deep as to the image of my larger hopes.

APPENDIX

NOTES ON THE ILLUSTRATIONS

Frontispiece.—Beinn Doireann.—This is the most impressive aspect of the hill. The view, which is taken from near the old main road to Glencoe, shows the normal direct line of ascent from Auch. On the right are the slopes of Beinn Odhar, and the railway runs a little higher up on that side before turning inwards along the semicircular viaduct which bridges the Allt Chonoghlais. The new road has been constructed on the other side of Glen Orchy, to the left, and so does not spoil the picture.

I. The Lochnagar Range from Beinn a Bourd.—This is taken from a point to the east of the north top. The general direction of the view is south-east, across the upper part of Coire nan Clach. The highest point on the ridge which forms the horizon is Lochnagar (the north top, Cac Carn Beag). To the right of this it is possible to make out successively the corrie of the White Mounth in which lie the Sandy Loch and Loch nan Eun, Carn an t-Sagairt, Fafernie and perhaps Carn an Tuirc. The Dee valley runs along the foot of the Lochnagar range, almost horizontally in the picture, and Braemar, out of sight, is slightly to the right of the direct line of vision towards Lochnagar.

As late as August this corrie sometimes holds extensive snow-drifts of 20 feet or more in depth. Although it appears at first sight to be a barren waste, it is a favourite

309

home, amongst other plants, of the Creeping Azalea (*Loiseluria procumbens*).

II. Glen Clova.—In this evening-photograph we are looking straight up Glen Clova from near Milton. The slopes in the left foreground belong to the Hill of Strone, those on the right to Boustie Ley. Beyond them, the point on the left is the northern wing of Driesh, and that in the centre is Craig Mellon. To the left of Craig Mellon is Glen Doll and ' Jock's Road ' over to Loch Callater ; to the right, Glen Esk, whence strike the routes to Loch Muick and Ballater and to Lochnagar.

III. Head of Glen Isla.—Looking south down Canness, the east branch of the forked head of Glen Isla, towards Tulchan Lodge, which is near the focal point of the picture. The camera is placed on a spur of the Carn na Glasha plateau, close to Badenjo Crag, an outstanding part of the cliffs extending westward to Caenlochan. On the left is Finalty Hill ; on the right, Monega Hill, across which the highest of all the Mounth-routes climbs from Tulchan by way of the Glas Maol into Glen Cluny. In the distance, behind Tulchan, are the Angus foothills, Badandan Hill occupying the central position.

IV. Loch an Eilein.—Showing the foot of the long spur leading to Sgoran Dubh, and the island-castle, from which the loch is named, and where, until a few years ago, there was a nest of ospreys.

V. The Carr Bridge.—This half-ruined bridge, which gives its name to the present village of Carrbridge, is possibly even older than the time of General Wade, who seems, however, to have put it into a better state of repair as part of his great road to Inverness.

The reader who is interested in General Wade's activities is advised to read a little book called *Wade in Scot-*

land, by J. B. Salmond.   Here I will content myself with recalling the familiar couplet (for which Governor Caulfeild must have the credit) :

> ' If you'd seen these roads before they were made,
> You'd lift up your hands and bless General Wade.'

VI. Loch Avon and Beinn Muichdhui.—The camera is pointed south-west from near ' the Saddle ' towards the summit of Muichdhui, which is the highest point on the sky-line.   Sharp on the extreme left is the angle of the Sputan Dearg precipice ; the two rocky bluffs below this and the summit respectively are the corner of Beinn a' Mheadhoin and Cairn Etchachan, and Loch Etchachan is between them, out of sight, at the back.   The square-topped mass of rock just to the right of Cairn Etchachan is the Shelter-stone Crag.   The hill-side to the right hand of the spectator (forbidding in appearance but far more so in fact) is of course part of Cairn Gorm.

It may perhaps make it easier for the imagination to create for itself the true atmosphere of the place to note that the level of the water below is nearly 2400 feet.

VII. Braeriach from the North.—Looking south-east from Aviemore.   From left to right, Creag an Leth-choin and (behind) Beinn Muichdhui, the Lairig Ghru, Sron na Lairige, and (below) Coire Gorm, Coire Beanaidh, the summit of Braeriach, Coire Ruadh, Coire Loch Coire an Lochain, the Eanaich Cairn, Glen Eanaich (with Coire Dhondail and Loch Eanaich just out of sight to left and right, and the edge of the Moine Mor plateau on the sky-line behind).   On the extreme right is part of the ridge leading to Sgoran Dubh.

VIII. Glen Lochay.—The Falls of Lochay.   The peak with the volcano-like streamer is Creag Mhor, and to the right of it can be seen part, but not the actual summit, of Beinn Heasgarnich.

Mr. Adam gives me the following additional note :

' The mountain-country is mainly built up from highly folded schists, and this material weathering to a fine friable soil, with rich mineral plant-food, explains why so many of the rarer Alpine species cling to the corries of this glen.'

IX. Grass of Parnassus and Cotton-grass.—Except to botanists, these explain themselves. The Grass of Parnassus is referred to in Chapter III ; Cotton-grass is common everywhere in the bogs.

X. The Central Grampians, from Beinn Lawers.—The general direction of this view is due north. Below lies Lochan a' Chait. The points in the foreground (forming part of Beinn Lawers itself) are, from left to right, Creag an Fhithich, Meall Garbh and Meall Cruaidh. The heavily shadowed range in the middle distance, across Glen Lyon, is that of Carn Mairg, with Shiehallion showing over it towards the right. In the left half of the photograph the slightly higher point on the level horizon of the Loch Ericht and Western Athole hills is Beinn Alder ; while the more considerable stretch of elevated country behind Shiehallion is the Cairngorm region.

XI. Shiehallion.—This is taken from the edge of the Tummel, between Kinloch Rannoch and Drumchastle.

XII. The Western Grampians, from Beinn Lawers.— Again the two points nearest to the camera are parts of Beinn Lawers, namely Beinn Ghlas and Meall Corranaich. Between them is Meall nan Tarmachan, the spiky projection on the left side of it being either Meall Garbh or Beinn nan Eachan, I am not sure which. Lochan na Lairige of course lies on the lower table-land connecting

312

Meall Corranaich and Meall nan Tarmachan ; the cliff of Creag an Loch betrays its position. The isosceles triangle behind Meall Corranaich is Meall Ghaordie. These preliminary identifications enable us now to place the most conspicuous of the hills in the far distance : on the extreme left, Stobinian and Beinn More ; behind Meall nan Tarmachan, Beinn Lui and Beinn Cruachan ; behind Meall Ghaordie, Beinn Doireann and Beinn Heasgarnich ; and on the very right, some of the Black Mount peaks.

XIII. Head of the Longest Glen in Scotland.—The head of Glen Lyon, from about two miles west of Pubil. Loch Lyon is in the hollow to the left. The dominant hill is Beinn Mhanach, with Beinn a' Chreachain behind, a little to the right. Right of these, Glen Mearan makes a low pass through the hills to Gortan ; it was probably this way that Campbell of Glenlyon started for the Massacre of Glencoe. On the right hand rise the less important slopes of Meall Daill.

This picture well illustrates the eastern aspect of the Drumalbain range, as described in Chapter XIX ; contrast Plate XIV. It is also suggestive of the very wet character of this country, where 70 inches of rain are not an abnormal annual allowance.

XIV. The Spine of Scotland, from Rannoch Moor.—Taken from a point close to the new road, beside the once lonely waters of Lochan na h-Achlaise, this comprises the best part of the Drumalbain range : Beinn a' Chreachain, the long ridge of Beinn Achallater, and Beinn an Dothaidh. Beinn Doireann is just out of sight to the right. The ruined Achallater Castle and the present farm lie at the foot of the great hollow in the centre of the picture. (Compare Plate XIII and note.)

XV. Loch Ericht and Beinn Alder.—From the head of the loch near Dalwhinnie. Beinn Alder is the bulky mass which holds the centre of the field, the part nearest the loch being Beinn Bheoil. It must be remembered that the distance from the camera is about ten miles as the crow flies, though it looks so much less.

The raising of the water-level by some 20 feet has done much to alter the appearance of Loch Ericht in point of detail, especially by causing subsidence and land slides which have done considerable damage to the growing timber along the road to Loch Ericht Lodge on the right-hand side.

INDEX

INDEX

318

PRINTED IN GREAT BRITAIN
BY ROBERT MACLEHOSE AND CO. LTD.
THE UNIVERSITY PRESS, GLASGOW

ON FOOT
IN THE
HIGHLANDS

By E. A. BAKER

Illustrated.   *5s. net.*

This book in 200 pages covers
Arran and Argyll, the Trossachs,
Lochaber, the country beyond the
Great Glen, besides the Cairn-
gorms and the Central and Eastern
Highlands.

"A most useful companion."
Times Literary Supplement

✦

ALEXANDER MACLEHOSE & CO.
58 BLOOMSBURY STREET, W.C. 1

MEMORIES
OF THE
MONTHS

First, Second and Third Series

6/- net each

BY

SIR HERBERT
MAXWELL

"A succession of most charming and original
volumes which have extremely pleased a
generation of Sportsmen, Naturalists and
Gardeners." SIR W. BEACH THOMAS

ALEXANDER MACLEHOSE & CO.
58 BLOOMSBURY STREET, W.C. 1